Oscar Aldred

GW00691529

Oscar Aldred

A View from the Air

Aerial Archaeology and Remote Sensing Techniques

Results and opportunities

Edited by

Marc Lodewijckx
René Pelegrin

BAR International Series 2288
2011

Published by

Archaeopress
Publishers of British Archaeological Reports
Gordon House
276 Banbury Road
Oxford OX2 7ED
England
bar@archaeopress.com
www.archaeopress.com

BAR S2288

A View from the Air: Aerial Archaeology and Remote Sensing Techniques. Results and opportunities

ISBN 978 1 4073 0865 4

Printed in England by 4edge Ltd, Hockley

All BAR titles are available from:

Hadrian Books Ltd
122 Banbury Road
Oxford
OX2 7BP
England
www.hadrianbooks.co.uk

The current BAR catalogue with details of all titles in print, prices and means of payment is available free from Hadrian Books or may be downloaded from www.archaeopress.com

Contents

A VIEW FROM THE AIR
AERIAL ARCHAEOLOGY AND REMOTE SENSING TECHNIQUES:
RESULTS AND OPPORTUNITIES

Preface

When we at the University of Leuven (K.U. Leuven) began to work with aerial archaeology in 1997, we had no idea as to where it all would lead. The contacts established with colleagues from both home and abroad led to us being entrusted with the organization of the *Aerial Archaeology Research Group's* (AARG) yearly congress in 2005. This congress took place at the University of Leuven from the 19th to 21st September of that year. It was organized by the Department of Archaeology, Art History and Musicology of the university, in consultation with the committee of the AARG, and with the support of the Research Foundation – Flanders (FWO – Vlaanderen) and K.U. Leuven. The large number of registered participants – from no less than 24 countries – was a great surprise. The countries of origin of the participants included; Belgium, the Netherlands, Germany, France, Italy, Austria, United Kingdom, Ireland, Denmark, Finland, Poland, Latvia, Estonia, Lithuania, Czech Republic, Slovakia, Slovenia, Switzerland, Romania, Turkey, Iceland, Mexico, United States and New Zealand. According to insiders, this made it one of the most interesting and best-attended congresses upon the subject of aerial archaeology to that date.

Following on from this positive experience, we decided to publish a book containing various contributions of the participants, as a memorial to the cordial collaborations of the congress. Naturally, such an undertaking is more complicated a task than it first appears. Not only were the participants quickly re-occupied by their day-to-day worries, but I myself was also assigned additional responsibilities within K.U. Leuven and given the task of overseeing the organization of large-scale excavations and long-term projects

Therefore, I needed to postpone the editing of the previously-submitted articles, much to my frustration. Eventually, in the spring of 2011, there was finally sufficient time to conclude the editing of the submitted articles. Fortunately, the authors were still prepared to allow the publication of – in some instances – somewhat dated articles. For this I sincerely wish to thank them, and again apologize for this delay for which I am solely accountable.

Due to the aforementioned heavy workload, I had to abstain from participating in later congresses. Fortunately, however, Rene Pelegrin has, through his constant and much-appreciated dedication, not only upheld the high standards of aerial archaeology at the University of Leuven, but also maintained contact with colleagues within this discipline, for which I genuinely thank him. Consequently, I am grateful for his involvement in the publication of the results of his work.

I also wish to heartfully thank all of the authors for their goodwill and their high-grade contributions; I hope that they take pleasure in this publication.

Marc Lodewijckx
Dept. Archaeology, Art History and Musicology
University of Leuven (K.U. Leuven)

ON THE PRECIPICE IN ICELAND

Oscar Aldred – Elín Ósk Hreiðarsdóttir

The setting and landscape

Iceland is located in the Mid-Atlantic, lying between Newfoundland, in the Americas, and the northern part of Norway, in Europe. Its land mass straddles the American and European tectonic plates along the Mid Atlantic Ridge, with the northern part lying about 50 km from the Artic circle. It is a landscape characterised by volcanoes, glaciers and a barren interior, but, as will be demonstrated in this paper, its lowland areas contains a rich archaeological record. For the landscape is one of great variety in topography and land features; valley and dale, upland ridges, highland plateaus, and open plains to name just a few. Features such as deserts, meadow land, heath, dwarf birch forests and extensive grasslands have encouraged a diversity of uses. Approximately twenty-five percent of the total land mass lies below the 200 meter contour line and within this zone much of the land is characterised by farming and a dispersed settlement of single farms. Iceland has a temperate climate, which is moderated by the North Atlantic Current, the summer days are bright, with twenty-four hour light on the solstice, but its winters are dark. Snow falls are common during winter, and often in the early and late parts of the day, low lying light gives rise to melting variations against earthworks producing good conditions for aerial photography.

Whilst the density of archaeological sites is less than in most other European countries, the remains are very well preserved. Iceland was colonised *de novo* in the late 9th century, though reference to Irish monks is made before this. In some places Viking age buildings are still visible as earthworks and many post medieval features are partially upstanding. The type of archaeological site is more often than not an earthwork, and may be amorphous in form but usually contain significant characteristics that help determine its particular function. For example, early sheep houses have a different shape, in general, to later ones, and Viking age long-houses are quite distinctive. Many farm sites that may have been established in the earliest settlement of Iceland are still occupied and the general assumption is that many of these lie on top of the earliest structures that are contained within a farm mound, which can be compared best to a small Middle Eastern *tell*.

Archaeological research in Iceland

Archaeological research has focused on the earliest periods of Iceland's history, in particular places that are associated with the Sagas that tell of stories relating to the settlement of Iceland in the Viking period. This has dictated the research agenda for many years, particularly for excavation, as well as generating the general public's perceptions of archaeology. In the last 30 years or so the agenda has widened, particularly in the last few years where an interest lies in more recent periods and other themes besides settlement, human burials and saga sites.

Archaeological survey has had a long tradition in Iceland, beginning in the 19th century (FRIÐRIKSSON 1994). More recent survey, driven by new legislation in 1989 has aimed to achieve total survey of districts and regions; between 1995-2005 the Institute of Archaeology, Iceland [www.instarch.is] has surveyed 70,000 sites using documentary sources and recorded 17,000 sites in the field. Although this underlying work has added much to the knowledge of archaeology it is particularly biased by written sources, contemporary oral knowledge and histories. Aerial photography is currently not a routine source in field survey, though the project looking at linear earthworks in the north-east of Iceland has demonstrated its valuable contribution to recording new sites and features (EINARSSON-HANSSON-VÉSTEINSSON 2002; ALDRED *et alii* 2004 and 2005).

Aerial photography in Iceland

The history of flight in Iceland is usually traced back to 1919 and the first aerial photographs were taken the same year. Over the next few years, oblique aerial photographs were sporadically taken, most often of the capital Reykjavik and its environs and usually by Icelandic portrait photographers. However, in the summers of 1937/38 the first aerial photographs of Iceland for cartographic purposes were taken. These photographs, which were mostly oblique shots, were of the interior and taken to complete the first detailed 1.100,000 maps of the country undertaken by the Danish cartography institute, (Geodætisk Institute) which began early 20th century.

Fig 1: The picture shows Dalatangi which is the outermost point between Mjóifjörður and Seyðisfjörður fjords in East of Iceland. Notice the small spread of farms on the coastal edge typical of a fjord landscape. The picture was taken by the Icelandic geologist Oddur Sigurðsson.

The Second World War marked the beginning of expansion in aerial photography in Iceland: German, British and American military aerial photographs of towns and the countryside are an invaluable resource on the landscape which has been enormously transformed in the last 50 years as many ruins have disappeared through levelling, new building and general development. The first Icelander to take up aerial photography in Iceland to any extent was Ágúst Böðvarsson. He worked as a guide for the Danish who were surveying Iceland in the 1930s and later studied surveying and cartography at the Danish cartography institute. For decades he was the leading authority in aerial photography in Iceland he held the position of Managing Director of the National Land Survey of Iceland from 1959 to 1976 (BRAGASON-GUÐMUNDSSON 1988). The National Land Survey of Iceland (Landmælingar Íslands – NLSI) was founded in the 1950s and part of its programme from the start has been to systematically take and collect vertical aerial photographs of the country. The NLSI continues this work today and each year, takes many photographs all over the country and now has a collection of over 150,000 images. Besides these, it also curates older photographs such as the Danish survey images and the German, British and American military aerial photographs. Since 1990 private companies have also started to build up an aerial photographic archive, particularly Hnit ehf and Loftmyndir ehf who have near national coverage of vertical shots in digital format. Both companies mainly take vertical (colour) aerials at 1400 to 8000 meters in altitude.

Over the last the last two decades, aerial photographs have started to be used in archaeological research. In the last quarter of the 20th century, the first systematic archaeological surveys of the country commenced and in the last decade, tremendous progress has been made and the number of sites registered, increased dramatically. In the same period, usage of aerial photography in archaeology survey multiplied such that the current situation is that most survey's now use aerial photographs at some stage in their work. In most cases the photographs are vertical aerial photographs, often from fairly high altitude, as their main purpose is for large-scale mapping. Such images are used to plot known ruins and show their location in reports. In rare cases, photographs are taken at low enough altitudes so that new and unknown sites can be identified from them. Consequently, archaeologists began to take low-level oblique photographs for their own purposes, though this has always been as part of specific projects. Recent developments have combined high resolution satellite imagery (SPOT 5 panchromatic 2.5m pixel resolution) with stereo-paired vertical aerial photographs, where extensive earthworks, such as linear boundaries, can be seen and matched on both sources. These features have then been integrated into a GIS and assigned attributes describing their type, condition, interpretation and identification number which then corresponds to an external database with matched records containing more metadata about the mapping process (ALDRED *et alii* 2004).

Aerial photography and survey in Iceland for archaeological purposes is circumscribed by rather specific conditions. On the one hand, arable farming is not a major element of the Icelandic landscape, where sheep and dairy farming dominates – therefore cropmarks and soilmarks do not constitute any appreciable component of aerial photography work in the country. Indeed, because of this, much archaeology survive as earthworks which remains the dominant type of site accessible through aerial sources. Although buried archaeology does exist, especially in the wake of homefield levelling after the war, such buried archaeology rarely constitutes infilled negative features (e.g. systems of ditches etc.) which are characteristic of lowland areas in other parts of Europe and thus parchmarks and related phenomena are also of limited value. On the other hand, much of the landscape that was settled at some period from the first settlement (Icel: *landnám*) and until the middle of 20th century have now been abandoned. Some of these areas are difficult to reach or see at ground level, and aerial survey would play a significant role for both discovering and mapping these sites and preparing the ground for a full field survey.

Archaeology and aerial photography

In the late 1970s and early 1980s Sveinbjörn Rafnsson used oblique aerial photography as an integral part of his survey of deserted valleys in the east of Iceland. This was the first practical use of aerial survey specifically for archaeology, and he took both conventional and infra-red images. However, the flights were largely directed at previously known sites in order to get a basic record, and no detailed transcription mapping was involved (RAFNSSON 1990) In the 1980s, Guðrún Sveinbjarnardóttir conducted regional studies of farm abandonment in Iceland which formed the basis of her doctoral thesis and during this, made occasional use of aerial photography (SVEINBJARNARDÓTTIR 1992). In the 1990s, the Institute of Archaeology began extensive field surveys in which they initiated aerial survey fly-overs with Garðar Guðmundsson taking many oblique shots in both conventional and infra-red format. This programme however was short-lived.

The first and probably only publication on the use of aerial photography in archaeology in Iceland was in 1995. The article discussed the use of the technique in relation to features on farms and land around Reykjavík and particularly highlighted the advantages of photography under conditions of light snow (ÍSAKSON-HELGASON 1995). Photographs had been taken of the same site under different conditions, using both conventional and infra-red film and these methods are discussed in the article.

The article also attempted to discuss the specific nature of aerial survey in Iceland as well as promote its more systematic use in archaeology.

None of the previously mentioned studies used aerial photography to map sites or features. However, the first use of aerial photographs to map features was conducted in 2001 (EINARSSON-HANSSON-VÉSTEINSSON 2002). The potential of vertical photographs showing an extensive system of earthworks in valleys and on heaths in the north east of Iceland was realised and this became a pilot study for a more detailed three year project that started in 2004. The objective was to map an area of 3,164 sq km with at least 267 km (2005 record) of linear earthworks in detail using both vertical and oblique photographs, in combination with ground survey and limited excavation. Concurrently, the project aimed to promote and develop the methodology of aerial survey in Iceland, as well as date the earthworks and relate them to early settlement patterns from 9th to 11th century AD (ALDRED *et alii* 2004 and 2005).

Fig. 2: Transcription of the boundary project directed by Árni Einarsson (after ALDRED et alii 2005). The figure shows the area which has undergone intensive aerial research, using a combination of vertical and oblique photographs as well as high resolution SPOT 5 satellite imagery to map the extensive boundary systems.

Fig. 3: Extensive boundaries on Fljótsheiði in north east Iceland. The boundaries can be seen as fine lines in the vegetation, running both parallel and cross contours on the heath. The picture was taken by Árni Einarsson in spring of 2004.

Fig. 4: Ruins of a weaning fold, several fishing booths and horse tracks seen to the left of the picture on the boundary between the þufa (frost-thaw hummocks) and the improved land. In Bakki, north of town Húsavík in northeast Iceland. Picture was taken by Árni Einarsson in the spring of 2006.

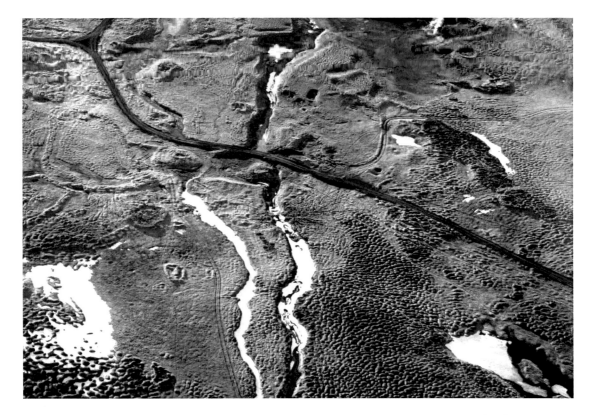

Fig. 5:   Þeistareykir in Aðaldælahreppi in north east Iceland, an active volcanic area. The farmstead is located highland (344 m. a.s.l.) and around it are various remains of buildings connected to the it as well as remains early of sulphur mining activity. The picture was taken by Árni Einarsson in the spring of 2006.

Archaeology on the edge ?

In the context of Europe Iceland's archaeological resource is similar to other countries in many ways. In terms of environmental variability, Iceland's archaeology is extreme. The human impact on the landscape as well as fluctuating climatic conditions has resulted in rapid changes in land cover and created the conditions for large areas of soil erosion (Edwards et al 2005). It is likely that these landscape changes, in the context of social upheaval and the colonisation of an unfamiliar and harsh landscape, created specific cultural responses, particularly in the regulation of land, as is suggested by the extensive system of linear earthworks in north-east Iceland (ALDRED *et alii* 2005). Natural agents have influenced the types of cultural responses, and this is evident in choices for the locations of settlement, routes, ritual and folklore, activity areas, industry and land markings. Cultural activity as seen in the archaeological record has a strong association with natural features and monuments, though this factor is particularly true of all the Scandinavian countries where the dichotomy of nature: culture is diffused within the perceptions of landscape (BRADLEY 2000; DESCOLA PÁLSSON 1996).

In the last part of this paper we would like to give examples of types of settlement and other archaeological features commonly found in Iceland and how aerial photographs can be used to illustrate both the archaeology and the landscape within Iceland.

Farm mounds

The earliest sites in Iceland date to the late 9th century and many of the first settlement farms are still lived on today, exhibiting continuity of occupation for over a thousand years. It was quite common for the farmhouses, which most of the time were built from stone, turf and timber even into the 20th century, to be built and rebuilt on the same location for centuries. In such cases large farm mounds now exist, containing the accumulated remains of buildings and middens of several centuries, mimicking urban stratigraphy – albeit writ small and in an emphatically rural context.

Destruction and survival of archaeology

From late 19th century, but especially since the middle of the 20th century Iceland, like other countries in Europe, experienced rapidly changing settlement patterns, with large parts of once flourishing countryside now abandoned. Since the introduction of agricultural machinery after the Second World War, levelling of homefields has damaged a large proportion of ruins on those farms still lived on. In these places the best

Fig. 6:   Remains of a homefield boundaries at Víkingavatn in Kelduneshreppur in north east Iceland. Furthest to right
          on the picture is the modern day farm on a much earlier farmmound. The boundaries have been flattened out
          during field levelling for land improvement. They are difficult to detect on the ground but appear well in the
          low spring sun when photographed from the air. Picture was taken by Árni Einarsson in the spring of 2006.

Fig. 7:   An abandoned farm close to a modern farm in Kelduneshreppur in north east Iceland. The farm has a double
          enclosure, with farm building and various outhouses inside it. Remains of similair farms are quite common in
          this area. The picture was taken by Árni Einarsson in the spring of 2006.

surviving archaeology is with few exceptions found outside the homefield for example in remains of shielings, shelters and sheep folds (fig 1 rdir), old tracks, cairns, boundaries, (both property boundaries as well as land use partitioning) and quarries (such as peat or turf cutting areas). Other factors, such as natural erosion have also contributed to destruction of archaeological remains, especially desertification, while urban and industrial development have had a much smaller impact on the archaeology than in many other European countries.

Abandonment

In contrast, those farms that were abandoned before the middle of 20th century often have substantial numbers of old turf and stone structures both in and around the homefield. Abandonment and/or relocation are among the main reasons for the preservation of ruins in Iceland. Although many of the first generations of settlers in Iceland seem to have chosen locations for their farms that remained stable throughout the centuries, in some instances the original/early location of settlement farms seem to have been abandoned, because of social or environmental factors. In these cases settlement remains of the 9th and 10th centuries can be seen on the surface and are not buried beneath later farm mounds. Later, as Iceland became more densely populated, the edges of settlement moved closer to the highlands. However, in later times as the population decreased and the climate deteriorated, these marginal settlements, often in the innermost parts of valleys or side-valleys or up on the edge of highland, were abandoned. Many such areas were never re-settled and thus remained undamaged by later activity.

Concluding remarks

Icelandic archaeology is, like any other, largely moulded by the land's location, its landscape and its environmental conditions. In that sense it does not differ from the rest of Europe. What makes it different is that the country has no prehistory and the history of settlement is consequently short compared to most of the rest of Europe. It is also different in the sense that a large part of marginal settlements that were once occupied on a permanent or seasonal basis have now been abandoned. The remains of these settlements are often visible on the surface and in many places no investigation has yet taken place. The role of aerial archaeology in locating, mapping and researching these remains in Iceland has great potential but so far has not been exploited. It is hoped that this will change, and that this paper, in a small way, will contribute to this change.

Oscar ALDRED (oscar@instarch.is) and
Elín Ósk HREIÐARSDÓTTIR (elin@instarch.is)
Institute of Archaeology, Iceland
Fornleifastofnun Íslands
Bárugata 3
101 REYKJAVÍK
Iceland
[www.instarch.is]

Apologizes

This article was written by the authors in 2005-06 but due to various difficulties it was only published in 2011, for which I want to apologize sincerely – Marc Lodewijckx (editor).

References

ALDRED Oscar, Elín Ósk HREIÐARSDÓTTIR, Birna LÁRUSDÓTTIR and Árni EINARSSON 2004. Forn garðlög í Suður Þingeyjarsýslu, *Fornleifastofnun Íslands FS257-04261*, Reykjavík.

ALDRED Oscar, Elín Ósk HREIÐARSDÓTTIR, Birna LÁRUSDÓTTIR and Árni EINARSSON 2005. Forn garðlög í Suður Þingeyjarsýslu – A System of Earthworks in NE Iceland, *Fornleifastofnun Íslands FS292-04262*, Reykjavík.

BRADLEY R. 2000. *An Archaeology of Natural Places*, London and New York, Routledge.

BRAGASON Þorvaldur and Magnús GUÐMUNDSSON 1988. *Fifty Years of Change and Development: Aerial Photographs from Iceland*, Hörpuútgáfan, Landmælingar Íslands.

DESCOLA P. and Gísli PÁLSSON 1996. Chapter 1 Introduction. In P. DESCOLA and Gísli PÁLSSON (Eds.), *Nature and Society. Anthropological Perspectives*, London, Routledge: 1 21.

EDWARDS K.J, I.T. LAWSON, E. ERLENDSSON and A.J. DUGMORE 2005. Landscapes of Contrast in Viking Age Iceland and the Faroe Islands, *Landscapes* 2005/2: 63-81

EINARSSON Árni, Oddgeir HANSSON and Orri VÉSTEINSSON 2002. An Extensive System of Medieval Earthworks in Northeast Iceland, *Archaeologia Islandica* 2: 61-73.

FRIDRIKSSON Adolf 1994. *Sagas and Popular Antiquarianism in Icelandic Archaeology*, Aldershot.

ÍSAKSON Sigurjón Páll and Þorgeir S. HELGASON 1995. Vetrarmyndir frá Nesi við Seltjörn og Laugarnesi, *Árbók hins íslenzka fornleifafélagi 1994* (with English summary).

RAFNSSON Sveinbjörn 1990. *Eyðibyggð í Hrafnkelsdal og á Brúardölum: Brot úr byggðarsögu Íslands*, Rit hins íslenzka fornleifafélags, Reykjavík.

SVEINBJARNARDÓTTIR Guðrún 1992. *Farm Abandonment in Medieval and Post-Medieval Iceland – An Interdisciplinary Study*, Oxbow Monograph 17.

THE 'ICCD-AEROFOTOTECA NAZIONALE' AERIAL PHOTO COLLECTIONS

M. FILOMENA BOEMI

Introduction

The activity of the *Istituto Centrale per il Catalogo e la Documentazione* – ICCD[1] is founded upon two interconnected operational services, the General Informative Catalogue System[2] and the Photography Area. Although it is one of the many subjects involved in the Catalogue System, photography alone is present in ICCD with truly consistent collections. This means that ICCD has to deal with many operations and problems connected with the management of visual heritage: conservation, restoration, cataloguing, digitisation and divulgation.

The ICCD photographic collection consists of the holdings of the National Aerial Photography Archives (*Aerofototeca Nazionale*)[3], the National Photographic Archives (*Fototeca Nazionale*)[4] and the Museum/ Archive of Historical Photography (*Museo/Archivio di Fotografia Storica* – MAFOS), summing up to a large number of images that constitute one of Italy's most important collections, both for its intrinsic quality and its sheer number. Dating from the invention of photography down to the 1950s, it comprises a thorough survey of subjects and processes. In addition, the Photographic Laboratory's highly professional activity contributes to the Institute's collections, as new photographic campaigns keep focussing on protected cultural heritage nation-wide.

A considerable effort is currently being made by ICCD to make photographs available for searching and purchasing through its Internet site. Searching can be carried out either in the entire photographic database or in single collections, but also through data contained in the *Photo Records* and *Subject/Object Records*. Through the e-commerce service it will be possible to buy copies of the selected images printed by colour laser, or a digital image on CD-ROM, or to download a file with the image. To the already available collection of historical images the Institute is now adding aerial photographs and a large collection of digital photos by its Photographic Laboratory, well illustrating Italian artistic and monumental heritage. Besides the output of digital-born images, the Institute is pursuing a consistent policy of digitization of earlier photographs on traditional support.

The importance of the photographic and catalographic collections, for a large part already available on the web, and its status as authority in the uniforming of Italian cataloguing methods have established ICCD as a main party both in the development of new technologies applied to cultural heritage and in the necessary training.

The Aerofototeca Nazionale

The *Aerofototeca Nazionale*, i.e. Italy's National Aerial Photography Archives, holds on its own over 2 million aerial photographs. These images, taken from the early 1900s up to the 1990s, constitute evidence of both an objective and historical kind. Thanks to the vast surveyed area the archives provide an excellent overview of the Italian landscape, outstanding in comparison with any traditional, symbolic cartographic representation.

The photographs are housed in the Negative (films and plates) Archive and in the Prints Archive, divided in collections and then in sections organized by geographic criteria. They include the earliest photographs of the Roman Forum, taken from a balloon by the Specialisti del Genio in 1889, by initiative of the archaeologist Giacomo Boni, and later in 1908 (fig. 1); the photos of the course of the river Tiber (1908) (fig. 2), of Pompeii (1910) and Venice (1911, 1913) (fig. 3), also taken by the Specialisti. The last two were used to produce the earliest photomaps, using point by point mapping technique.

One of the main collections is that of World War II aerial reconnaissance images by the British Royal Air Force (RAF), dated 1943-1945 and focussed on the main strategical targets, at scales of approximately 1.10.000 or 1:50.000 according to the lenses employed, the size of photographs is 24x24 cm or 18x24 cm. These photos were taken during reconnaissance missions (the s.c. *sorties*) that departed from the military base of S. Severo (Puglia); they cover only a limited part of Southern Italy (figs. 4-5). Reconnaissance flights by the U.S.A. Air Force (USAAF, today USAF) cover only limited areas of Northern Italy in 1945 (fig. 6).

Fig. 1:   Rome, early 1900s. The Engineer Corps specialized in aerial photography (Brigata Specialisti dell'Arma del
Genio, Sezione Fotografica) prepare the air balloon in front of Maxentius' Basilica, in the Roman Forum. The
photographic camera was suspended to the balloon, anchored to the ground by a strong rope. The first aerial
photos of the Roman Forum were taken in 1889.

Fig. 2: 1908. Aerial photomosaic of the Tiber north of Rome. To the right: the special raft used by the Brigata Specialisti as an anchoring point for the balloon.

Fig. 3:   *Venice, 1913. The first large scale aerophotogrammetric plan produced by the Brigata Specialisti. This time the photographs were taken from an airship, the 'Parseval'.*

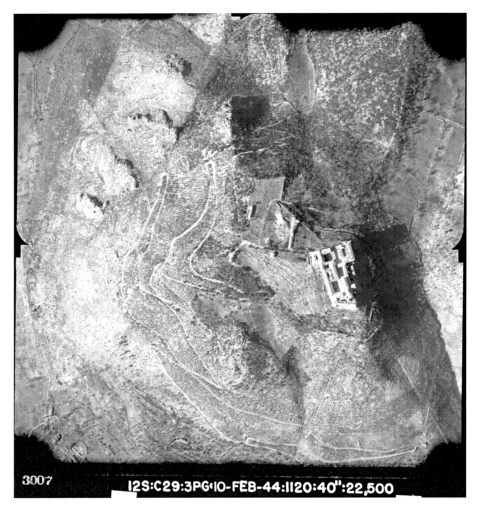

Fig. 4:   *Central Italy, February 10, 1944. Aerial photo of the Montecassino Abbey by the British Royal Air Force (RAF). At this time the mountain area of Cassino was the battlefront during the advance of the Allied army.*

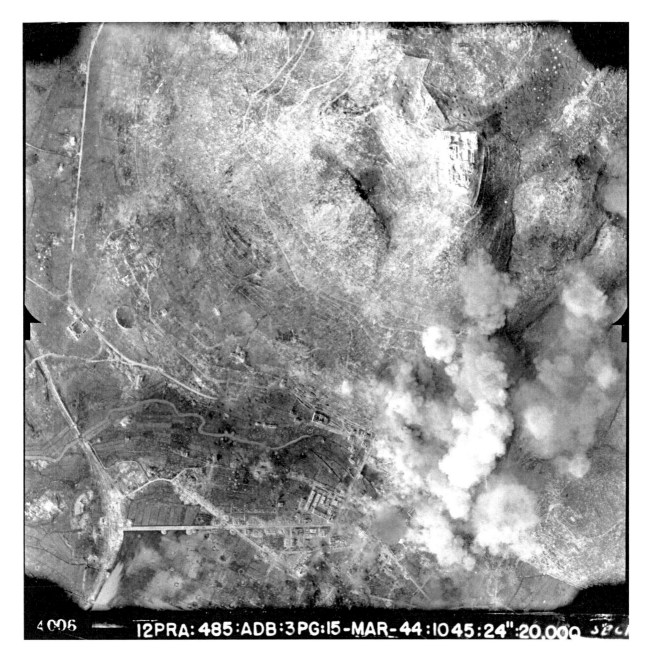

Fig. 5: Central Italy, March 15, 1944. Aerial photo of the Montecassino Abbey by the British Royal Air Force (RAF), during its bombing by the Allied army.

Also present is the s.c. GAI flight, also called 'base flight', dating from 1954-1956 and showing the whole national territory in stereoscopy. The negative plates measure 24x24 or 20x20 cm; the scale is 1:33.000 in the peninsular part of Italy, lower in the Alpine region (fig. 7).

The so called 'integrative flights' are a number of sets of vertical photographs taken over the Italian territory from the early 1900s up to 1991, in different scale and with partial coverage. These photographs, besides the 24x24 cm format traditional to the vertical views, are also in a special 24x48 cm format, employed by the Italian Air

Force (fig. 8), or a 30x30 cm one used in war time both by the Italian Royal Air Force and the German Luftwaffe (fig. 9). Among the integrative material the richest collections are those transferred to the Aerofototeca by the Italian Air Force and those by private firms such as EIRA, ESACTA, Aerotop-Lisandrelli and Aerofoto Consult (fig. 10).

Also represented in the Aerofototeca collections are oblique photographs produced by the Italian Air Force and by firms such as Fotocielo (colour and b/w), Aerotop and I-BUGA (colour), with coverage's over many years and different areas (fig. 11).

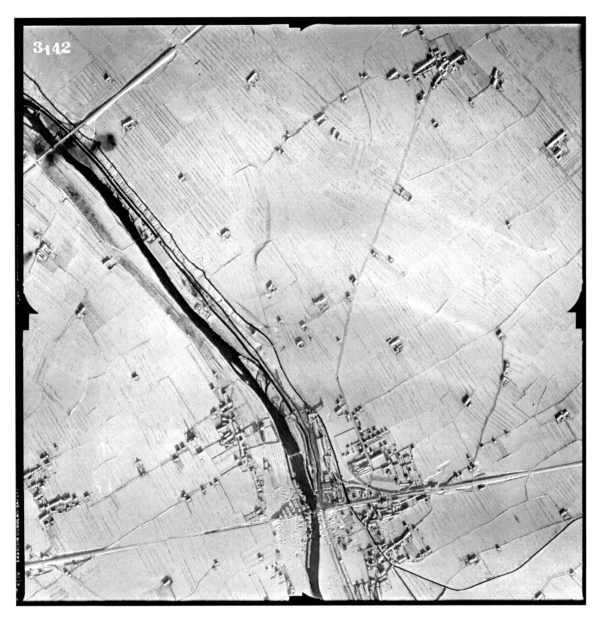

Fig. 6:   Ponte di Cividino, Lombardia, January 29, 1945. Aerial photo by the USAAF of the land under the snow. Traces of bombing of the railway bridge (bottom) on the river Oglio are visible, as well as those of an earlier bombing around the bridge to the north.

Aerial photos in the Aerofototeca Nazionale have been used, from the very first, to support research by officers and specialists in the Italian Ministry for Cultural Heritage, especially for archaeological purposes (fig. 12). A new use of this material is made today by means of digital photogrammetry and georeferencing.

The Aerofototeca is currently availing itself of three different software applications:

1. ArcView 8.3 for georeferencing raster images;
2. Archie, an ArcView application that allows the management of large-sized archives;
3. GestArc, a module integrated in Archie that creates vectorial reference layers from existing graphics;
4. Geodos, a sw that creates vectorial graphics directly from aerial photographs or from existing graphics.

Fig 7: Lucca, Tuscany, 1954. Aerial photo from the Volo Base collection, showing the Tuscan city inside its medieval walls and the surrounding territory. Traces of the Roman division of land (the regular plots of cultivated land) and of the ancient course of the river Auser (dark curving area, bottom r.) can also be detected.

Managing the Aerofototeca Archive, today

Archie is an ArcView application that allows the management of large-sized archives (with vectorial reference layers) so as to be able to select photograms or strips of specific areas and with particular characteristics. Archie manages archives in which information is stored that describes both the strips and the individual photograms of one or more aerial film.

Archie allows.

1. screen displays of the geographical area on which users want to make consultations and overlay on video the edges of the photograms;
2. spatial queries. The efficiency of spatial queries very much depends on how appropriate they are for a particular application domain and on which layers they lay.

Fig. 8: Tavoliere, Puglia, 1968. Large dimension (24x48) aerial view by the Italian Air Force showing the area of Trinitapoli with the salt pans of Margherita di Savoia (bottom).

The main functions of Archie are:

1. setting selection criteria, based on the technical characteristics of the photograms so as to obtain the list of the photograms that satisfy a preselected criteria (e.g. all the photograms taken before 1985 on scale < 1:10000 can be selected);

2. identifying one or more objects in the territory (e.g. an area with particular constraints) to get the list of photograms that regard totally or partially that area;

3. combining in cascade the previous operations (e.g. selecting the photograms that relate to a particular area and subsequently selecting from them only those that were filmed on a certain date);

4. identifying, after selecting a photogram, all the photograms with a common characteristic (e.g. all those with the same date, or the same flight height).

To simplify consultation Archie offers auxiliary functionalities that allow users to find easily and quickly the geographical area of interest. These functionalities allow users to:

1. identify a zone on the basis of a toponym;
2. add toponyms to facilitate subsequent searches;
3. save the status of a search with a name;
4. recall a previously saved and identified status so as to be able to continue the search.

If the photograms (or some of them) have been rasterized, Archie allows users to display the selected ones for video consultation. However if the photograms have not been rasterized, print functions can be activated for reports containing the list of photograms currently selected, with the relative characteristics or maps scaled suitably for the zone in question and the photograms selected.

The organization of the descriptors of the photograms in one or more information layers depends exclusively on the organizational criteria chosen by the body that manages the archive of aerial photographs. Archie can thus operate both on one archive and on different archives in which the manager has divided the descriptors according to his/her own criteria.

An archive generally has aerial photographs from many strips and from several filming flights. This implies that, in addition to the overlay of photograms belonging to a certain strip, there are overlays between strips belonging to the same flight and to different flights. Overlaying a great number of photograms creates display problems and makes it difficult to select with a mouse the photograms that are of interest. To resolve this problem, Archie allows one to adopt a hierarchical approach by making a series of restrictions on the data selected, both spatial and alphanumerical.

The availability of descriptors of aerial photographs with data processing support entails a data digitizing process, both for the alphanumerical part and for the graphic part. In most cases today for newly produced material suppliers companies are required to provide descriptors in numerical format. Archie allows the digitization of descriptors via the Gestarc module.

Digitizing the geographical part consists in 'outlining' the edges of the photograms on a reference background. Typically this involves using a scanner-acquired image of the flight graphic, on which the edge of the photograms have already been outlined and that has georeferenced (with ArcView or other sw).

Before starting digitizing, GestArc asks the user to set the characteristics that are common for a series of photograms belonging to the same strip (collection, strip number, date period, height). When the edges of the photograms are digitized the characteristics of the strip are automatically reported in the descriptor of the photogram.

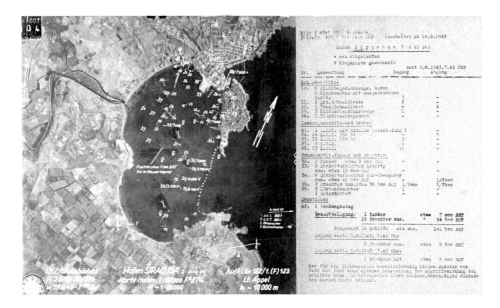

Fig. 9:   *Siracusa, Sicily, August 8, 1943. Aerial photo of the harbour by the German Luftwaffe, with the corresponding*
intelligence annotations on the right, assessing the number, type and force of the anchored ships.

Fig. 10· Rome, 1986. View of the center of the city with the Roman Forum by the Italian aerophotography firm
Aerofoto Consult, now in the collections of the Aerofototeca Nazionale.

Fig. 11: Venice, 1979. Aerial view by the Italian aerophotography firm I_BUGA, now in the collections of the Aerofototeca Nazionale.

When the digitizing of the area covered by a photogram has terminated, a Photogram window appears so that the technical characteristics of the current photogram can be inserted, such as the number of the photogram, scale, notes. If necessary, users can in any case access another window that allows them to insert or modify the value of the other attributes.

The number of the photogram is proposed by the system but can be modified. GestArc checks that number is unique within a strip. The settings of the scale, orientation of the label (reporting the photogram number) the notes and any other attributes, are maintained for subsequent photograms, until they are expressly modified. The position and orientation of the writing are determined when digitizing takes place, following a predetermined and suitable order. If errors are found, the orientation of the writing can be modified, without having to redigitize the edges of the photogram; however, in order to insert the correction in the alphanumeric data base the position must be cancelled and reacquired.

Both when consulting and acquiring, operators act in a logical window, or work area, defined as the geographical area within which some data are active (descriptors and reference background). The description of a work area can be stored via a symbolic name and when the work area is called the same situation is presented as when it was saved (e.g. with reference background, selection and zooms). It is thus possible to interrupt the work to begin it again later, or to save the information related to a geographical area and the reference data for re-use in other work sessions.

An example of consultation

The area on which the consultation is to be made can be identified via successive zooms on a reference map or via a toponym; it is advisable to proceed by removing records that are not relevant to the research.
1. Select a broader area presumably containing the research area (fig. 13);

Fig. 12a-b: Rome, April 3, 1953. Aerial view of the Centocelle airport (a). In this photo archaeologists were able to
              detect the traces of a large Roman villa (b, corresponding to the area with an asterisk).

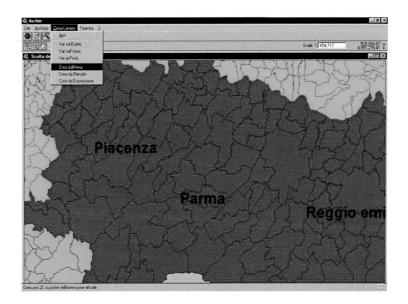

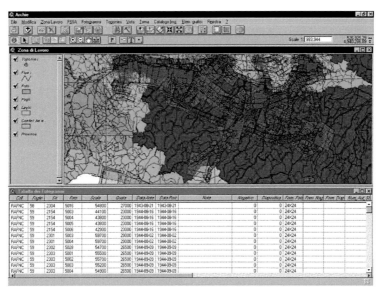

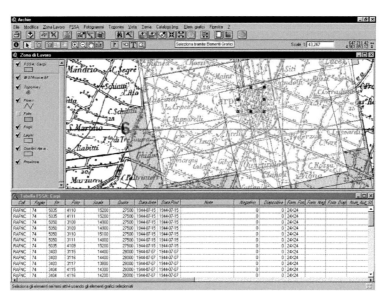

Figs. 13-15: Examples of the use of sw Archie in cataloguing and researching aerial photographs in the Aerofototeca Nazionale collections.

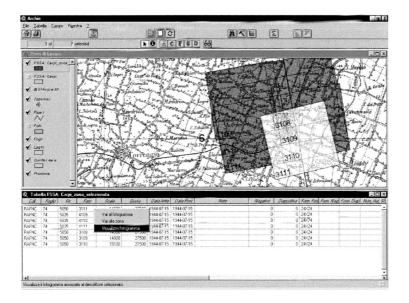

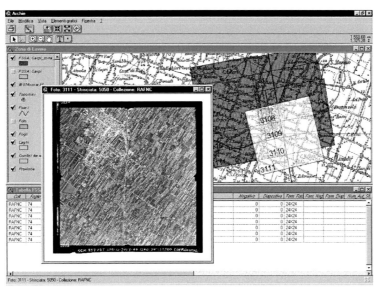

Figs. 16-17: Examples of the use of sw Archie in cataloguing and researching aerial photographs in the Aerofototeca Nazionale collections.

2. Select all photos contained in the broader area (fig. 14);
3. Load the informative layers supporting the consultation (e.g. IGM Raster maps, toponyms, etc.),
4. Locate the research area using the loaded informative layers;
5. Select those intersecting the research area (fig. 15);
6. Remove all unnecessary records on the basis of their parameters;
7. Load the photogram numbers as they appear on the image;
8. Select the matching record/s (fig. 16);
9. Display images, if available (fig. 17); otherwise, print the first four record descriptors to detect the required images in the archive.

Looking ahead

The Aerofototeca is currently developing a project to make its collections available to the public through Internet, allowing it to browse or to make different kinds of geographical research in the collections. Theoretically a simple project, it requires however some effort on the part of the Aerofototeca and its financing authorities, as it will constitute the means of recovering both the large quantity of material produced in a traditional way (photo prints on paper, graphs on paper or film), the rasterized images produced in the past decade and the databases presently in use.

The new system is based on two main archival levels:

1. the catalogued photo archive, containing the description of photos in a numerical form; this enables the research of images on the basis of coverage, date and technical characteristics of the images;
2. the raster photo archive, containing raster images in different resolutions, each with a small descriptive record.

The two archives will be linked so that starting from an identified image in the catalogued photo archive it will be possible to reach the raster photo or vice versa.

The system is composed by a Back Office, engaged in the flow from primary archive to operative archives, and a Front Office, offering access to the operative archives for the public. The users are the Aerofototeca staff, acting in a local net logic; guests (external users, also acting in a local net logic); Web users. In principle, the approach to the archive is the same for all users, apart from the possibility of limiting access via Web to restricted material or for SW development and upkeep.

We feel sure that it will be possible, in a hopefully near future, to access the Aerofototeca collections in a range of easy and constructive ways, always with the highest degree of scientific skill.

M. Filomena BOEMI
Director ICCD-Aerofototeca Nazionale
Via di San Michele 18
ROMA 153
Italy

Apologizes

This article was written by the author in 2005-06 but due to various difficulties it was only published in 2011, for which I want to apologize sincerely – Marc Lodewijckx (editor).

Mariella Boemi retired in 2009. Since then many changes have been undertaken. However, the present text is still largely valid – Elizabeth J. Schepherd (Aerofototeca Nazionale).

[1] http://www.iccd.beniculturali.it
[2] In Italian: *Sistema Informativo Generale del Catalogo.*
[3] http://aerofototeca.iccd.beniculturali.it
[4] http://aerofototeca.iccd.beniculturali.it

HERITAGE STEWARDSHIP: A NEW TOOL FOR OLD HERITAGE

KARL CORDEMANS

In all aspects of its assignment to care of the open space, the Flemish Land Agency is confronted with cultural historical elements of various kind and importance. In order to assure the conservation and proper management of these elements, a new tool is being developed: the heritage stewardship. The mechanism and framework is largely inspired by the current agri-environmental agreements, in execution of the Rural Development Plan and Council Regulation 1257/1999. The frameset is to financially compensate farmers or private persons for the loss of income, the work invested and costs maid by managing cultural historical heritage.

1. Introduction

The Flemish Land Agency (VLM) is a public company assigned to 'take care of the open space'. To achieve its goal, the agency has five 'tasks': land-use planning, land consolidation, nature development, regulation of the manure problem and a support centre GIS Flanders. This paper only focuses on the first three instruments.

Rural development projects responding to the various claims on the open space and trying to meet with the integration of functions in the open space and sustainable development are of vital importance. One of these functions is cultural history. Whenever possible, the cultural historical identity of a project area is conserved or when possible enhanced by using heritage as an inspiration. One of the problems encountered in the merging of past and present is guaranteeing the future management. Up to now, the agency bought or obtained archaeological valuable parcels or monuments. Maintenance, conservation or reconstruction are carried out in the case of monuments, fields are evaluated and appreciated in the case of archaeological sites and afterwards, the monument or field is bestowed to a public administration to ensure an appropriate management. This is an expensive, time consuming and often impossible procedure. In partial answer to this burden, the heritage stewardship – before November 2005 it was called *cultural historical stewardship* – is being developed.

2. Stewardship ?

2.1. Definition

A stewardship can be defined as a voluntary contract between a public authority and a private person or a company for a specified time, in which one party undertakes himself to fulfil a number of acts: the management measures. In return for these acts, the other party pays a compensation. The intention of a stewardship is to raise, maintain or create a certain value (nature, environment, cultural history, etc).

2.2. Other measures offered by the Flemish Land Agency

At present, the measures offered by the agency mainly focus on the protection of meadow birds, buffer strips, the management of 'small landscape elements' such as ponds and hedgerows, botanical management and the reduction of manuring. In the near future erosion management end measures for the protection of hamsters will apply. All measures are in execution of chapter 6 of the Rural Development Plan complying with Council regulation n° 1257/1999 on support for rural development from the European Agricultural Guidance and Guarantee Fund (EAGGF) of the Council of the European Union. Other measures in the Flemish Rural Development Plan are a/o investment support for farmers, measures for green coverage, mechanical weeding, genetic diversity, reduction of pesticide use in ornamental horticulture...

2.3. Heritage stewardship

The heritage stewardship complies with the regular and overdue maintenance and necessary measures for the safeguarding of immovable rural heritage. A first category of heritage aimed at are artificial landscape features such as dykes, raised fields, mottes and duck decoys. A second category is the build rural heritage such as chapels, pillboxes, baking houses and ice cellars. Thirdly, the soil record in all its aspects is intended. This includes archaeological sites (crop mark sites, moated sites and occupation sites) and palaeo-ecological or geomorphological heritage such as creek ridges, peat layers or mires. Also 'woody' heritage is eligible such as ancient solitary trees, hedges... Finally, traditional crops who have a large impact on identity (such as hop) can be preserved. The stewardship is only directed to local rural heritage that doesn't receive funding of any kind for the maintenance. Regionally important sites and features will still be acquired.

2.4. Demand for heritage stewardship ?

The development of this new stewardship is a consequence of the growing need in the field for an instrument to ensure the management of rural heritage. A quick scan of the agency's project of the past 4 years shows at least 40 features that might as well have been managed by a heritage stewardship. Most features are archaeological sites (especially moated sites and Roman villa's), but also a chapel, an orchard, a crop mark site, a duck decoy, a redoubt, a sheepfold and a little bridge. A better turn to account of the available budget could be obtained with the new stewardship. A few sites selected on regional, scientific and/or recreational importance are acquired, while the management of the others is arranged by the stewardship. At the same time, the number of heritage features taken in account will go up. Archaeological crop mark sites are up to now rarely managed. With a flexible and easy instrument to manage this type of sites, they will become much more appreciated and incorporated.

2.5. Inspiration

Without going into much detail, it is worthwhile noting that interesting examples can be found in many countries, like for instance the U.S.A. The State of Florida offers easements to private persons in order to preserve and manage their heritage. These are 'made to fit' arrangements in which the protection and management is registered. The owner is assisted by non-profit organizations. In exchange for this, a tax benefit is granted. In New Zealand, the *Historic Places Trust* makes covenants with owners to ensure proper management. These covenants are bound to the ground and remain legitimate when the owner sells his property.

The United Kingdom has already a long tradition in stewardship-like heritage management. As early as 1972, acknowledgement Payments were maid for taking archaeological sites out off cultivation (OXFORD ARCHAEOLOGY 2002). In execution of the Rural Development Regulation, the Countryside Stewardship Scheme was set up in 1991. One of the eligible measures in this scheme is buffer strip management for the protection of archaeological sites. Other measures for the managing of the historic landscape included in the scheme are maintenance of orchards, ditches and dykes (PATERSON-WADE-MARTINS 1999).

In 2001, the Rural Enterprise Scheme became active. This scheme also holds a package for the protection and management of rural heritage (MAFF 2000). In 2003, the new Entry Level Scheme was introduced (DEFRA 2003). The scheme offers a series of management options designed to prevent further damage and to improve the condition of many archaeological sites and historic buildings and features. Even more recent, several 'Countryside Archaeological Advisers' were employed to advise farmers in archaeology friendly farming and to help them through the different Schemes. The Advisers are jointly paid for by the Department for Environment, Food and Rural Affairs, English Heritage and the County (ESSEX COUNTY COUNCIL 2003).

In the Netherlands several projects on the management of archaeological sites have taken place or are ongoing. Most of these projects are about the use of non-tillage or minimum-tillage techniques, the conversion of farmland into meadow or the adjustment of groundwater levels (VAN HEERINGEN-THEUNISSEN 2002). Recently, a study was made about archaeological stewardship modules, how to finance these and where to find support for it (TERWAN 2004). Some attention is paid to wider aspects of cultural heritage. In the community of Meerssen, management plans are drown for the management of chapels, trees, baking houses, archaeological sites etc. (oral communication R. VAN DER ENDEN).

3. Cultural heritage management in Flanders

3.1. Legal framework

The Flemish legislation offers some opportunities on subsidizing the management of rural heritage. The Decree on the Protection of Monuments and Landscapes of 1976 provides in financial support for managing heritage features. However, this is limited to protected heritage. The Decree on the Protection of Archaeological Heritage of 1993 is similar to the first, but is focused on protected archaeological sites. Up to now, no sites are protected yet. Even if a site is protected, correct management is not guaranteed: an archaeological site located on farmland is only protected in so far that the normal agricultural practice is not disturbed: a site that has been deep ploughed before, can continue to be deep ploughed.

In 1999, a Decree on Small Historical Heritage was issued. This decree foresaw a subsidy of 40% to non-protected heritage and for amounts even below 1250 EUR. Its application range was very wide: from fountains over statues to trees and fences. Unfortunately, due to the lack of interest induced by the administrative and regulatory burden, it was ended in 2000. Recently, a Decree on Heritage landscapes was voted. This will also provide possibilities for the subsidising of management of heritage features. The disadvantage of this regulation however, is the restriction to designated heritage landscapes and the rather complicated procedure. A management plan has to be drawn up and for each landscape a commission has to be installed. None of the above regulations proved to be an answer to the urgent need for an adequate instrument in the management of non-protected rural heritage.

3.2. Other frameworks

More structural attention to rural heritage is paid by the Regional Landscapes. These non-governmental organisations established by the Decree on Nature Conservation of 1997, take care of nature and landscape in large areas. The last few years, some projects have been initiated for the conservation of rural heritage elements. They maintain chapels, field crosses, field roads, orchards, etc.

Recently, several Rural Development projects focusing on non-protected rural heritage, were approved. Especially the provinces of East-Flanders and West-Flanders and more recently the province of Limburg are active in this field. In their Provincial Rural Development Plan, attention is paid to the preservation of small cultural historical heritage, the management of valuable, non-protected buildings in the countryside and how to deal with cultural historical heritage.

4. Heritage stewardship

4.1. Set up

A first set up dates back to 2000, when an internal working group of landscape specialists and archaeologists of the Flemish Land Agency assembled a number of heritage features often encountered in projects and suggested management actions for each of these elements. This included archaeological elements, build heritage and landscape features. In continuation of this work, an extensive study on the stewardship was set up. This included a literature review, a more detailed elaboration of the stewardship itself and a start of legislative, organisational and financial framework.

4.2. Elaboration of the stewardship

In order to create a flexible and widely applicable instrument, over 20 heritage features are described in detail. This included archaeological sites, geomorphological phenomena and cultural historical features of different nature (*cfr.* 2.3.). For each of these features the threats are identified and combined with possible mitigations therefore. A distinction was made between management measures that can be done by farmers and specialized measures, only executable by trained professionals. This last category is not included in the heritage stewardship. Listing and combining of all possible measures result in five different stewardship modules: Management of the soil record, Management of cultural historical landscape heritage, Management of cultural historical build heritage, Management of 'woody' heritage and Preservation of traditional crops. For each heritage element, the relevant management options are selected and integrated in a specific stewardship module. We call this the *à-la-carte* approach. This assures for each element the necessary management with respect for the individual characteristics of the monument. To enable this, five modules with an explicit citation, description and corresponding payment of each set of measures will be offered to the European Commission. The selection and combination of measures by experts within modules renders it possible to offer a heritage stewardship to a heritage type that was not included in the starting list.

Management measures are often identical for similar elements. This *a-la-carte* approach will provide us with a flexible instrument with a high performance and the insurance of a correct management.

4.3. Legislative framework

In search for a fitting legislative framework to offer heritage stewardship, four options were investigated: the Decree on heritage landscapes, European projects, the European State Aid Regulation (EU Reg. 659/1999) and the European Regulation on Rural Development (EU Reg. 1257/1999 and following). This last one was retained for several raisons. The EU-commission (FISCHLER 2001) itself indicated the importance of the farmers in the fulfilment of their duty as stewards of the rural heritage. The most important argument is the familiarity of the agency with the procedures of the Rural Development Regulation. The current agro-environmental measures fit into chapter 6 of this regulation. Chapter 9 offers the possibility to install the cultural historical stewardship. Article 33 states that support shall also be granted for measures concerning 'the protection and conservation of the rural heritage'. Also the new regulation 1698/2005 for the second rural development plan states in art. 57, that support is eligible for *the conservation and upgrading of the rural heritage*.

A major advantage of using the Rural Development Regulation as a framework is the spreading of the financial burden (Europe, Flemish Community): indeed measures approved by the European Commission are co-funded for 50%. On the other hand, a lot of rules and regulations have to be followed, which are meticulously controlled by various audits etc. A major issue up to now is the limitation of the measures to farmers and other professionals. The new regulation however does not exclude private persons from receiving financial support. This possibility then has to be foreseen in the new Flemish Rural Development Plan for 2007-2013. For this reason, the choice was made to further develop, tweak and test the heritage stewardship and to effectively start only in 2007. This indicates straightaway one of the major drawbacks: the rather short term of the rural development programme i.e. only 6 years. Never the less, to maximize the management period the land agency is considering an contract duration of 10 years. This means that management agreements have to be regularly renewed and that management is not ensured in the long run. In view of the greater importance of the second and third pillar of the Common Agricultural Policy, approval of the new stewardship by the European Commission is very likely.

4.4. Financial framework

Managers who enter the stewardship receive a compensation for the loss of income caused by the loss of product, extra costs and labour, increased with a small encouragement bonus. For each management measure, an appropriate compensation must be calculated and agreed.

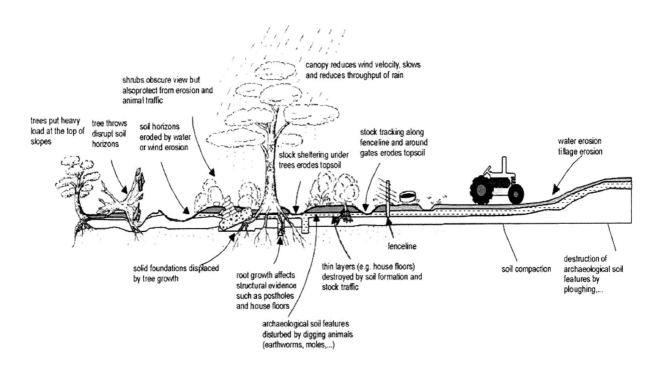

Fig. 1: Overview of common threats to archaeological heritage features (OXFORD ARCHAEOLOGY 2002).

Some measures are fairly easy to calculate. Agronomists for instance can work out the conversion of farmland into meadow. Less evident is the calculation of the compensation for the painting of the woodwork of a chapel or the removal of overgrow on the roof of a baking house. If the 'a-la-carte' system will be applied, the European commission has to approve with the calculations of all measures. This is taking place in a working group with specialists in the field of monument management, Regional Landscapes, etc. As mentioned above, half of the stewardship fee will (hopefully) be financed by the European Union. The other half will be paid for by the Flemish Community. A possible source is the Administration of Monuments and Landscapes who already have a budget line, now only used to pay for the maintenance of small landscape elements. Other possible funding sources are communities and provinces.

4.5. Organisational framework

All farmers can apply for the current agro-environmental measures. However, this will not be possible for the new stewardship. Due to the large amount of rural heritage features of various qualities, the agency will only offer the cultural historical to owners of selected elements. In most cases, this will be determined by the location in a project area and the nature of the element. In a further stage, application for the stewardship by local munici-palities or societies is considered. To make a selection of the heritage elements and to determine the appropriate composition of the stewardship module and other requirements, an expert group will be installed. Possible members of this group are government officials of the

Administration of Monuments and Landscapes, the Nature Department, heritage or nature conservation societies, the academic world, Regional Landscapes... Thus a correct estimation of historical, archaeological, ecological and economical values will be ensured. Communication with the Flemish government and other Flemish administration has started, and the reactions are very positive. The cabinet of the Flemish minister responsible for Monuments and Landscapes even asked the Flemish Land Agency to further develop the heritage stewardship and ordered all related administrations and departments to cooperate.

5. Management of archaeological heritage by means of stewardship ?

A large part of our heritage is buried in the ground and therefore needs special ways of detection, management and monitoring. The Flemish Land Agency uses several sources to assess the archaeological potential of an area. Desktop study is completed with field survey, aerial photographs and very accurate DEM data (by LIDAR). To ensure that all selected archaeological sites are properly managed, a study was commissioned to investigate the soil environment in order tot quantify the effects of land use and land management on archaeological traces in Flanders. This study was part of the Interreg IIIb project 'Farmers for Nature' and was co-funded by the Administration of Monuments and Landscapes, the Flemish Land Agency and Interreg North Sea Region. The final report was delivered October 2005. The main part of this study was a literature review, but some analyses of soil samples on selected archaeological sites were made. Purpose of the samples was to check data coming from the scientific literature and to give some guidelines concerning monitoring.

Firstly, archaeological traces in all its varieties were identified and described. In general it can be said that traces are discrete disturbances in the soil, that can be recognised by it's different colour, texture, structure or proportion of organic and mineral compounds. Secondly, all threats for these characteristics were listed. Three types were recognised: physical degradation (erosion, disturbance by agricultural practises, compaction, bioturbation, shrink), chemical degradation (acidification, complexation & mobilisation, redox processes, eutrofication) and microbiological degradation. Most of these threats are visible on figure 1.

Thirdly, possible measures to counter or minimise the identified threats were listed. Measures countering the physical disturbance of the archaeological remains are a/o direct drilling, minimum cultivation, reburial, maintaining plough depth, reversion to grassland, reduce grazing population, tree and shrub control... Erosion can be reduced by applying permanent cover, reburial, direct drilling, minimum cultivation, mulching, reseeding, set-aside or buffer strip management. Bioturbation is ideally remedied by reburial or possibly low nitrogen fertilization. Chemical degradation is a lot more difficult to minimise: reducing manure levels and stabilising water table are the most practical options. Finally, to reduce microbiological degradation a high C/N ratio is vital.

For all of these measures a correct payment must now be established and politically approved. By applying the correct measures to selected archaeological sites (by expert judgement), a great deal of our archaeological heritage can be sustained for at least the stewardship term of 10 years.

6. Prospect

So far, the possibilities for the new heritage stewardship have been explored. The framework and the outline are determined. Still, a lot remains to be done. The elaboration of the modules and compensations for each of these measures have to be established. The procedure has to be formalized and approved by all partners involved. During 2006, the heritage stewardship will be tested on selected heritage features. This is part of the Interreg IIIb project 'Farmers for Nature'.

Evaluation data have to be incorporated and the stewardship need to be tweaked. Furthermore, the complete procedure must be translated in Flemish legislation and incorporated in the Flemish Rural Development Plan 2007-2013. The possibility of offering a heritage stewardship is already inscribed in the Flemish Strategy. A good begin of a long administrative trajectory.

The stewardship will hopefully be applicable in Flanders from 2007 onwards.

7. Conclusions

A scientifically funded and widely endorsed heritage stewardship, modelled after the current agro-environmental measures can offer a powerful instrument for the management of the Flemish rural heritage in projects such as land-use planning, land consolidation and nature development. The *à-la-carte* approach guarantees a high efficacy and appropriate management. Also, the stewardship is flexible and the procedure ensures a well guided application. Finally and complying with the European vision, the conservation and management of the rural heritage is partly paid for with European funds.

Karl CORDEMANS
Flemish Land Agency (Vlaamse Landmaatschappij)
Gulden Vlieslaan 72
1060 BRUSSELS
Belgium
karl.cordemans@vlm.be
http://www.farmersfornature.org

Acknowledgements

The Interreg IIIB project 'Farmers for Nature' is financed with support of the ERDF.

Apologizes

This article was written by the author in 2005-06 but due to various difficulties it was only published in 2011, for which I want to apologize sincerely – Marc Lodewijckx (editor).

References

DEFRA 2003, *Entry Level Agri-environment Scheme Pilot. Scheme Guidance Booklet 2003*, London, Department for Environment, Food and Rural Affairs, http://www.defra.gov.uk/erdp/reviews/agrienv/pdfs/elspilotschemebooklet.pdf, march 2004.

ESSEX COUNTY COUNCIL, 2003. *Essex Past & Present* 5, November 2003.

FISCHLER F 2001. *The European Union's Rural Development Policy: Protecting our Heritage*, Naturopa 95. European Rural Heritage, Council of Europe, Strasbourg.

MAFF 2000. *The Rural Enterprise Scheme* (leaflet) Ministry of Agriculture, Fisheries and Food Publications, http://www.defra.gov.uk/erdp/pdfs/promo/respromo.pdf, March 2004.

LOUWAGIE G., G. NOENS and Y. DEVOS 2005. *Onderzoek van het bodemmilieu in functie van het fysisch-chemisch kwantificeren van de effecten van grondgebruik en beheer op archeologische bodemsporen in Vlaanderen*, University Ghent, Vakgroep Geologie en Bodemkunde and Vakgroep Archeologie en Oude Geschiedenis van Europa, Interreg IIB Project 'Farmers for Nature'.

OXFORD ARCHAEOLOGY 2002. The Management of Archaeological Sites in Arable Landscapes BD1701, Final Project Report Supporting Documentation Appendix C: Legislation and Policy for Archaeological Conservation, http://www2.defra.gov.uk/research/Project _Data/More.asp?I=BD1701&M=KWS&V=bd1701&SU BMIT1=Search&SCOPE=0, March 2004.

PATERSON P. and P. WADE-MARTINS 1999. Monument Conservation in Norfolk – The Monument Management Project and Other Schemes. In J. GRENVILLE (Ed.), Managing the Historic Rural Landscape, Issues in Heritage Management, Routeledge in Association with English Heritage, London/New York: 137-147.

TERWAN P. 2004. *Beschermingspakketten voor archeologische vindplaatsen in boerenland. Notitie in opdracht van agrarische natuurvereniging 'Tussen Y en Dijken'*, unpublished document.

VAN HEERINGEN R.M. and E.M. THEUNISSEN 2002. Desiccation of the Archaeological Landscape at Voorne-Putten, *Nederlandse Archeologische Rapporten* 25, Rijksdienst voor het Oudheidkundig Bodemonderzoek, Amersfoort.

Interreg North Sea Region   European Community European Regional Development Fund   F4N   Farmers for Nature

ACCESSING IRELAND'S GROWING AND DIVERSE AERIAL ARCHAEOLOGICAL RESOURCES

ANTHONY CORNS – ROBERT SHAW

Introduction

Ireland has a longstanding and well-established archaeological tradition within which aerial survey is very much a lesser known component. However, as will be shown through the discussion in this paper, aerial archaeology has generated a significant volume of images, data and interpretation in the past which is increasing as exciting new approaches are being researched and implemented. All of this information is a potentially valuable resource, and it should be incorporated into archaeological research to help shape the understanding of our cultural landscape. The insights delivered would aid and improve planning and management processes, and would also be of great interest to the general public, but only if we can provide the means to access and interact with the data. New technology, in particular web-based services can provide the potential solution to this problem, and have been subject to detailed research by the Discovery Programme in collaboration with Irish and international partners.

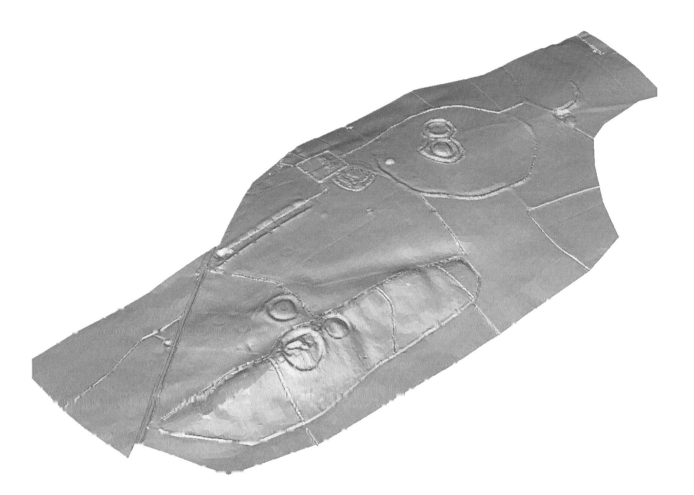

Fig. 1: Perspective view of the 3D model generated from the total station survey of the Hill of Tara, completed in 1996.

1. Ireland's Aerial Archaeology Resources

Contrary to the general perception of international archaeology (MUSSON-HORNE 2007), Ireland is a country where aerial archaeology has in fact been widely applied. Ireland has a rich aerial archaeological legacy and there is currently a vibrant aerial research community applying new aerial sensors and techniques.

1.1. Historic collections

In 2008 the Heritage Council (Ireland) published *Air and Earth, Aerial Archaeology in Ireland* by George Lambrick. This is a wide-ranging review of the past, present and future of aerial archaeology in Ireland and presents a comprehensive catalogue of the sources of aerial photography available in Ireland. A paragraph in its summary provides a concise history of Irish aerial archaeology and a list of the legacy of resources that exist.

> "The first application of aerial archaeology in Ireland was a 1927 initiative of the Ancient Monuments Board in Northern Ireland working with the RAF. Raftery (1944) cited the first use of archaeological air photography in the Republic in 1934, and called for "proper collaboration in surveying... archaeological sites all over this country". In the 1950's, the National Monuments Advisory Council commissioned aerial archaeological surveys by the Air Corps. J.K. St Joseph undertook two main campaigns of flying in Ireland – in 1951-5, and more particularly 1963-73. From the 1970's onwards, much has been done by the Ordnance Survey Ireland (OSi), Geological Survey of Ireland (GSI), the Office of Public Works (now the National Monuments Section/NMS of the Department of the Environment, Heritage and Local Government), and individuals (the late L. Swan, D. Pochin Mould, G. Barrett and others). From the 1980's onwards, aerial archaeology has been carried out increasingly in the context of research through the Discovery Programme and some academic initiatives, enhancement of the National Sites and Monuments Record (SMR), and development-led archaeology for pipelines and road schemes." (LAMBRICK 2008).

Most of these resources are not readily accessible having been the result of discrete initiatives. A fragmented record has resulted, held in the individual archives of the source organisations, hence they are largely underutilised resources. This is a reflection of the fact that Ireland has never undertaken a programme of systematic aerial archaeology survey.

1.2. A decade of advancement – the Discovery Programme's contribution

Established in 1991, the Discovery Programme is a state-funded archaeological research company that aims to enhance the understanding of Ireland's past through strategic long-term projects. Included in this remit is the requirement to investigate new archaeological methods and techniques, and in recent year's considerable research has been undertaken in 3D surveying and modelling. Ironically it was through the success of its own ground based surveys that the Discovery Programme became involved in aerial survey and researching new aerial technologies.

For over thirty years archaeological surveyors have been using ground based instruments such as total stations and differential GPS (dGPS) to record the cultural components of the landscape in three dimensions (3D); (REMONDINO 2011). This has provided the opportunity to record the subtle micro-topographical evidence of human activity on the landscape, a powerful tool to help archaeological investigators unravel the evolution and functions of historic and prehistoric sites using non destructive methods (BOWDEN 1999). The topographic survey of the Hill of Tara completed in 1996 highlights the effectiveness of this technique in identifying new monument features (NEWMAN 1998). In this survey over 60,000 height points covering 60ha provided a more naturalistic visualization of the archaeological complex in comparison to traditional hachure approach (HALE-HEPHER 2008). The Tara model (fig. 1) was considered ground breaking at the time, but from a present perspective its limited extent provides little of the archaeological landscape context to its features, and the artificial nature of the defining boundary give the impression of a surface model floating in space.

To significantly extend the modelled area by ground survey techniques is not viable; it is too expensive to put survey teams in the field for weeks on end. For this reason the Discovery Programme began to look at alternative aerial survey approaches to enable more extensive landscape modelling and recording.

1.2.1. Aerial Photogrammetry

Aerial photogrammetry is a well established survey and mapping technique which has been used for decades by national mapping agencies in the production of cartographic products (MIKHAIL *et alii* 2001).

The principle of this method is that through complex pixel matching processes within the overlap area of adjacent stereo digital images, a Digital Elevation Model (DEM) is extracted which, through the process of orthoprojection is used to generate orthophotographs. (CORNS-SHAW 2008). Repeated for large block of overlapping stereo imagery seamless DEM's and orthoimagery can be generated for complete survey areas. The Discovery Programme investigated the potential of aerial photogrammetry through a number of pilot projects, in a variety of archaeological landscapes employing a range of flying heights and photo-scales. Whilst the orthophotographs proved to have enormous potential for

*Fig. 2:   Top: orthoimage draped over DEM generated by photogrammetric processing.
Bottom: oblique aerial photograph of the prehistoric site, Mullaghfarna, Co. Sligo, Ireland.*

landscape analysis, it was concluded that the derived DEMs were generally too coarse to reflect the micro-topographic features required for modelling small-scale or complex archaeological sites (fig. 2).

Following discussions with photogrammetric experts it became clear this was a result of difficulties with the automatic pixel matching routine, a core component of photogrammetric processing software we were using (PCI Geomatica 9). These algorithms use matrices to analyse the adjacent pixels on overlapping images in order to 'match' the pixels, from which parallax measurement enable the height component and resulting

DEM to be extracted. The automated pixel matching routines, configured for high resolution DEM output, often failed because most of our project areas contained a predominance of grass or pasture land coverage – totally indistinct areas of green. To resolve this larger pixel correlation matrices had to be employed, significantly lowering the resolution of the final 3D models. However, recent experiments with a new multi-ray path matching algorithm for the automatic extraction of high resolution terrain surfaces (ERDAS LPS eATE) appears to radically reduce this effect and result in a vastly superior resolution and quality of DEM. (see *www.erdas.com* and *http://labs.erdas.com/blog_view.aspx?q=6074*).

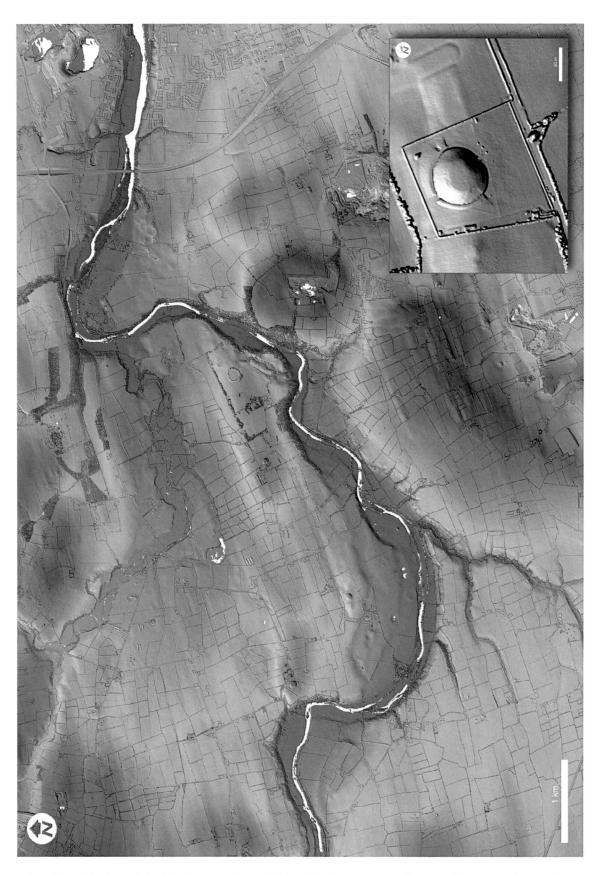

Fig. 3: Hillshade model of the Bru na Boinne DSM, with enlargement to illustrate limitation of resolution.

Fig. 4: The Hillshade DSM of the Hill of Tara, inset enlargement to illustrate high resolution.

There were other factors that negatively impacted on our experience of using photogrammetry. Although field survey time was significantly reduced – only photo control points need to be surveyed – considerable computer-based processing effort was required to create and edit the DEMs. The issue of mapping sites located in areas of forest or woodland was an additional problem, requiring a field completion programme using total stations.

1.2.2. LiDAR (Light Detection And Ranging)

Many research projects (DONEUS-BRIESE 2006a; BEWLEY *et alii* 2005) have already powerfully demonstrated the potential for LiDAR to record the archaeological landscape in 3D, including those areas of terrain beneath tree cover (DONEUS-BRIESE 2006b; BOFINGER-HESSE 2011; GEORGES-LEROY 2011).

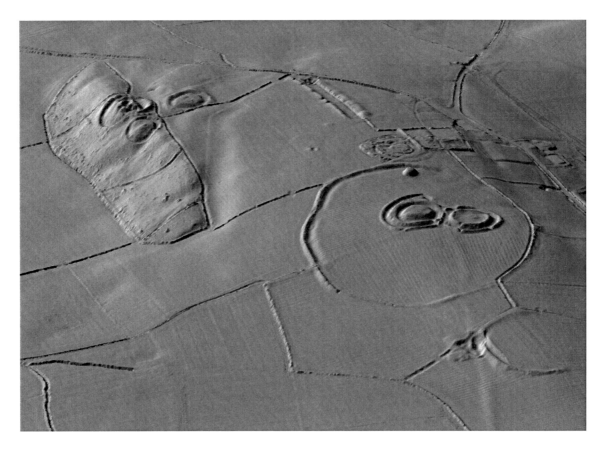

Fig. 5: Perspective view of the Hillshade DTM illustrating vegetation penetration.

The typical horizontal and vertical accuracies of the final data models are quoted at 0.6m and 0.15m respectively (BOYDA-HILLB 2007), values which are clearly appropriate for topographic modelling of archaeological landscapes.

To examine the potential of LiDAR we were given access by Meath County Council to a recently gathered block of data for the Brú na Bóinne World Heritage Site. The data was supplied processed and filtered by the data capture organisation to give a first return Digital Surface Model (DSM), and a last return Digital Terrain Model (DTM) data set respectively.

From these ASCII data sets simple GIS processes were applied to generate both DSM and DTM grids and their associated hillshade models. Figure 3 graphically illustrates the powerful landscape models which can be generated in a remarkably short time period between the commissioning of a survey and creation of the final functioning DSM/DTMs. However, with a typical ground resolution of 0.5m – 1m the ability of this technology to successfully depict the subtle micro-topography or identify possible phasing of an individual monument is questionable (CORNS-SHAW 2009). To generate DSM /DTM's that enable this level of research requires the application of an enhanced variation of the LiDAR explained in the following section.

1.2.3. High Resolution LiDAR - FliMAP

The FLI-MAP 400 LiDAR system was designed and developed primarily to meet the survey requirements of infrastructural projects including, railways, highways and electricity distribution networks; situations where point accuracy and resolution specifications exceed those possible from conventional fixed wing LiDAR systems. Our research aimed to investigate whether such a system could provide the solution for the 3D modelling of small-scale archaeological features.

The FLI-MAP 400 system can be mounted on a range of helicopter types. The system consists of the following components which are all contained within a modular rigid frame that is attached to the cargo mounting point positioned on the fuselage beneath the helicopter:
- A single Class I laser scanner operating at a frequency of 150Khz that scans through a cycle inclined 7° forward to nadir and 7°aft along the line of flight;
- Two GPS receivers to supply accurate positional information when used in conjunction with ground-based GPS base stations;
- An Inertial Navigation System (INS/IMU) to continuously track the orientation and rotational elements of the sensor;
- An RGB digital line scanner to supply virtual colour attribution to the acquired LiDAR data and;

• Forward oblique and nadir facing medium format digital cameras and videos.

Unlike fixed-wing aircraft that are constrained by a minimum airspeed before which stalling occurs, the slower speed and lower flying heights at which a helicopter can operate, facilitates the collection of data at a much higher resolution.

In 2008 the Discovery Programme commissioned a survey of one of Ireland's iconic archaeological sites, the Hill of Tara, which provides a showcase for the enhanced capabilities of the FliMAP system. The data was acquired on a single day and generated in excess of 150 million individual LiDAR points to cover the survey area of 2.38 km²; equating to a point density in excess of 50pts per m², (or a point spacing approximately 16cm on the ground).

A sequence of GIS processes converted the supplied DSM and DTM ASCII datasets into DSM and DTM grids which are most effectively visualised using hill-shade processing, based upon multiple light sources correlated to the frequency of relief features (LOISIOS *et alii* 2007).

The resulting model has optimal lighting conditions to enable the identification of archaeological features. The exceptional detail of these hill-shaded models is readily apparent even at a cursory glance. Figure 4 displays the DSM (first return) for the whole survey area, with an enlargement of the conjoined earthworks of the iconic Forrad and Tech Cormaic to illustrate the extraordinary detail and high level of resolution that exists throughout the whole model. This surface model includes all the vegetation and man-made features in the landscape, such as houses and barns and even captures overhead power-lines. By contrast, the DTM provides a 'bare earth' representation of the terrain and enables us to view the topographic detail of the ground surface beneath the obscuring vegetation (fig. 5).

In addition to the Hill of Tara the Discovery Programme has undertaken FliMAP surveys of two sites; Dún Ailinne royal site, Co. Kildare, and Newtown Jerpoint, Co. Kilkenny. The publicity these surveys generated resulted in a number of other Flimap projects being commissioned in Ireland. They include a number of sites in Northern Ireland commissioned by the Dept. of Environment (NI),

Fig. 6: LiDAR data for Bru na Boinne was a crucial resource during the development of a Research Framework for the World Heritage Site.

Monastic site, see inset plan

Monastic site

Fig. 7: DSM generated from the first-return FLiMAP data for Skellig Michael, 60pts per m² density. Inset shows plan view of monastic structures.

sites for contract archaeology companies, and sites for other archaeological researchers. In total 15 Irish archaeological locations have been surveyed by this high resolution LiDAR system.

1.3. Low cost solutions

Beyond these increasingly complex and expensive data capture systems lower cost aerial imagery has been captured for a number of archaeological sites using elevated platforms, kite systems and balloons. The Discovery Programme has used a helium kite balloon system extensively for excavation recording, taking overlapping images to generate orthophoto plans of ground surface. Recent tests with a low cost unmanned aerial vehicle (UAV) system (http://www.sensefly.com/) indicate a huge potential for wider area surveys generating high resolution mapping quality imagery.

2. Resources for research frameworks

An important application of the new aerial resources, particularly LiDAR hillshade models has been in the drafting of research framework documents. Our FliMAP survey of the Hill of Tara has been identified as a core resource for the Tara/Skryne Landscape Conservation project initiated by Meath County Council.

(www.meath.ie/LocalAuthorities/Planning/TaraSkryneLa ndscapeProject/). Even in the early consultation phase FliMAP maps and images were used in public meetings and presentations to engage with local residents and stakeholders.

The LiDAR data for the Brú na Bóinne has subsequently become an important resource during the development of a Research Framework for the World Heritage Site (SMYTH 2009). It was identified as a vital data source particularly given the shift of research emphasis from sites to landscapes, and featured extensively in the final publication (fig. 6).

A FliMAP survey of Skellig Michael, one of the three sites in Ireland currently on UNESCO's list of World Heritage Sites, was commissioned by the National Monuments Service, with the Discovery Programme giving advice on the specification and carrying out the data modelling for the project. The DSM generated (fig. 7) was regarded as a primary resource for a project considering the maintenance and stabilisation of the islands heritage sites. It was used as the baseline survey by contractors working on the restoration of the monastic structures to tie in conventional surveys and drawn plans, and has been used to identify possible additional step structures across the island.

3. Infrastructure and policies to fulfil the potential of resources

3.1. The General Problem

The discussions thus far highlight the rich, diverse and growing collection of aerial archaeology resources in Ireland. The Discovery Programme is not alone in applying new technologies to gather aerial resources for archaeological research. Universities, state agencies and the private sector are all active in this process. The result is increasing volumes of spatial data which been gathered at much financial and professional effort, but in a fragmented manner by a number of stakeholders over a number of years. The gathering, cleaning and processing of these datasets has been carried out at great financial expense and effort often for specific research projects. There are a number of issues and factors which need to be overcome if we are to find the solutions to re-use these resources and fulfill their potential.

Once datasets have been used for their original research purpose they are often stored in an unstructured way on the source organization's server, or back-up tapes. This may be deemed an acceptable form of storage from the source organization point of view, but even then it is vulnerable to a number of serious archiving problems such as obsolete formats and software, corruption, loss of knowledge. (CCSDS 2004). Furthermore, the datasets are being hidden from and have become inaccessible to other potential users, eliminating any possible knowledge transfer. The result of this approach is the creation of fragmented and discrete data silos – vaults of information containing non-standardized data types. This approach essentially locks away data from the wider research community, and as a result the risk exists of replication of effort in creating, processing or cleaning data by other researchers.

Often there exists an intensely competitive environment between research institutions resulting in understandably protectionist attitudes, and a reluctance to share resources. However, if creators of data look beyond their own field of study, the data may be of great value in different field of scientific study. For example, a LiDAR dataset collected for landscape archaeology could prove invaluable to a geomorphologist, and vice versa.

Internationally, there are often very different strategies for accessing data and there are currently no agreed mechanisms to explore and share data across geographic boundaries. There is generally less exposure to, and awareness of international datasets beyond individual researchers' special interests, and researchers rarely establish formal cross border relationships unless structured within an EU or international scheme.

Semantic barriers are also a major issue as sites and features may be described and represented in very different ways. National archaeological inventories will use classifications, structures and terminology appropriate to the specific country. Harmonizing the inventories of more than one country is highly complex, mapping across cultural themes and requires huge effort.

3.2. The problem in Ireland

In Ireland, in recent years, much financial and professional effort has been invested in the collection and analysis of spatial archaeological data by government, research and commercial sectors. Within this digital asset aerial survey data forms a substantial component and includes: aerial photography; topographic surveys created by both LiDAR (Light Detection and Ranging) and digital photogrammetry. Once this data is recorded and interpreted, the printed report is often seen as the final deliverable, while the digital assets created frequently remain hidden and unused within the source organizations, eliminating any possible knowledge transfer to the wider archaeological community. In the current economic climate, particularly with the contraction in private sector archaeological consultancies, the possibility for the loss of archaeological information is great as the digital data collected and held by these companies could potentially disappear.

Recently reports (COONEY 2006; REENERS 2006) reviewing the current archaeological research framework within Ireland highlighted concerns that exist within the archaeological community. Some major problems to the successful development of the knowledge society in Irish archaeology were identified including:

- Underdeveloped and poorly resourced research infrastructure.
- The disconnected nature of archaeological information and key resources within the archaeological research community.
- A lack of accessible and sustainable digital archives for archaeological data, conforming to established standards and metadata.
- An inadequate return on the investment in primary data collection, from both development-led and grant-funded archaeological practice, resulting in the production of hidden archaeological material.

A potential solution to these problems lies in the creation of an effective complimentary ICT infrastructural strategy to provide easy access to primary research information whilst offering a sustainable and robust digital archive that adheres to recognised international standards.

3.3. Solutions

Traditionally, the GIS technology used to view and interrogate spatial data (such as LiDAR DSMs and DTMs) has been expensive desktop-based software solutions but, in recent years, technological developments and the adoption of open standards has enabled the delivery and exploration of spatial data within a Spatial

Data Infrastructure (SDI). SDI is the collective name for a group of technologies and supporting measures that enables access to spatial data. It is more than a single data set or database, and incorporates geographic data and attributes, documentation (metadata), a means to discover, visualise, and evaluate the data and provides access to data through web services.

To help understand the concept of SDI a useful definition is found in the SDI 'cookbook':
"...the relevant base collection of the technologies, policies and institutional arrangements that facilitate the availability of access to spatial data" (NEBERT 2004).

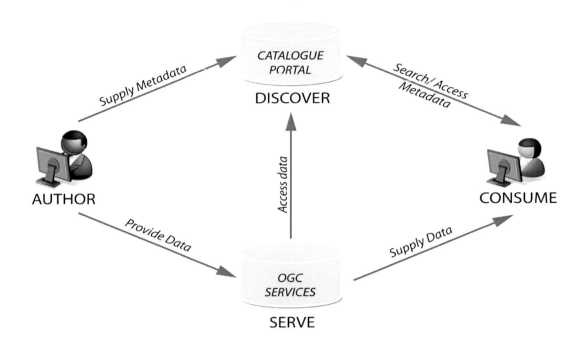

Fig. 8: Schematic diagram of the components of SDI.

Figure 8 shows a schematic diagram of the basic concepts of SDI.

- An author creates a spatial dataset or map using the convention approach, such as a desktop Geographical Information System (GIS), but in addition generates two extra key components.
- Firstly the author creates and publishes a metadata record that references the new spatial dataset, conforming to internationally recognized standards. (eg INSPIRE, ISO19115)
- The author then publishes the spatial data or map via web mapping services utilizing the interoperability standards defined by the Open Geospatial Consortium (OGC).
- A consumer wishing to discover this dataset will utilize a metadata catalogue or geo-portal and finds appropriate data using free or agreed theme search criteria.
- Once data is discovered its web mapping service is exposed and the user can consume it within a provided web application or on their desktop software.

There are important additional elements which should be considered along with the development of SDI. The organizational structure and commitment needs to be in place to keep the cycle of knowledge reuse in operation

and a trusted digital repository is necessary, ideally based on the principles of the OAIS (CCSDS 2004).

3.3.1. SHARE-IT

In 2008 the Discovery Programme undertook a detailed feasibility study to examine the potential development of an SDI for cultural heritage spatial data in Ireland, including DSM/DTM's derived from LiDAR data. Entitled the Spatial Heritage and Archaeological Research Environment using IT (SHARE-IT) this study examined the long term access to digital spatial data within the cultural heritage domain. Potential solutions including open archives, metadata, data standards and the construction of an SDI were outlined. One of the components of an SDI – a web mapping application – was piloted during the project (fig. 9). Another key research challenge was to identify a suitable digital archiving strategy for spatial landscape data and this was approached by reviewing the current best practices that have been adopted within the cultural heritage sector and within the wider professional community. Standards organizations specific to cultural data such as the Archaeological Data Service (ADS) and ARENA (Archaeological Records of Europe Networked Access) were consulted on their prescribed policy.

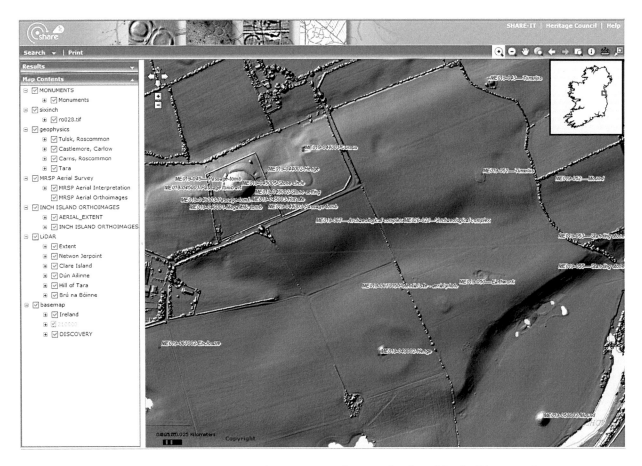

Fig. 9: Screen image of the prototype web mapping application developed by the Discovery Programme.

3.3.2. ArchaeoLandscapes

Another network through which the Discovery Programme hopes to further the development of an archaeological SDI is the EU ArchaeoLandscapes project.

The target of ArchaeoLandscapes is to address existing imbalances in the use of modern surveying and remote sensing techniques and to create conditions for the regular use of these strikingly successful techniques across the Continent as a whole. It aims to create a self-sustaining network to support the use throughout Europe of aerial survey and 'remote sensing' to promote understanding, conservation and public enjoyment of the shared landscape and archaeological heritage of the countries of the European Union. The project represents the culmination of a growing European cooperation from the mid-1990's onwards. Now federating 42 prestigious institutions in the field of archaeology and heritage protection from 26 separate countries, it will bring that process to a sustainable and self-supporting future as the long-term legacy of this and earlier EU-assisted initiatives.

As part of the project a European wide SDI will be implemented in conjunction with other project activities. A schematic project architecture is shown in figure 10.

A geodatabase approach is proposed for the truly spatial data, with associated INSPIRE compliant metadata which will be accessed via a web service. The project will assess both open source and proprietary software solutions, documenting the processes to enable other partners to establish conforming archives.

The Fedora Commons open archive model is seen as the best solution to the storage and access of the non-spatial datasets such as the important historic and legacy photo collections outlined at the beginning of this paper. Further activities are planned into the potential to migrate these datasets into spatial data through georectification. An additional venture beyond the ArcLand project aims to digitise and deposit many of the historic aerial collections within Ireland.

The project's long-term legacy will be better appreciation of the landscape and archaeological heritage of Europe, closer contact between heritage professionals and the general public, more effective conservation of the shared cultural heritage, the international sharing of skills and employment opportunities, better public and professional education, the wider use of archive resources and modern survey techniques, and higher professional standards in landscape exploration and conservation.

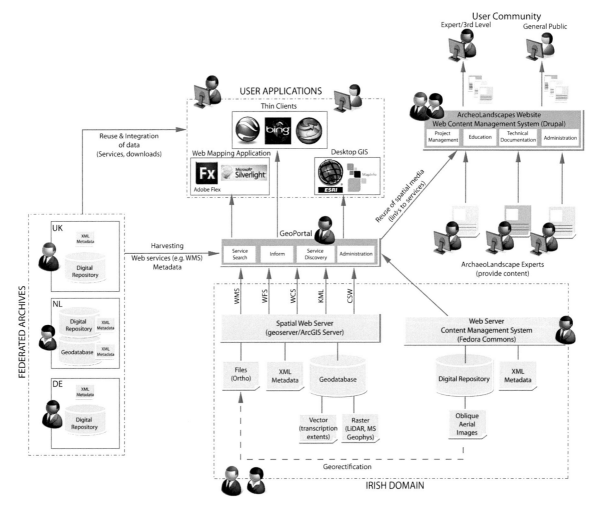

Fig. 10: Schematic diagram of the components and interactions of the proposed ArchaeoLandscapes SDI.

4. Conclusions

With a solid legacy of early aerial archaeology photography and a vibrant archaeological sector generating new aerial resources it is vital that the mechanisms for archiving, exploring and accessing be established in Ireland. It is only by putting in places such infrastructure that these collections will be protected into the future and the full value of the resources invested realized. A consensus is building to provide solutions through pan-European networks which should ensure robust, high quality systems become available to the wider European archaeology community. Further technological advances will inevitably impact on the design and implementation in future years but the core principles – the benefits in opening access and sharing data – should remain.

Anthony CORNS – Robert SHAW
The Discovery Programme
63 Merrion Square
DUBLIN D2
Ireland

Bibliography

BEWLEY R.H., S. CRUTCHLEY and C.A. SHELL 2005. New Light on an Ancient Landscape: Lidar Survey in the Stonehenge World Heritage Site, *Antiquity* 79/305: 636-647.

BOFINGER J. and R. HESSE 2011. As Far as the Laser can reach…: Laminar Analysis of LiDAR Detected Structures as a Powerful Instrument for Archaeological Heritage Management in Baden-Wurttemberg, Germany. In *EAC Occasional Paper No. 5 Remote Sensing for Archaeological Heritage Management*, Europae Archaeologia Consilium (EAC): 107-115.

BOWDEN M. 1999. *Unraveling the Landscape: Inquisitive Approach to Archaeology*, NPI Media Group, London.

BOYDA D.S. and R.A. HILLB 2007. Validation of Airborne Lidar Intensity Values from a Forested Landscape Using Hymap Data: Preliminary Analyses, *International Archives of Photogrammetry and Remote Sensing (IAPRS)* XXXVI/3: W52.

CCSDS – Consultative Committee for Space Data Systems 2004. *Reference Model for an Open Archival Information System (OAIS)*, CCSDS 650.0-B-1 Blue Book, Washington DC, USA.

COONEY G. 2006. *Archaeology in Ireland: A Vision for the Future*, Dublin, Royal Irish Academy.

CORNS A and R. SHAW 2008. The Application of Digital Vertical Aerial Photogrammetry in the Recording and Analysis of Archaeological Landscapes. In O. BENDER, N. EVELPIDOU, A. KREK and A. VASSILOPOULOS (Eds.), *Geoinformation Technologis for Geocultural Landscapes: European Perspectives,* Abingdon, UK.

CORNS A and R. SHAW 2009. High Resolution 3-Dimensional Documentation of Archaeological Monuments & Landscapes Using Airborne LiDAR, *Journal of Cultural Heritage*: doi:10.1016/j.culher.2009.09.003.

DONEUS M. and C. BRIESE 2006a. Digital Terrain Modeling for Archaeological Interpretation within Forested Areas Using Full-Waveform Laser Scanning. In M. IOANNIDES, D. ARNOLD, F. NICCOLUCCI and K. MANIA (Eds.), *The 7th International Symposium on Virtual Reality, Archaeology and Cultural Heritage VAST 2006*: 155-162.

DONEUS M. and C. BRIESE 2006b. Full-Waveform Airborne Laser Scanning as a Tool for Archaeological Reconnaissance. In S. CAMPANA and M. FORTE (Eds.), *From Space to Place. Proceedings of the 2nd International Conference on Remote Sensing in Archaeology.* BAR International Series 1568, Archaeopress, Rom: 99-106.

GEORGES-LEROY M. 2011. Airborne Laser Scanning for the Management of Archaeological Sites in Lorraine (France). In *EAC Occasional Paper No. 5 Remote Sensing for Archaeological Heritage Management,* Europae Archaeologia Consilium (EAC): 107-115.

HALE A. and J. HEPHER 2008. 3D Data Fusion for the Presentation of Archaeological Landscapes: A Scottish Perspective. In A. POSLUSCHNY, K. LAMBERS and

I. HERZOG (Eds.), *Layers of Perception. Proceedings of the 35th International Conference on Computer Applications and Quantitative Methods in Archaeology (CAA), Berlin, April 2-6, 2007*: 145.

LAMBRICK G. 2008. *Air and Earth: Aerial Archaeology in Ireland, a Review for the Heritage Council,* The Heritage Council.

LOISIOS D., N. TZELEPIS and B. NAKOS 2007. A Methodology for Creating Analytical Hill-Shading by Combining Different Lighting Directions, *Proceedings of 23rd International Cartographic Conference,* Moscow, August 2007.

MIKHAIL E., J. BETHEL and C. McGLONE 2001. *Introduction to Modern Photogrammetry*, John Wiley & Sons, Inc., New York.

MUSSON C. and P. HORNE 2007. *European Landscapes Past, Present and Future*, Culture 2000 Project Ref. No. CH-A2-UK-2007, Final Report, Culture 2000 and English Heritage.

NEBERT D. (Ed.) 2004. *Developing Spatial Data Infrastructures: The SDI Cookbook*, available at: http://www.gsdi.org/docs2004/Cookbook/cookbookV2.0.pdf.

NEWMAN C. 1998. *Tara: an Archaeological Survey*, Discovery Programme Monographs 2, Royal Irish Academy, Dublin.

REENERS R. (Ed.) 2006. *Archaeology 2020. Repositioning Irish Archaeology in the Knowledge Society*, Dublin: University College Dublin.

REMONDINO F, 2011. 3D Recording for Cultural Heritage, In *EAC Occasional Paper No. 5 Remote Sensing for Archaeological Heritage Management*, Europae Archaeologia Consilium (EAC): 107-115.

SMYTH J. (Ed.) 2009. *Brú na Bóinne World Heritage Site: Research Framework*, The Heritage Council, Kilkenny Tara Skryne Landscape Project, http://www.meath.ie/LocalAuthorities/Planning/TaraSkryneLandscapeProject/ (accessed 19th April 2010).

METHODOLOGIES FOR THE EXTRACTION OF ARCHAEOLOGICAL FEATURES FROM VERY HIGH-RESOLUTION IKONOS-2 REMOTE SENSING IMAGERY, HISAR (SOUTHWEST TURKEY)

Véronique DE LAET – Etienne PAULISSEN – Marc WAELKENS

Abstract

From the very start the archaeological research on the territory of Sagalassos evolved into a multidisciplinary research project supported by various scientific disciplines such as archaeology, anthropology, zoology, geomorphology, palynology and geology. In contrast to disciplines traditionally linked to archaeology also new technologies are embraced. Since the development of very high-resolution images with a sufficient radiometric and spatial resolution (<2.5 m), also remote sensing can be used for the detection, mapping and analysis of archaeological matters. One such sensor is Ikonos-2, launched in 1999.

This research emphasizes on the evaluation of GIS-, pixel- and object-based techniques for automatic extraction of archaeological features from very high-resolution Ikonos-2 satellite imagery and will confront them with a visual interpretation of ancient structures. Whereas a visual interpretation is based on differences in hue intensity, shape, shade and associations between different features, the automatic methodologies are based on spectral and/or shape characteristics. This study was carried out on the archaeological site of Hisar (southwest Turkey) where no excavations have taken place (VANHAVERBEKE-WAELKENS 2003).

Although all techniques were able to detect archaeological features from very high-resolution Ikonos-2 imagery, none of them succeeded in extracting features in a unique class. Various landscape elements, including archaeological features, can be automatically classified when their spectral characteristics are different. However, a major difficulty arises when extracting and classifying archaeological features like remnants of walls, which are composed of the same material as that of the surrounding geologic substrate. Additionally archaeological structures do not have unique shape or colour characteristics, which could make the extraction more straightforward.

In contrast to the automatic extraction methods, a simple visual interpretation performed rather well. It is expected that only very detailed hyperspectral and lidar images could improve objective automatic classification methods because of their more elevated spectral and topographic information.

The methodologies presented in this paper can be applied with variable success to archaeological structures composed of the same material as the surrounding substrate. It is expected that these methods will better perform when the composition of the archaeological structures is different from the surroundings or when trees and shrubs are absent.

1. Introduction

"Remote sensing is the acquisition of data about an object without touching it" (JENSEN 2000). Such a broad definitions encompasses all forms of remote sensing, including sub-surface remote sensing, aerial photography, aerial spectroscopy and satellite remote sensing. Hence in its broadest sense and in relation to archaeology, remote sensing encompasses major methods to discover and map remnants of past civilisations, whether or not they are situated sub-surface (e.g. crop marks, buried archaeological remains, traces of ancient industrial activity and above ground architectural remnants). Remote sensing is also very useful in preparing an intensive survey campaign or to direct fieldwork. Viewing archaeological features from ground level generally does not clearly identify the spatial significance of archaeological remains or the relationship to surrounding archaeological sites. In some cases ancient features are not apparent from ground level but become obvious from bird view.

Since the beginning of the 20th century, aerial photography has been used in archaeology primarily to view features on the earth surface, which were difficult, if not impossible to visualize from ground level (SEVER 1995; VERMEULEN-VERHOEVEN 2004). With the launch of the first Landsat satellite in 1972 (http://landsat7.usgs.gov/), satellite remote sensing also became

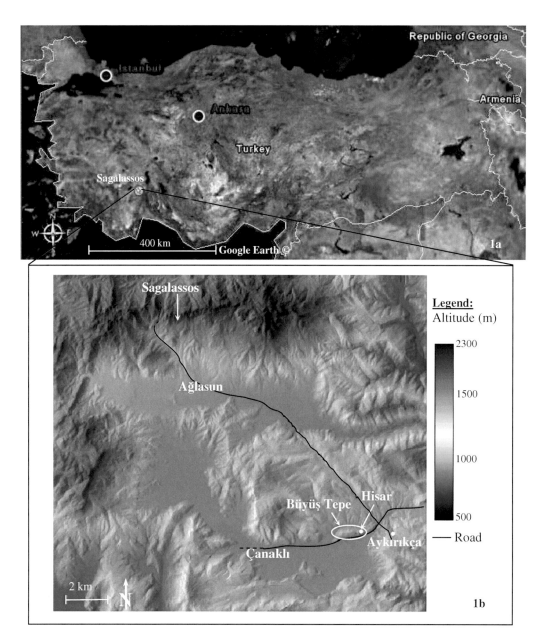

Fig. 1: Location of the study area (fig. 1a: Situation of the study area in Turkey; fig. 1b: Physical setting of the archaeological site of Hisar (20 m resolution DEM derived from 1:25.000 topographic map).

accessible to the wider archaeological community. However, much of these satellite images did not provide more and probably even less information than aerial photography for archaeological surveys, due to ground resolution constraints. Indeed, even the most recent Landsat ETM[+] images have a resolution of 15 m for the panchromatic band, which is not detailed enough for the identification of most archaeological structures. Therefore the launch of the first commercial very high-resolution satellite Ikonos in 1999, was a major step forward for application in archaeological research. This satellite platform provides panchromatic images with 1 m spatial resolution. Fusing the 1 m panchromatic and 4 m multispectral bands, a 1 m false or natural colour image can be generated. Recently, also aerial hyperspectral imagery is used in archaeology (EMMOLO *et alii* 2004).

Hyperspectral imagery is characterised by their enormous number of wavebands and by their (not necessarily) very high spatial resolution defined by the operator (RICHARDS-XIUPING 1999). Until now very few geoarchaeological studies have applied images with such a high spatial resolution (PAVLIDIS 2005; GEORGOULA *et alii* 2004; CHANGLIN *et alii* 2004; EMMOLO *et alii* 2004).

Fig. 2: Büyüş Tepe seen from the South (fig. 2a); archaeological features at Hisar (figs. 2b and 2c).

Within this study three satellite remote sensing images with varying ground resolution (ASTER and SPOT), including very high-resolution imagery (Ikonos-2), were applied in order to test their potential for the automatic extraction of archaeological features, by means of GIS-, pixel- and object-based methods and to confront them with a visual interpretation.

2. Study Area

The study area covers the archaeological site of Hisar, located in southwest Turkey, roughly 100 km to the north of Antalya (fig. 1a). In ancient times, the Western Taurus Mountains, in which Hisar is set, was known as the region of Pisidia (BRACKE 1993). On the 1.25.000 topographic map any information is available concerning the Hisar site. The archaeological site of Hisar was chosen for this study because of its large size and occurrence of many vertical, well visible archaeological remains.

The Hisar site is situated on an isolated hill (Büyüş Tepe, Turkish for magic hill) bordered with steep slopes – altitude between 1050 and 1200 m a.s.l. – and situated 150 m above the Çanaklı plain (fig. 2). The site, surveyed in 1993, is a well-fortified stronghold, roughly 14 km

southeast of the ancient metropolis Sagalassos (fig. 1b). Because of its heavy defence walls and the building techniques used, the site probably dates back to the late Iron Age and early Hellenistic period (VANHAVER-BEKE-WAELKENS 2003). Hisar may have had an important strategic function during Hellenistic times, because of the situation at the intersection of important roads (fig. 1b). Remnants of ancient houses and the Hellenistic defence wall are also depicted in figs. 2b and 2c. Hisar is the successor of the Early Iron age site Aykırıkça, located some 2 km to the east (fig. 1b) (WAELKENS *et alii* 1997).

The substrate of the Büyüş Tepe is composed of autochthonous limestone of the Boy Dağları formation, surrounded by sand, silt and clay stone of the same geologic formation (MTA 1997). The site overlooks the western part of the large, fertile Çanaklı basin, filled with alluvial and colluvial deposits of Quaternary age (fig. 1b). Today, in combination with rainfed agriculture, irrigated agriculture only occurs in the southern part of the Çanaklı plain. North of the Hisar site a mixture of rainfed agriculture and degraded *Quercus coccifera* maquis occurs whereas to the east of Hisar the land cover consists of alternating *Pinus brutia* and *Pinus nigra* forests.

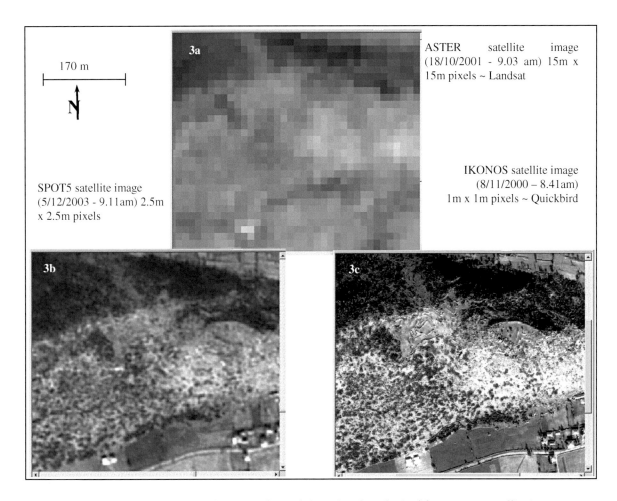

Fig. 3: The effect of spatial resolution on the visibility of archaeological features on satellite imagery.

3. Methodology

3.1. Available satellite imagery

In advance of the visual interpretation of remote sensed imagery, the minimum spatial resolution, necessary to detect the archaeological features under study had to be defined. All the images in fig. 3 show the Hisar site and her surroundings.

All these images cover the same area and have the same scale, but their spatial resolution and thus their level of information is quite different. ASTER images have a moderate resolution and record data in 14 spectral bands: 3 bands in the Visible Near InfraRed Region (VNIR) with a spatial resolution of 15 m, 6 bands in the Short Wave InfraRed Region (SWIR) with a spatial resolution of 30 m and 5 bands in Thermal InfraRed Region (TIR) with a spatial resolution of 90 m (ABRAMS 2000). The ASTER image used in this analysis is a 1B image, taken at 18th October 2001 at 9.03 am (fig. 3a).

The SPOT5 image was acquired at 5th December 2003 at 9.11 am (fig. 3b). Spot5 imagery has a high spatial

resolution of 2.5 m for the panchromatic band, 10 m for the 3 VNIR wavebands and 20 m spatial resolution for the SWIR band (http://spot5.cnes.fr). Finally also a very high-resolution Ikonos-2 image taken at 8th November 2000 at 11 am was used (fig. 3c). Ikonos-2 imagery, launched in 1999, contains 1 panchromatic band with a spatial resolution of 1 m and 4 multispectral bands with a spatial resolution of 4 m (table 1) (http://www.space imaging.com/products /ikonos/index.htm).

From fig. 3, it is concluded that a minimum spatial resolution of 1 m is required for an adequate visual interpretation and inferred automatic extraction of archaeological features from remote sensed imagery. For the time being only five types of imagery accomplish this requirement: commercial satellite imagery of Ikonos-2 and Quickbird, aerial photographs, Russian Corona imagery and aerial hyperspectral imagery. Because aerial photographs or hyperspectral imagery were not at our disposal and the cloud coverage of corona was too high, only Quickbird and Ikonos-2 were left. Until now no Quickbird archive images were available for our study region. Fortunately there was one Ikonos-2 archive image covering the Hisar site and surroundings.

	Bandwidth (μm)	*Spatial resolution (m)*
Panchromatic	0.45 – 0.90	1
Band 1	0.45 – 0.53 (blue)	4
Band 2	0.52 – 0.61 (green)	4
Band 3	0.64 – 0.72 (red)	4
Band 4	0.77 – 0.88 (near infrared)	4

Table 1: Spectral characteristics of Ikonos-2 imagery
(http://www.spaceimaging.com/whitepapers_pdfs/IKONOS_Product_Guide.pdf).

Attributes	*Archaeological description*
Tone	Tonal differences in soil may indicate buried structures (crop marks)
Texture	Different vegetation textures may indicate buried features (crop marks)
Shape	Knowledge of shape of archaeological features can assist with determining whether a feature can be recognised as archaeological or not
Size	The dimensions of the feature are also important in order to regard the feature as archaeological or not
Spatial patterns	The spatial patterns among different features may represent an ancient settlement
Orientation	Some archaeological features are consistently orientated in a certain direction
Shadows	Positive archaeological features appear in an imagery through the shadows they cast
Spatial relationships	Ruins which have been abandoned for hundreds or thousands of years are sometimes located in isolated areas. Depending on the state of the ruins, they may be still associated with other nearby ancient features

Table 2: Ikonos-2 visual archaeological interpretation (modified after PAVLIDIS 2005).

Preceding the automatic extraction of archaeological features from Ikonos-2 imagery the high resolution panchromatic and low resolution multispectral bands were fused, using an IHS (Intensity Hue Saturation) transformation in Envi® to produce a pan-sharpened colour image. This pan-sharpened image was further rectified in PCI Geomatics® using 2 GCPs (ground control points) derived from a 1:25.000 topographic map and the Ortho Kit supplied by the image provider, in order to get a spatial accuracy of 3 to 4 m (fig. 7) (PCI 1998). With the intention not to bias the classification results, no radiometric corrections were applied.

3.2. Extraction of archaeological features from Ikonos-2 imagery

In the first place a visual interpretation of the Ikonos-2 image was carried out by digitising all supposed archaeological remains based on shape, tone, linearity and spatial patterns between different features as set out in Table 2.

The main aim of this research was to evaluate the contribution of an automatic extraction of archaeological features versus a visual interpretation from very high-resolution remote sensing imagery. Therefore three different methods were tested:

- a GIS-based method: (an edge enhancement filtering technique)
- a pixel-based method: (a maximum-likelihood classification)
- an object-based method: (a segmentation and nearest neighbourhood classification)

These methods were already used for the extraction and classification of various landscape elements in geology, geomorphology and ecology (HOFMANN 2001; MASUOKA 2003; JORDON *et alii* 2005), but no analogies are known to us for the classification and extraction of archaeological features.

Various landscape elements can be automatically classified when their spectral characteristics are different.

However, a major difficulty that arises when extracting and classifying archaeological features like remnants of walls is that these are often composed of the same material as that of the surrounding substrate. At Hisar the spectral characteristics of the archaeological features are identical to those of the surrounding substrate as both are composed of white limestone. Moreover archaeological structures do not have unique shape or spectral characteristics, which could make the extraction more straightforward. Regarding their shape, width and length of ancient walls are very different. Neither do they form a straight line in the landscape. With relation to their spectral characteristics, archaeological walls are often degraded by surface weathering or covered with mosses causing a change in reflection.

3.2.1. GIS-based method: edge enhancement filtering technique

Because no analogies for automatic archaeological feature extraction were found in literature, filtering techniques used for automatic road extraction from high resolution remote sensing images and filtering methods used for lineament extraction in geology were evaluated (NEAWSUPARP-CHARUSIRI 2004; MOORE-WALTZ 1983). The application of an edge enhancement filtering technique available in Idrisi® gives the best results. Edge enhancement techniques accentuate areas of abrupt change in continuous surfaces and a new pixel value is derived from the original pixel value and the surrounding pixel values by moving a window with a specific kernel size (3 by 3, 5 by 5 or a user specified kernel size).

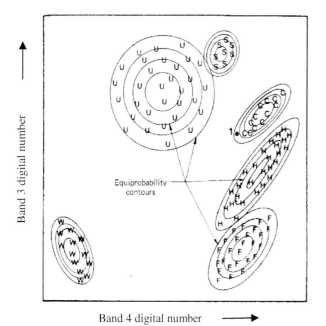

Fig. 4: Class division defined by a maximum likelihood classifier (LILLESAND et alii 2004).

3.2.2. Pixel-based method

Pixel-based methods only take into account the spectral characteristics of pixels in the image. Various pixel-based methods (SAM, Parallelepiped, Minimum Distance, Maximum Likelihood) were evaluated and eventually a maximum likelihood classification was selected, because of the incorporation of both variance and covariance of the spectral classes (fig. 4) (LILLESAND et alii 2004). This classification method assigns a pixel to the class with the highest probability.

To apply a maximum likelihood classification, different types of land cover training samples were selected to guide the classification and to test the class separability using the Transformed Divergence value Eq. (1) and Eq. (2) (SWAIN-DAVIS 1978).

$$TD_{ij} = 2000(1 - \exp\left(\frac{-D_{ij}}{8}\right)) \qquad \text{Eq (1)}$$

$$D_{ij} = \frac{1}{2}tr((C_i - C_j)(C_i^{-1} - C_j^{-1})) + \frac{1}{2}tr((C_i^{-1} - C_j^{-1})(\mu_i - \mu_j)(\mu_i - \mu_j)^T) \qquad \text{Eq (2)}$$

i and j= the two signatures (classes being compared)
C_i= the covariance matrix of signature I
μ_i= the mean vector of signature I
tr= the trace function (matrix algebra)
T= the transposition function

As archaeological remains of the Hisar site mainly consist of limestone walls of about 0.5-1 m high and were also detectable by their shadows, only those two classes (walls and shadows of walls) were selected for the extraction of archaeological features.

Due to atmospheric absorption of carbon dioxide, ozone and water vapour, only the 3-5 µm, 8-9 µm and 10-14 µm regions of the thermal infrared band are useful in remote sensing. Other pronounced absorption features are present at 1.4 and 1.9 µm. As such, these regions are not used in remote sensing of the earth surface (MATHER 2004). With relation to limestone, a low contribution to the red part of the electromagnetic spectrum is observed. Limestone possesses typical CO_3^{-2}-ion absorption features in the 1.8-2.5 µm region.

Two strong absorption features occur at 2.3-2.35 µm and 2.50-2.55 µm and three weaker bands are present at 1.85-1.97 µm, 1.97-2.00 µm and 2.12-2.16 µm (VAN DER MEER-DE JONG 2003). Areas under shadow modify significantly the value of the surface signature. Shadow reduces the reflectance and standard deviation value of the surface reflectance (MASSALABI et alii 2004).

Because for some land cover classes no normality could be achieved – a requirement for using a maximum likelihood classification – classification problems occur.

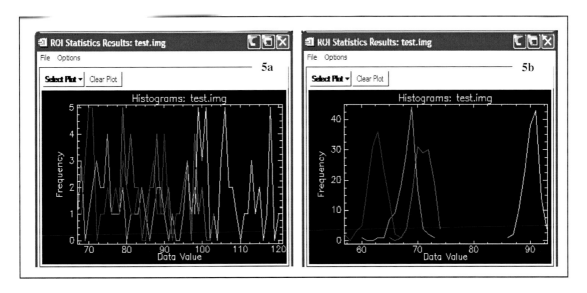

Fig. 5: Signature distribution of limestone outcrops (fig. 5a) and wasteland (fig. 5b).

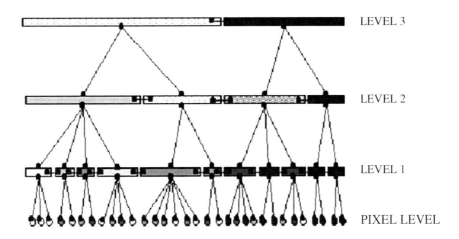

Fig. 6: Pixel aggregation within the segmentation procedure (WILLHAUCK 2000).

For instance, limestone signatures do not show a normal distribution in contrast with wasteland (fig. 5). Except for four class-combinations the separability index did not provide any problems: all values were higher than 1.9, the critical separability threshold (JENSEN 1996). Class-combinations with values between 1.9 and 1.7 are difficult to distinguish; while it is impossible to differentiate combinations with values lower than 1.7 (JENSEN 1996).

3.2.3. Object-based remote sensing

Conventional pixel-based techniques do not always work, as a pixel is not related to the characteristics of an object or an area as a whole, but to components of it (BLASCHKE STROBL 2001). An object-based method is considered as very useful for heterogeneous land cover, common in very high-resolution satellite imagery because of their high spatial and low spectral resolution.

An object-based technique in eCognition® starts with a segmentation step: the image is subdivided into homogenous regions based on their spectral characteristics, shape, scale (maximum allowed heterogeneity) and object hierarchy level (GIADA *et alii* 2003). A high shape value corresponds with a low colour or spectral value because of the importance of shape compared to spectral characteristics and visa versa. With relation to shape, a weighting should be made between smoothness and compactness. The latter is high for objects with similar spectral characteristics that are very different in shape.

Discrete land cover types often show a difference in internal heterogeneity and as a result various segmentation levels with specific scale values should be used. Hence, a high internal heterogeneity corresponds with a high scale value. Segmentation starts at pixel level where each pixel is a separate object (fig. 6).

Level	Scale factor	Homogeneity criteria		
		Shape factor	Compactness factor	Smoothness factor
1	5	0.023	0	1
2	10	0.07	0.85	0.15

Table 3: Segmentation parameters (increasing pixel aggregation level from top to bottom).

Fig. 7: Visual interpretation of archaeological features on Ikonos-2 imagery.

Next, different pixels are grouped according to the parameters defined and a new level is generated based on the previous level (level 1, fig. 6). The segmented regions become larger from one level to the next so that the internal heterogeneity of the objects increases (level 3, fig. 6). As a consequence segmentation assumes that more heterogeneous surfaces are stretched out over larger areas.

In a second step -the classification step- training objects are selected to train the classification in analogy to the pixel-based classification, but instead of using pixels as training samples, objects (the result of the segmentation step) are used. Next, classification parameters are defined. In comparison to a pixel-based classification not only spectral parameters, but also shape and hierarchical parameters are taken into account (table 3). Finally a nearest neighbourhood classification is carried out (BAATZ-SCHÄPE 2000; BAATZ *et alii* 2002).

4. Results

4.1. Visual interpretation

Fig. 7 shows the visual interpretation of remains of the Hisar site on the Ikonos-2 satellite image, where a distinction was made between archaeological features and inferred archaeological features. Only the main visual features are indicated in fig. 7. With relation to the inferred walls the association with other architectural features is less obvious, also the colour and shape of these inferred archaeological structures are less characteristic. The identified objects are remnants of a Byzantine and Early Hellenistic defence wall and some pre-roman house constructions (pers. comm. M. Waelkens). The perimeter of the mostly inferred defense wall elements that could be identified by visual interpretation, amounts to 510 m. Remnants of this ancient defense wall could be delineated in all directions. Other ancient wall structures derived from the very high resolution Ikonos-2 image are ascribable to remnants of ancient houses and cover an area of 3785 m², subdivided into three zones.

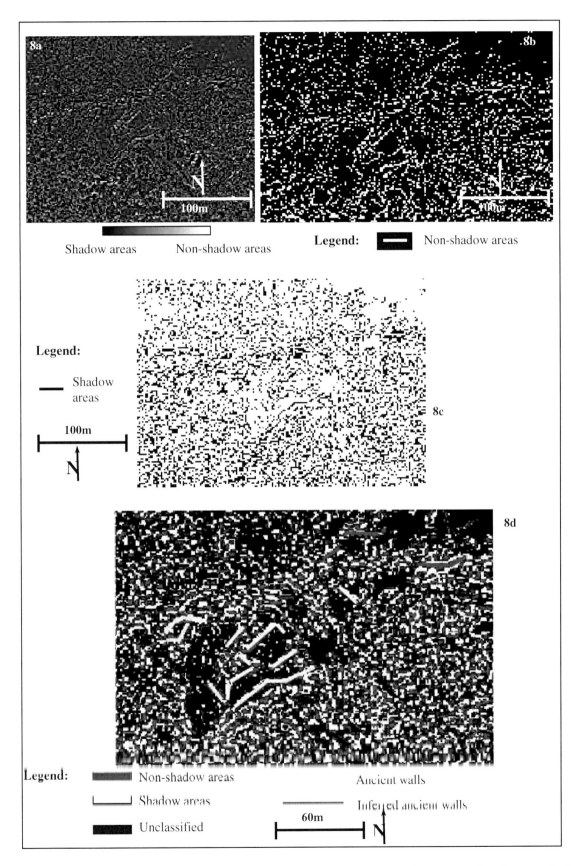

Fig. 8: Result edge enhancement filtering technique (fig. 8a: Initial result edge enhancement; fig. 8b: non-shadow areas classification; fig. 8c: shadow areas classification; fig. 8d: final result edge enhancement filtering).

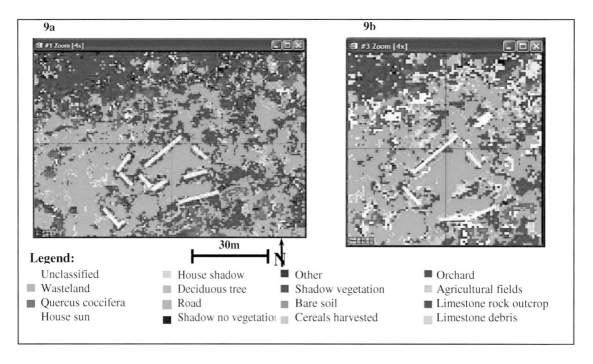

Legend:

Unclassified	House shadow	■ Other	■ Orchard
■ Wasteland	Deciduous tree	■ Shadow vegetation	Agricultural fields
■ Quercus coccifera	Road	■ Bare soil	■ Limestone rock outcrop
House sun	■ Shadow no vegetation	Cereals harvested	Limestone debris

Fig. 9: Pixel-based maximum likelihood classification result (fig. 9a: hard classifier version; fig. 9b: soft classifier version).

This visual interpretation of the Ikonos-2 image was used to evaluate the information level of the various automatic extraction techniques (see 4.2., 4.3., 4.4.). The advantage of a visual interpretation derived from very high-resolution satellite imagery over a field survey is the facility to correlate archaeological features and the ability to construct a city ground plan. Such an interpretation is very useful in advance of an intensive field campaign, to direct the fieldwork.

4.2. Edge enhancement filtering technique

The initial result of the automatic extraction of archaeological features by edge enhancement is a greyscale image (fig. 8a). In a second step this initial result was reclassified according to values corresponding to archaeological features: 100 - 400 for non-shadow linear features and -70 till -400 for shadow linear features (figs. 8b and 8c). The definition of these values was based on the visual interpretation of the Ikonos-2 image. The final result is an image showing lineaments in red and yellow. Unfortunately, not only archaeological features were extracted (fig. 8d). Edge enhancement filtering clearly does not provide a unique class for archaeological features, due to the presence of too many small linear features (e.g. trees and shrubs intermingled with archaeological features, a very normal situation for most archaeological sites in the Mediterranean) that provide a quick spectral transition. One may suggest that filtering is not the best option for adequate archaeological feature extraction.

4.3. Pixel-based classification

After evaluation of several pixel-based techniques, the maximum likelihood classification provides the best results. Fig. 9 shows the results for both the soft (fig. 9a) and hard (fig. 9b) version of the maximum likelihood classifier. By using a decision rule we were able to separately set the minimum membership value for each class and steer the classification result in contrast with the hard classifier version. For classes with a high separability index, the application of a rule classifier generates good results. The results of shadow areas are acceptable although a post classification threshold – e.g. on area – is necessary to extract areas under shadow directly connected to archaeological features.

Fig. 10 shows the membership value distribution of limestone outcrops. A membership value indicates for each pixel assigned to a certain category, how well that pixel matches the training sample of that category. If training sites are well chosen, many pixels will have the highest membership value. This is not the case for limestone as the peak is shifted to the left and the signature mean is off-centre from the pixels it represents. There are two explanations for this kind of distributions: poor training samples or class heterogeneity. With relation to limestone we suggest that the latter is the case. The spectral characteristics of limestone in the vicinity of Hisar are very divers, due to surface weathering, moss growth or internal chemical composition.

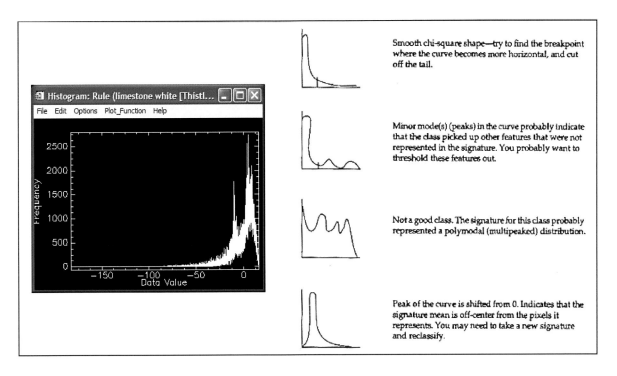

Fig. 10: Membership value distribution of limestone rock outcrops.

Because of separability index problems the application of a rule (soft) classifier does not yield better results for classes that experienced separability problems (e.g. many areas are assigned to crops although they are not). Also a mixture between oak -mainly shrubs- and deciduous trees occurs. Additionally, archaeological features are visible but they do not belong to a unique class as they should.

4.4. Object-based classification

To cope with the imperfections of pixel-based methods, an object-based remote sensing technique, particularly developed for very high-resolution images, was used (BLASCHKE-STROBL 2001; KIEMA 2002; GIADA *et alii* 2003).

In analogy to the pixel-based method limestone rock outcrops and shadows of walls and other landscape structures were selected to classify archaeological features. For the segmentation of archaeological features composed of limestone, we used a first segmentation level. For areas under shadow a second segmentation level was used, because they are more homogenous and less segment demanding. Segmentation parameters are presented in table 3. Fig. 11 shows the results of the object-based classification of both limestone outcrops and areas under shadow for the Hisar site. The results of the segmentation procedure of limestone rock outcrops (level 1, table 3) and areas under shadow (level 2, table 3) are represented in respectively, figs. 11a and 11b.

The results of the classification procedure are represented in fig. 11c. From fig. 11 it is concluded that many of the archaeological features are segmented very well. Archaeological features are segmented as separate objects.

The classification results show that the differentiation between roads and limestone and between *Quercus coccifera* and deciduous trees works very well. For most landscape elements on very high-resolution images, an object-based classification works very well compared to other automatic extraction methods. Unfortunately, the features within the classification category shadows of walls and other landscape structures (fig. 11c) do not only belong to archaeological structures, but also to other objects, such as trees. In analogy we observed that the category limestone rock outcrops (fig. 11c) encloses more than only archaeological features. Also fresh limestone is assigned to this category.

Because of the non-unique spectrum or shape characteristics of archaeological remains object-based classification seems impossible. We were not able to achieve a unique class for archaeological features under shadow and a class for archaeological features consisting of limestone.

However, the segmentation procedure within the object-based methodology is a valuable means to limit the digitalisation of individual archaeological structures as carried out in a visual interpretation.

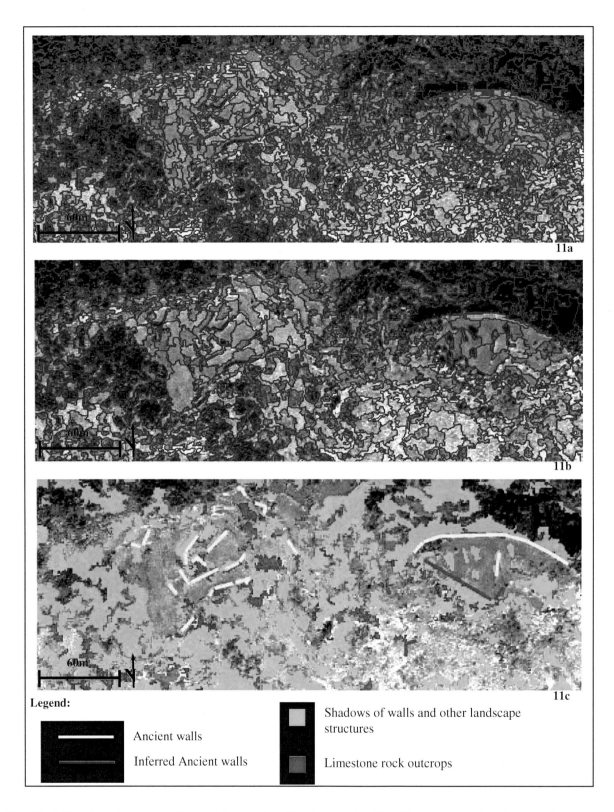

Fig. 11: Object-based segmentation and image classification results (fig. 11a: segmentation level 1: limestone rock outcrops ~ archaeological features; fig. 11b: segmentation level 2: shadows of walls and other landscape structures; fig. 11c: classification result of both limestone rock outcrops and shadows of walls).

5. Discussion and conclusion

The different classification methods applied, are able to classify archaeological features based on very high-resolution images, however with variable success. For most landscape elements pixel-based techniques and especially object-based classification techniques provide reasonable results. None of the demonstrated techniques however results in a unique class for archaeological features on the Hisar site. In the case of pixel-based techniques, this is due to the large spectral heterogeneity of archaeological structures. Most Archaeological features do not have uniform shape or spectral characteristics compared to modern houses or trees. The spectral characteristics of archaeological structures correspond with natural elements making them different from all other landscape elements. As a result, object-based classification methods do not yield satisfying results. Finally, due to the occurrence of many linear features at Hisar, with various lengths and irregular plan form, the contrast of archaeological structures with their surroundings is less obvious. As a consequence filtering does not contribute more than other techniques and does neither provide a unique class for archaeological features.

In case the archaeological structures at the archaeological site of Hisar consisted of materials different from those present in the natural environment, although this is only seldom the case, the automatic extraction of archaeological features from very-high resolution remote sensing images could be more successful. Since the archaeological site of Hisar is protected by the Turkish government, the lack of vegetation management and the interdiction of herding flocks causes an expansion of shrubs and trees. If some vegetation maintenance would occur in the area, much of the areas under shadow ascribed to shadows of natural vegetation would disappear and the classification of archaeological features would be more straightforward. Moreover, if the archaeological site should be located in an open field area, the automatic extraction of archaeological features would be less complicated.

In contrast to the automatic classification techniques, a visual interpretation of very high-resolution images presents excellent results. Such a visual interpretation of very high-resolution images could therefore provide much information for site location, site extension or site planning and should precede an archaeological prospection. It is also recommended to visually interpret very high-resolution imagery before executing automatic extraction techniques. Although the automatic extraction techniques are not fully satisfied, this should however not distract us from refining automatic extraction methods since these are less time consuming, are applicable on a large scale, and are much less subjective compared to a visual interpretation.

Possibilities for refining automatic extraction methods are the application of lidar and hyperspectral imagery with a very high spatial resolution (at least 1 meter) (DEVEREUX *et alii* 2005; CHALLIS in press). Spectroscopy measurements in the vicinity of the Hisar area and literature showed that hyperspectral imagery is able to identify locations with high ceramic densities so that the areas for archaeological field surveys can be limited (BUCK *et alii* 2003). It is assumed that many archaeological features undergo weathering processes with varying degree and typology compared to fresh limestone outcrops: for instance fungi and mosses growing on monumental structures are observed to be different from those on natural limestone. Such differences should be detectable much easier with hyperspectral imagery. Lidar provides very detailed and accurate information on micro topography, which is not available by any other means. Without lidar or hyperspectral images, it will be extremely difficult to extract less visible or small-unknown archaeological sites.

Véronique DE LAET and Etienne PAULISSEN
Physical and Regional Geography Research Group,
K.U. Leuven
Geo-Institute, Room 03.212
Celestijnenlaan 200 E
3001 HEVERLEE
Belgium

Marc WAELKENS
Eastern Mediterranean Archaeology, K.U. Leuven
Blijde-Inkomststraat 21, bus 3314
3000 LEUVEN
Belgium

Acknowledgments

This research is supported by the Belgian Programme on Interuniversity Poles of Attraction initiated by the Belgian State, Prime Minister's Office, Science Policy Programming (IUAP P5/09).

Apologizes

This article was written by the authors in 2005-06 but due to various difficulties it was only published in 2011, for which I want to apologize sincerely. Marc Lodewijckx (editor).

References

ABRAMS M. 2000. The Advanced Spaceborne Thermal Emission and Reflection Radiometer (ASTER): Data Products for the High Spatial Resolution Imager on NASA's Terra Platform, *International Journal of Remote Sensing* 21 (5): 847-859.

BAATZ M. and A. SCHÄPE 2000. Multi Resolution Segmentation: an Optimization Approach for High Quality Multi-Scale Image Segmentation. In J. STROBL and T. BLASCHKE, *Angewandte Geographische Informations Verarbeitung* XII, Wichmann Verlag, Heidelberg: 12-23.

BAATZ M., M. HEYNEN, P. HOFMANN, I. LINGENFELDER, M. MILMER, A. SCHAEPE, M. WEBER and G. WILLHAUCK 2002. *eCognition. Object Oriented Image Analysis. User guide (3.0)*, Definiens AG, Munich.

BLASCHKE T.S. and J. STROBL 2001. What's Wrong with Pixels ? Some Recent Developments Interfacing Remote Sensing and GIS, *GIS – Zeitschrift für Geoinformationssysteme* 6: 12-17.

BRACKE H. 1993. Pisidia in Hellenistic Times (334-25 B.C.). In M. WAELKENS, Sagalassos I, First General Report on the Survey (1986-1989) and Excavations (1990-1991), *Acta Archaeologica Lovaniensia, Monographiae* 5, Leuven University Press, Leuven: 15-37.

BUCK P.E., D.E. SABOL and A.R. GILLESPIE 2003. Sub-Pixel Artifact Detection Using Remote Sensing, *Journal of Archaeological Science* 30: 973-989.

CHALLIS K. in press. Airborne Laser Altimetry in Alluviated Landscapes, *Archaeological Prospection*.

CHANGLIN W., Y. NING, N. YUEPING and Y. LIN 2004. Environmental Study and Information Extraction of Archaeological Features with Remote Sensing Imagery in Arid Area of Western China, *Proceedings of the International Conference on Remote Sensing Archaeology*, Beijing.

CLARK C.D., S.M. GARROD and M.P. PEARSON 1998. Landscape Archaeology and Remote Sensing in Southern Madagascar, *International Journal of Remote Sensing* 19 (8): 1461-1477.

DEVEREUX B.J., G.S. AMABLE, P. CROW and A.D. CLIFF 2005. The Potential of Airborne Lidar for Detection of Archaeological Features under Woodland Canopies, *Antiquity* 79: 648-660.

EMMOLO D., V. FRANCO, M. LO BRUTTO, P. ORLANDO and B. VILLA 2004. Hyperspectral Techniques and GIS for Archaeological Investigation,

Proceedings of the XXth ISPRS Congress on Geo-Imagery Bridging Continents, Istanbul, Turkey.

LEICA 2002. *Erdas Field Guide (6th Edition)*, Leica Geosystems, Atlanta.

GEORGOULA O., D. KAIMARIS, M. TSAKIRI and P. PATIAS 2004. From the Aerial Photo to High Resolution Satellite Image. Tools for the Archaeological Research, *Proceedings of the XXth ISPRS Congress on Geo-Imagery Bridging Continents*, Istanbul, Turkey.

GIADA S., T. DE GROEVE and D. EHRLICH 2003. Information Extraction from Very High Resolution Satellite Imagery over Lukole Refugee Camp, Tanzania, *International Journal of Remote Sensing* 24 (22): 4251-4266.

HOFMANN P. 2001. Detecting Informal Settlements from Ikonos Image Data Using Methods of Object Oriented Image Analysis – an Example from Cape Town (South Africa). In C. JÜRGENS, Remote Sensing of Urban Areas – Fernerkundung in urbanen Räumen. *Regensburger Geographische Schriften*: 107-118.

JENSEN J.R. 1996. *Introductory Digital Image Processing: a Remote Sensing Perspective*, Prentice Hall, New Jersey, 526 pp.

JENSEN J.R. 2000. *Remote Sensing of the Environment. An Earth Resource Perspective*, Prentice Hall, New Jersey, 544 pp.

JORDAN G., B.M.J. MEIJNINGER, D.J.J. VAN HINS-BERGEN, J.E. MEULENKAMP en P.M. VAN DIJK 2005. Extraction of Morphotectonic Features from DEM's: Development and Applications for Study Areas in Hungary and NW Greece, *International Journal of Applied Earth Observation and Geoinformation* 7 (3): 163-182.

KIEMA J.B.K. 2002. Texture Analysis and Data Fusion in the Extraction of Topographic Objects from Satellite Imagery, *International Journal of Remote Sensing* 23 (4): 767-776.

LILLESAND T.M., R.W. KIEFER and J.W. CHIPMAN 2004. *Remote Sensing and Image Interpretation*, John Wiley & Sons, New York, 763 pp.

MASSALABI A., D.C. HE, G.B. BÉNIÉ and E. BEAUDRY 2004. Restitution of Information Under Shadow in Remote Sensing High Space Resolution Images: Application to Ikonos Data of Sherbrooke City, *Proceedings of the XXth ISPRS Congress on Geo-Imagery Bridging Continents*, Istanbul, Turkey.

MASUOKA P.M., D.M. CLABORN, R.G. ANDRE, J. NIGRO, S.W. GORDON, T.A. KLEIN and H. KIM

2003. Use of Ikonos and Landsat for Malaria Control in the Republic of Korea, *Remote Sensing of Environment* 88: 187-194.

MATHER P.M. 2004. *Computer Processing of Remotely Sensed Images: An Introduction,* John Wiley & Sons, Chichester, 324 pp.

MOORE G.K. and F.A. WALTZ 1983. Objective Procedures for Lineament Enhancement and Extraction, *Photogrammetric Engineering and Remote Sensing* 49: 641-647.

MTA 1997. *Geological Survey of Turkey Geological Maps,* vol. 4, MTA, Ankara, Isparta.

NEAWSUPARP K. and P. CHARUSIRI 2004. Lineaments Analysis Determined from Landsat Data Implications for Tectonic Features and Mineral Occurrence in Northern Loei Area, NE Thailand, *Science Asia* 30: 269-278.

PAVLIDIS L. 2005. High Resolution Satellite Imagery for Archaeological Application, www.fungis.org/files/news_mar05_archaeology.pdf.

PCI Geomatics OrthoEngine Reference Manual 1998. PCI Geomatics, Ontario.

RICHARDS J.A. and J. XIUPING 1999. *Remote Sensing Digital Image Analysis. An Introduction.* Springer Verlag, New York, 363 pp.

SEVER T.L. 1995. Remote Sensing. In P.E. McGOVERN *et alii* (Eds.), Science in Archaeology, *American Journal of Archaeology* 99 (1): 83-84.

SWAIN P.H. and S.M. DAVIS 1978. *Remote Sensing: the Quantitative Approach,* McGraw Hill Book Company, New York, 396 pp.

VAN DER MEER F.D. and S. DE JONG 2003. *Imaging Spectrometry. Basic Principles and Prospective Applications,* Kluwer Academic Publishers, Dordrecht, 403 pp.

VANHAVERBEKE H. and M. WAELKENS 2003. *The Chora of Sagalassos (Pisidia, Southwest Turkey). The Evolution of the Settlement Pattern from Prehistory until Recent Times,* Brepols Publishers, Turnhout, 362 pp.

VERMEULEN F. and G. VERHOEVEN 2004. The Contribution of Aerial Photography and Field Survey to the Study of Urbanization in the Potenza Valley (Picenum), *Journal of Roman Archaeology* 17: 57-82.

WAELKENS M., E. PAULISSEN, H. VANHAVERBEKE, I. ÖZTÜRK, B. DE CUPERE, H.A. EKINCI, P. VERMEERSCH, J. POBLOME and R. DEGEEST 1997. The 1994 and 1995 Surveys on the Territory of Sagalassos. In M. WAELKENS and J. POBLOME (Eds.), Sagalassos IV, Report on the Survey and Excavation Campaigns of 1994 and 1995, *Acta Archaeologica Lovaniensia, Monographiae* 9, Leuven University Press, Leuven: 11-103.

WILLHAUCK G. 2000. Comparison of Object Oriented Classification Techniques and Standard Image Analysis for the Use of Change Detection between SPOT Multispectral Satellite Images and Aerial Photos, *Proceedings of the XIXth ISPRS Congress on Geo-Imagery Bridging Continents,* Amsterdam.

Fig. 2:   The 'portable antiquity' of the Moscow ABM system: a Galosh (A-350) missile in its canister on parade in Moscow.

2.2. The response

The response of the Soviet authorities to this emerging threat has been described recently by V. Gobarev (GOBAREV 2001) and P. Podvig (PODVIG 2001: 412-418) drawing on Russian language sources. Ballistic missile defence was identified as a task of high national priority in the mid 1950s and between 1955 and 1959 an experimental system, known as System 'A', was developed at the Sary Shagan proving ground west of Lake Balkhash in Soviet Kazakhstan based on an anti-missile interceptor designated the V-1000. The first successful test of System 'A' as a whole took place on 4 March 1961 when the V-1000 interceptor engaged an R-12 medium range ballistic missile (known as the SS-4 Sandal by the US) launched from the Kapustin Yar Missile Range. In subsequent testing, the experimental System 'A' successfully intercepted similar missiles 11 times and demonstrated to the Soviet authorities that it was possible to develop and employ an ABM system that could intercept ballistic missiles.

Even before the results from the final stage of their experiments with System 'A' were known, the Soviet authorities decided to begin the development of a missile system, designated System 'A-35', to defend Moscow against ballistic missile attack. The main requirement of the system was the ability to intercept several ballistic missiles attacking Moscow simultaneously with each missile having a single warhead. A new interceptor missile, designated the 'A-350', was developed and practical work on the construction of the installations associated with System 'A-35' around Moscow began in 1962. The intention was for the system to be placed on

combat duty on 7 November 1967. However, by that date only a test model of the system was ready at the Sary Shagan test range and experimental launches of the 'A-350' interceptor missile indicated that the Moscow system would not be capable of defending the capital in the event of a massive nuclear attack. The primary problem was its inability to intercept the new generation of US ballistic missiles that were being equipped with multiple warheads (MIRVs) and improved defensive countermeasures. A new goal was therefore designed for the system of repelling a single or limited missile attack.

Acceptance tests of the Moscow ABM system were conducted in 1971 with the first section of System 'A-35' being approved for experimental use in June 1972 and the facilities of the second section being put on duty in 1974. The system as then deployed comprised a main command centre near Akulovo, approximately 70 km from the centre of Moscow and eight 'battle stations' situated in pairs along the Moscow Major Ring road near Bereya, Solnechnogorsk, Kiln and Zagorsk. A total of 64 'A-350' missiles were deployed across the 8 'battle stations', with each station comprising 8 launchers, two precision tracking radars and a single battle management radar (rather than a pair as reported by P. Podvig (PODVIG 2001: 416) – see below). In addition, the system included two very large phased-array early warning radars; one modelled on the Dunay-3 radar which was co-located with the command centre at Akulovo and a second, more modern Dunay-3U radar near Chekhov. Long-range warning of attacking missiles was provided by a number of Dnestr-M radars (nicknamed dual Hen House by the US) located on the periphery of the FSU (PODVIG 2002).

Component	Latitude	Longitude	Comments
Dog House radar	55.58N	36.65E	Transmitter
	55.49N	36.68E	Receiver
Cat House radar	55.20N	37.29E	Transmitter
	55.23N	37.29E	Receiver
Try Add complex	55.35N	36.48	E24 (Bereya)
	56.16N	36.50E	E31 (Solnechnogorsk)
	56.34N	36.79E	E33 (Klin)
	56.40N	38.19E	E05 (Zagorsk)
Support facility	55.30N	36.55E	Borovsk
Training facility	55.54N	38.19E	Kubinka (approximate location)

Table 1: Geographic locations of components of the first generation Moscow ABM system as determined from Google Earth.

2.3. The intelligence

Descriptions of the installations associated with the Moscow ABM system can be found in a number of intelligence assessments (e.g. CIA 1970; 1971; 1982) that have been released into the public domain as part of the CIA's Historical Review Programme. By the time it was considered to have achieved initial operating capability in the early 1970s, the system was assessed to comprise of the following components (fig. 1):

- Two acquisition and tracking radars nicknamed Dog House and Cat House located at Naro Fominsk and Chekhov. These correspond to the Dunay-3 radar and command centre at Akulovo and the Dunay-3U radar near Chekhov as described previously. Each radar comprised separate transmitter and receiver installations located some distance apart.
- Eight ABM launch sites deployed in pairs at 4 complexes around Moscow. Each site was composed of one large tracking radar and two smaller defensive missile tracking and guidance radars (the set of 3 being nicknamed Try Add) together with eight launchers for an antimissile missile nicknamed Galosh. These correspond to the 'battle stations' referred to above.
- A support facility at Borovsk that was used to prepare the Galosh missiles for deployment at the launch sites.
- A Galosh training facility located near Kubinka.

The 'portable antiquity' of the system, the A-350 interceptor missile (designated the ABM-1 'Galosh' missile by the US), was first observed in its canister (fig. 2) during the November 1964 Moscow parade. The intelligence assessed that the missile was most likely to be armed with a nuclear warhead (subsequently confirmed by Russian language sources (PODVIG 2001: 413)), and had an estimated maximum operational range of 650 km, a speed of 3,500-4,4000 m sec[-1] and a maximum effective altitude of 370-550 km (CIA 1969: 39). It was intended to intercept an attacking missile outside of the atmosphere and whilst the CIA initially assessed that a second intercept could possibly be achieved within the atmosphere (CIA 1970), by 1982 the assessment had reduced the system to a single-layer defence (CIA 1982).

3. Imaging the materiel culture

3.1. Imagery

Because of the large sizes of the structures associated with the Moscow ABM system, it is relatively easy to locate the identified components on geographically referenced, medium resolution imagery provided over the Internet by *Google Earth* (http://earth.google.com/) (see Table 1). Based on these locations, declassified KH-7 GAMBIT and KH-9 intelligence satellite photographs covering representative examples of the system's components were purchased from the US Geological Survey (USGS) (http://edcsns17.cr.usgs.gov/EarthExplorer/) at relatively modest cost in the form of scanned digital TIFF images provided on DVD. The spatial resolutions of the images were estimated to be of the order of 2m for the KH-7 photographs and 10m for the KH-9 photograph. In addition, three KH-4B CORONA photographs acquired by Mission 1111 were purchased, but, because of their high contrast, the scanned images were found to be

Fig. 3:   *KH-7 GAMBIT satellite photograph of the Dunay-3/Dog House acquisition and tracking radar acquired by mission 4038 on 11 June 1967. Key to annotations: A – transmitter complex; B – area cleared of woodland in front of the northwest phased array; C – receiver complex; D – support area. Data available from US Geological Survey, EROS Data Center, Sioux Falls, SD, USA.*

Fig. 4:   *KH-7 GAMBIT satellite photograph of the Dunay-3/Dog House transmitter complex acquired by mission 4028 on 15 May 1966. Key to annotations: A – security fence enclosing the transmitter complex; B – northwest phased array; C – southeast phased array. Data available from US Geological Survey, EROS Data Center, Sioux Falls, SD, USA.*

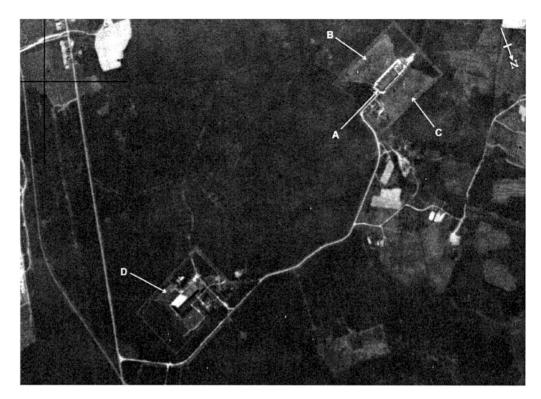

Fig. 5:   KH-9 satellite photograph of the Dunay-3/Dog House acquisition and tracking radar acquired by mission
          1215-5 on 25 May 1979. Key to annotations: A – transmitter complex; B and C – areas of cleared woodland in
          front of phased arrays; D – receiver complex. Data available from US Geological Survey, EROS Data Center,
          Sioux Falls, SD, USA.

Fig. 6:   KH-7 GAMBIT satellite photograph of the Dunay-3/Dog House receiver complex acquired by mission 4028
          on 15 May 1966. Key to annotations: A – security fence enclosing transmitter complex; B – northwest receiver
          face; C – southeast receiver face; D and E – construction cranes and their shadows; F – main command centre
          of the ABM system. Data available from US Geological Survey, EROS Data Center, Sioux Falls, SD, USA.

Fig. 7:   KH-9 satellite photograph of the Dunay-3U/Cat House acquisition and tracking radar acquired by mission 1215-5 on 25 May 1979. Key to annotations: A – transmitter complex; B – receiver complex; C – support complex. Data available from US Geological Survey, EROS Data Center, Sioux Falls, SD, USA.

unsuitable for detailed interpretation. This was surprising since the Photographic Evaluation Report for the mission (NRO 1971) indicated that the quality of the photographs was 'good overall' with 'generally medium' contrast. Clearly a significant reduction in quality has occurred between the original negatives and the scanned images provided by the USGS.

For ease of use, the digital images, each comprising approximately 1.2 Gbyte file segments of the original photographic negatives that had been digitised at 7µm (3600 dpi), were compressed using the ER Mapper freeware ECW JPEG 2000 compressor (http://www. ermapper.com) and viewed with the freeware ER Viewer 7.0 as described previously for digital CORONA images (FOWLER 2005). Once areas of interest were identified on the compressed, extracts were made from the original files for interpretation. Manipulation of these extracts, including image rotation, contrast stretching and enhancement, were achieved using Adobe PhotoShop Elements.

3.2. Acquisition and tracking radars

3.2.1. Dunay-3/Dog House radar

KH-7 GAMBIT photography acquired in June1967 (fig. 3) shows the Dunay-3/Dog House acquisition and tracking radar to comprise of two main components: a transmitter complex and a receiver complex, separated by

some 2.4 km in dense woodland and connected by an access road. Enclosed by a rectangular security fence, the transmitter complex (fig. 4) comprises a large central building together with two parallel, phased array, transmitter antennae orientated approximately northwest/ southeast. Additional smaller buildings are located within the enclosed area. Comparison of photography acquired in 1966 (fig. 4) with that acquired some 13 months later (fig. 3), shows the woodland in front of northwest phased array to have been removed by 1967. This was presumably in order to reduce the attenuation of the radar signal by the nearby trees and broadly coincides with the first interception by the US of signals associated with the radar in the summer of 1968 (BROWN 1969). By 1979, when the whole complex was operational, a low resolution KH-9 photograph of the Dog House radar (fig. 5) shows that the woodland in front of the southeast face of the transmitter array had likewise been cleared.

The receiver complex comprises an A frame structure rising to nearly 100m above the surrounding area, together with a large L-shaped building, all of which are enclosed by a security fence (fig. 6). The two flat faces of the receiver are essentially square and over 100 m on a side and, like the transmitter, are orientated approximately northwest/southeast. The L-shaped building probably corresponds to the main command centre of the system and additional, smaller, buildings are present in the enclosed area. Evidence that the structure was still under construction can be seen by the presence of two

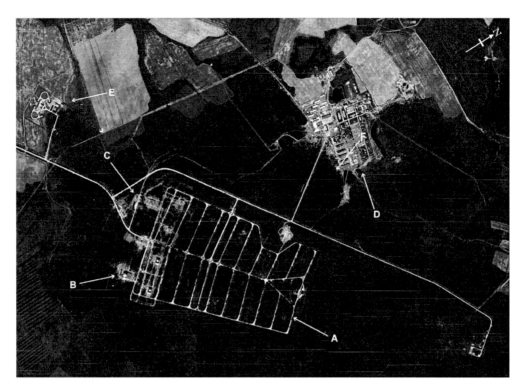

Fig. 8: KH-7 GAMBIT satellite photograph of ABM launch site E24 acquired by mission 4028 on 15 May 1966. Key
to annotations: A – 'herringbone' road network of former SA-1 Guild antiaircraft missile site; B – southern
Try Add complex; C – northern Try Add complex; D – support area; E – SA-3 Goa SAM complex. Data
available from US Geological Survey, EROS Data Center, Sioux Falls, SD, USA.

Fig. 9: KH-7 GAMBIT satellite photograph of E24 Try Add complexes acquired by mission 4038 on 11 June 1967.
Key to annotations: A – large tracking radar apparently externally complete; B and C – small tracking and
guidance radars apparently externally complete; D – large tracking radar under construction; E and F – small
tracking and guidance radars under construction; G, H and I – radomes under construction; J – possible
launch positions for Galosh missile interceptors. K – unidentified star-shaped feature. Data available from US
Geological Survey, EROS Data Center, Sioux Falls, SD, USA.

Fig. 10: KH-7 GAMBIT satellite photograph of the E24 support complex acquired by mission 4028 on 15 May 1966.
Key to annotation: A – road leading to 'herringbone' complex; B – possible multi-storey accommodation
buildings; C – cleared area on which 5 buildings were constructed by June1967; D – garden; E – possible
headquarters building; F – sports track; G – two buildings located within a possible enclosed area. Data
available from US Geological Survey, EROS Data Center, Sioux Falls, SD, USA.

large cranes adjacent to the receiver faces. However, by 1967 external work on the northwest face appears to have been completed as the crane is no longer present on a KH-7 image acquired at this time (fig. 3).

Approximately halfway between the transmitter and receiver complexes a support area comprising a number of rectangular buildings can be seen on the 1967 KH-7 image (fig. 3). The buildings in this area are absent on the KH-9 photograph acquired in 1979 (fig. 5) suggesting that it was associated with the construction of the Dog House complex rather than with its subsequent operation.

3.2.2. Dunay-3U/Cat House radar

Construction of the Dunay-3U/Cat House radar did not commence until 1968 (CIA 1970: 9) and therefore it is not covered by available KH-7 photography. As noted above, the 1971 CORONA imagery that was purchased for this study has a very high contrast and cannot be interpreted to any great extent. However, the KH-9 photograph acquired in 1979 (fig. 7) shows the radar to comprise a transmitter and receiver complex, both orientated approximately east/west and located approximately 2.8 km apart. With the exception of a possible support complex that could serve the two complexes, further interpretation is unfortunately constrained by the relatively low spatial resolution of the image.

3.3. ABM launch sites

Eight Try Add ABM launch sites we built in pairs at four previously constructed SA-1 antiaircraft SAM sites located in an arc around Moscow from the northeast to southwest. KH-7 photography of the southeastern site at Bereya, designated E24 by the US, shows clearly the characteristic 'herringbone' road network of the SA-1 SAM launch site (CIA 1961: fig. 4) as well as the structures associated with the two ABM launch sites (fig. 8). These comprise two Try Add complexes and a support area to the north of the 'herringbone' road network. In addition, on the basis of its characteristic shape (ZALOGA 1989: 84), a launch site for a SA-3 Goa SAM battery providing low level air defence can be identified to the southwest of the 'herringbone' complex.

Oblique KH-7 photography acquired in 1967 clearly shows the southern-most Try Add complex (fig. 9) to comprise three buildings on which radomes were located, the larger corresponding to the tracking radar and the two smaller buildings corresponding to the missile tracking and guidance radars for the Galosh interceptor. Adjacent to southeastern small domed structure is a star-shaped feature of unknown function and which is absent on the 1966 photograph (fig. 8). Six small rectangular features, each possibly comprising two vertical objects, can also be seen located on the two parallel roads either side of the smaller domed structures and a further two such features

Fig. 11: KH-9 satellite photograph of the Borovsk ABM support facility acquired by mission 1215-5 on 25 May 1979. Key to annotation: A – security fence enclosing the support facility; B – large building. Data available from US Geological Survey, EROS Data Center, Sioux Falls, SD, USA.

are conjectured to be obscured by trees. On the basis of a poor quality illustration in a contemporary intelligence memorandum (CIA 1966), these features may represent the launch positions for the Galosh missile interceptors. The missile appears to have been launched from within its canister and these features may represent pairs of trunnions that were used to elevate the canister into its launch position (ZALOGA 1989: 131).

By way of contrast, the northern-most Try Add complex is in a mid stage of construction with the radomes yet to be installed and in the process of being assembled beside each of the three buildings (fig. 9). The image gives some indication of what was located within the completed radomes with vertical structures on the roofs of the buildings most likely representing components of the radar antennae that were subsequently covered by the radomes.

Additional buildings associated with the complexes appear to be under construction beside the road leading away to the northwest and an extensive support area is connected to the road network of the herringbone complex (fig. 10). Features that can be identified in this area include: at least five probable multi-storey accommodation buildings, a possible headquarters building, a garden, a sports track and two large buildings

located within a possible enclosed area. In addition, by 1967 five large buildings had been constructed on a cleared area that was visible on the satellite image acquired one year earlier.

3.4. Support and training facilities

A number of the intelligence estimates (e.g. CIA 1971; 1982) depict a support facility located to the northeast of Borovsk and a training facility at Kubinka on maps of the Moscow ABM system. No further information is, however, provided for either of these facilities. A rectangular feature that encloses a complex of roads and buildings can be seen on low-resolution the KH-9 photography (fig. 11) and probably represents the Borovsk support facility. Further interpretation is constrained by the low spatial resolution of the KH-9 photograph. On higher resolution KH-7 photography, the facility is unfortunately obscured by an aircraft condensation trail and the poor quality of the CORONA photography precludes more detailed interpretation.

Positive identification of the training facility at Kubinka is more problematic. Two possible candidates for the facility can be seen on a KH-7 photograph acquired in 1966 (fig. 12), although it is not possible to say so with any degree of certainty.

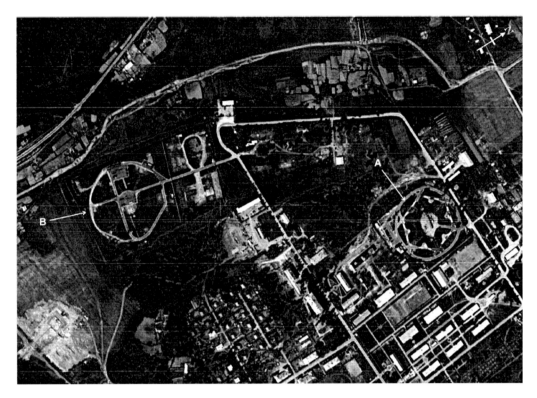

Fig. 12: KH-7 GAMBIT satellite photograph of the possible Kubinka ABM training facility acquired by mission 4028 on 15 May 1966. Key to annotations: A and B – candidates for possible Galosh training complex. Data available from US Geological Survey, EROS Data Center, Sioux Falls, SD, USA.

4. Putting the picture together

4.1. Operational concept

By combining the historical, intelligence and satellite photography evidence, the operational concept of the first generation ABM system can be described (fig. 13). Firstly, large, high-powered, Dnestr-M/dual Hen House phased-array radars located on the periphery of the FSU provided initial detection and tracking of incoming ballistic missiles at long range. The Dunay-3/Dog House and Dunay-3U/Cat House acquisition and tracking radars subsequently provided accurate trajectory information to the ABM launch sites deployed around Moscow. The Dog House radar was orientated to provide coverage of all potential ICBM trajectories from the continental US to Moscow but only a very small portion of the Polaris SLBM threat. The Cat House radar was orientated to provide coverage against SLBMs launched from the North Atlantic and intermediate range missiles launched from Europe. Once within range, the large Try Add radars at each of the ADM launch sites then provided accurate tracking information to the Galosh interceptor that was then tracked and guided to the intercept point by the small Try Add radars. Destruction of the incoming missile would take place outside the atmosphere at slant ranges out to 650 km from the Try Add launch sites through the detonation of the nuclear warhead carried by the interceptor.

Whilst each Try Add site was capable of guiding two Galosh interceptors, the relatively slow acceleration of the interceptor limited the system to essentially a single layer of defence. As such, the system could provide only limited defence against a massive US missile attack but could provide some protection against a small accidental, or unauthorised, US launch, or against a small unsophisticated attack by a third country.

4.2. Subsequent development of the system

The enormous technical problems that were encountered in developing the system prompted a cardinal change in the Soviet political leadership's attitude towards missile defence in the late 1960s (GOBAREV 2001: 38). Recognising that it would be impossible to provide absolute protection from US ballistic missiles, they decided to seek a legal ban on the creation of ABM systems whilst shifting priorities towards developing strategic offensive weapons as opposed to strategic defences. On 26 May 1972, the Soviet Union and the US signed the ADM Treaty that limited both sides to one ABM system deployment area centred on its national capital and another deployment area defending ICBM silo missiles.

In June 1975, a decision was made to develop a new generation ABM system to defend Moscow, codenamed A-135, within the limitations of the ABM Treaty

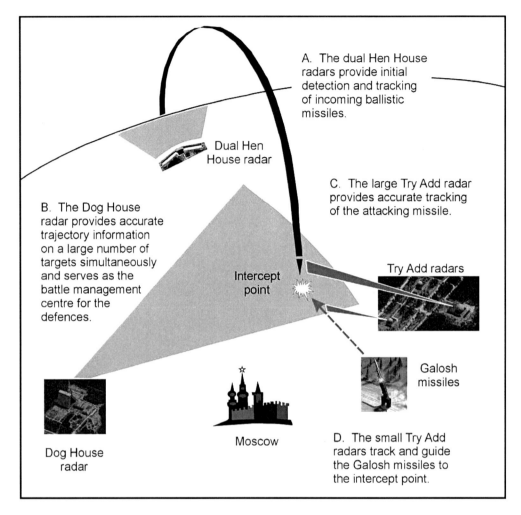

Fig. 13: Operational concept of the first generation Moscow ABM system (modified from CIA 1970).

(ZALOGA 1989: 138-141). The system was to be a two-layer defence similar to the US Safeguard ABM system of the time (BERHOW 2005: 30-36) and comprised two missile systems: a new hypersonic endoatmospheric interceptor missile and an exoatmospheric interceptor missile based on the Galosh missile, both types being launched from hardened silos. In addition, a new phased-array battle management radar, designated Don-2N and known as Pill Box by US intelligence, with four faces providing 360° coverage was built near the Moscow suburb of Pushkino. The A-135 system continues in service to the present day but appears to be suffering from benign neglect with its battle management radar operating less and less (ZALOGA 1999).

5. Discussion

This initial study has demonstrated that declassified US intelligence satellite photographs represent a unique source of overhead photography of FSU that can be used by the Cold War aerial archaeologist. Guided by the recently declassified US intelligence assessments and the low resolution imagery of *Google Earth*, the declassified

satellite photographs can be used to describe in relatively fine detail the fixed Cold War installations of the FSU that have hitherto not been considered in any degree of detail.

Whilst KH-7 GAMBIT photographs represent the highest quality images that are available to the Cold War aerial archaeologist, their temporal coverage is limited to the period 1963 to 1967. Notwithstanding the poor quality of the photographs from CORONA Mission 1111 purchased for this study, other photographs acquired by the KH-4B CORONA system that became operational in 1967 are of sufficient quality to be used to investigate Cold War installations and extend the temporal coverage up to 1972. From 1973 to 1980 the aerial archaeologist is limited to the lower quality photographs acquired by the KH-9 mapping cameras, but, as demonstrated in this paper, they nonetheless can have some use in respect of larger installations. Since over 900,000 photographs were acquired by these systems (FOWLER 2004: 121-122), the majority of which covered the FSU and China, for a significant part of the Cold War the aerial archaeologist has a vast resource of readily available satellite images available for use in studies.

Further work is required to characterise the Moscow ABM system in more detail in order to better understand the nature of the materiel culture of the system. In this respect, the large number of satellite photographs of the system's components (estimated to be in excess of 800 although approximately half can be expected to be cloud covered) allows the possibility to virtually 'excavate' many of the installations – much as the CIA analysts did some 40 years ago when the satellite photographs were first acquired (c.f. CIA 1963). By comparing a range of photographs of a site acquired over time, it will be possible to gain some understanding of both the order of construction and the internal layouts of the buildings associated with the installations as the various images document their construction. This can be seen in the present study in a number of examples including the clearance of trees in front of the transmitter arrays of the Dog House radar, the removal of buildings presumably associated with the construction of the radar by 1979 and the buildings of the two Try Add radar complexes being at different stages of construction.

Based on the scope of the English Heritage study of Cold War remains in England (COCKROFT-THOMAS 2003), the present study has but touched the tip of the iceberg of the FSU's Cold War materiel culture. Further areas for study include the Hen House strategic early warning radars mentioned above, airfields used by strategic bomber and air defence forces, fixed launch sites for ICBMs, atomic energy facilities and other installations. Declassified intelligence satellite photographs will provide a unique source of aerial photography to take forward such studies in a cost-effective manner.

Martin J.F. FOWLER
Les Rocquettes, Orchard Road
South Wonston
WINCHESTER SO21 3EX
United Kingdom
Email: satarchuk@btinternet.com

Acknowledgements

The assistance of the Information Access and Released Center of the US National Reconnaissance Office in providing a copy of the photographic evaluation report for CORONA mission 1111 is gratefully appreciated.

Apologizes

This article was written by the author in 2005-06 but due to various difficulties it was only published in 2011, for which I want to apologize sincerely Marc Lodewijckx (editor).

References

BAKER F. 1993. The Berlin Wall: Production, Preservation and Consumption of a 20th Century Monument, *Antiquity* 67: 709-733.

BECK C.M. 2002. The Archaeology of Scientific Experiments at a Nuclear Testing Ground. In J. SCHOFIELD *et alii* (Ed.): 65-79.

BERHOW M.A. 2005. *US Strategic and Defensive Missile Systems 1950-2004*, Osprey Publishing, Oxford.

BROWN D.C. 1969. On the Trail of Hen House and Hen Roost, *Studies in Intelligence* 13 (1): 11-19 (approved for release 1994, US National Archives and Records Administration, Research Group 263).

CIA 1961. *Soviet Technical Capabilities in Guided Missiles and Space Vehicles*, NIE 11-5-61 dated 25 April 1961, Central Intelligence Agency, Washington DC (released as sanitized 1996, CIA FOIA website).

CIA 1963. *Chronological Development of the Kapustin Yar/Vladimirovka and Tyuratum Missile Centers, USSR, 1957 Through 1963*, reproduced in K.C. RUFFNER 1995, *CORONA: America's First Satellite Program*, 191-196, Central Intelligence Agency, Washington DC.

CIA 1966. *Intelligence Memorandum: USSR Pushing Ahead with Antimissile Defenses for Moscow*, dated 18 May 1966, Central Intelligence Agency, Washington DC (released as sanitized 2003, CIA FOIA website).

CIA 1969. *Intelligence Handbook: Soviet Guided Missiles*, SR IH 69-2 dated May 1969, Central Intelligence Agency, Washington DC (released as sanitized 1998, CIA FOIA website).

CIA 1970. *Intelligence Memorandum: Soviet ABM Defenses – Status and Prospects*, SR IM 70-27 dated August 1970, Central Intelligence Agency, Washington DC (released as sanitized 1999, CIA FOIA website).

CIA 1971. *National Intelligence Estimate: Soviet Strategic Defenses*, NIE 11-3-71 dated 25 February 1971, Central Intelligence Agency, Washington DC (released as sanitized 1995, CIA FOIA website).

CIA 1982. *Soviet Ballistic Missile Defense: Volume 1 – Key Judgments and Summary*, NIL 11-15-82 dated October 1982, Central Intelligence Agency, Washington DC (released as sanitized 1996, CIA FOIA website).

CLARKE B. 2005. *Four Minute Warning – Britain's Cold War*, Tempus, Stroud.

COCROFT W.D. and R.J.C. THOMAS 2003. *Cold War: Building for Nuclear Confrontation 1946-1989*, English Heritage, Swindon.

DOLFF-BONEKAMPER G. 2002. The Berlin Wall: an Archaeological Site in Progress. In J. SCHOFIELD *et alii* (Ed.): 236-248.

DOBINSON C., J. LAKE and A.J. SCHOFIELD 1997. Monuments of War: Defining England's 20th-Century Defence Heritage, *Antiquity* 71: 288-299.

FOWLER M.J.F. 2003. The Archaeological Potential of Declassified KH-7 and KH-9 Intelligence Satellite Photographs, *AARG-News* 26: 11-16.

FOWLER M.J.F. 2004. Archaeology Through the Keyhole: the Serendipity Effect of Aerial Reconnaissance Revisited, *Interdisciplinary Science Reviews* 29: 118-134.

FOWLER M.J.F. 2005. An Evaluation of Scanned CORONA Intelligence Satellite Photography, *AARG-News* 31: 34-37.

GADDIS J.L. 2006. *The Cold War,* Allen Lane, London.

GOBAREV V. 2001. The Early Development of Russia's Ballistic Missile Defense System, *Journal of Slavic Military Studies* 14(2): 29-48.

ISBY D.C. 1988. *Weapons and Tactic of the Soviet Army*, Jane's, London.

JAMES N. 2002. The Cold War, *Antiquity* 76: 664-665.

McDONALD R.A. 1997. Potential New Applications for Declassified Early Satellite Reconnaissance Imagery. In R.A. McDONALD (Ed.), *CORONA between the Sun and the Earth: the First NRO Reconnaissance Eye in Space*: 245-254, American Society for Photogrammetry and Remote Sensing, Bethesda MD.

NRO 1971. *Photographic Evaluation Report Mission 1111*, Record 5/E/0041 of the Collection of CORONA,

ARGON and LANYARD Records Declassified on 26 November 1997, National Reconnaissance Office, Chantilly, VA.

PODVIG P. (Ed.) 2001. *Russian Strategic Nuclear Forces*, MIT Press, London.

PODVIG P. 2002. History and the Current Status of the Russian Early-Warning System, *Science and Global Security* 10: 21-60.

RICHELSON J.T. 2003. A 'Rifle' in Space, *Air Force Magazine* 86(6): 72-75.

SCHOFIELD J. 2005. *Combat Archaeology: Material Culture and Modern Conflict*, Duckworth, London.

SCHOFIELD J. and M. ANDERTON 2000. The Queer Archaeology of Green Gate: Interpreting Contested Space at Greenham Common Airbase, *World Archaeology* 32(2): 236-51.

SCHOFIELD J., W.M. JOHNSON and C.M. BECK (Eds.) 2002. *Materiel Culture: the Archaeology of Twentieth Century Conflict*, Routledge, London.

TUCK C. and W.D. COCROFT 2005. Digging up the Space Age, *British Archaeology* 81: 26-31.

WHORTON M. 2002. Evaluating and Managing Cold War Era Historic Properties: the Cultural Significance of US Air Force Defensive Radar Systems. In J. SCHOFIELD *et alii* (Ed.): 216-226.

ZALOGA S.J. 1989. *Soviet Air Defence Missiles: Design, Development and Tactics*, Jane's Information Group, London

ZALOGA S.J. 1999. Moscow's ABM Shield Continues to Crumble, *Jane's Intelligence Review* 11(2): 10-14.

MANAGING ARCHAEOLOGY IN AN AGRICULTURAL LANDSCAPE A SCOTTISH PERSPECTIVE

MOIRA GREIG

This paper is intended to show another use that aerial photography is being put to in a wider field – by using it as a tool to inform and educate farmers and landowners what archaeology survives on their land, and show how their current agricultural practice is damaging it, and how best to protect it for the future. Archaeology and agriculture have never sat easily together, with generations of farmers and landowners perceiving archaeology as something taking up a useful space – or in the local vernacular 'It's jist a pickle o'stanes – so git rid o't'.

Since the start of the great agricultural revolution in the late 18th/early 19th century agriculture has been responsible for the destruction of many archaeological sites, many disappearing especially in the early – mid 19th century. I work for Aberdeenshire Council, which also provides a service for the two neighbouring council areas, Moray & Angus, covering an area of 4200 sq miles (6759 sq kms) (fig. 1). In Aberdeenshire alone we lost nearly 330 out of 1078 recorded burial cairns, which is almost a third, and 92 out of a recorded 223 stone circles, almost half, and that is not counting the ones that were never recorded. The convenient 'pickles o'stanes' were used for building the farms and dykes. But the destruction didn't stop there. Unfortunately Government Policy over the years since the war must also take some blame for encouraging farmers to grow more.

Agriculture has continued to destroy sites up into the late 1990's with drainage and land reclamation, and with bigger machinery available and deeper ploughing, the sites that survived beneath the ground in the more fertile areas as crop marks, have continued to suffer from erosion over the years (fig. 2). Something had to be done to stop the destruction.

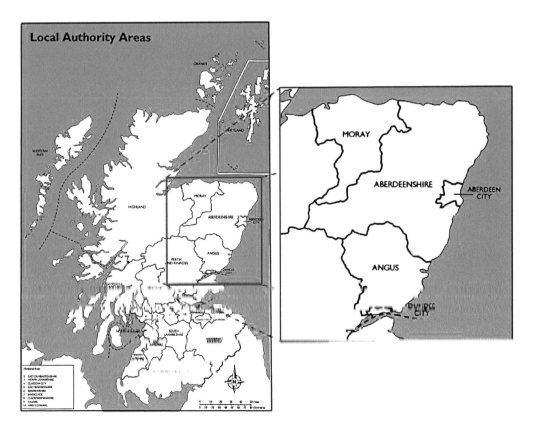

Fig. 1: Map of Scotland, with Aberdeenshire, Moray & Angus highlighted.

Fig. 2:   Newbigging, Angus: ring ditches being eroded by ploughing.

Fig. 3: Glenbardy, Aberdeenshire: extensive remains of a prehistoric settlement and field system,
overlain by medieval and later cultivation and settlement.

Fig. 4: Dun, Angus: Roman camp showing as a crop mark along with ring ditches and enclosures.

Farmers have often been described as a mercenary lot, with little interest in the historic environment. Their main interest being the yields of a crop and how much money they could make from it. In some cases this may well be the case, but I have found on the whole that most farmers do take an interest in the history of their farm, especially if their family has farmed the same land for several generations. Lack of understanding is probably one of the main problems, and just not knowing what they had on their land. To stop the destruction means showing farmers and landowners what they have surviving, and to help explain why it is important.

In Scotland the Government body for the protection of ancient monuments and historic buildings is called Historic Scotland, the equivalent of English Heritage. By an Act of Parliament of 1979, called the Ancient Monuments and Archaeological Areas Act, sites of national importance have a form of protection. It is an offence to damage a Scheduled Ancient Monument. There are some management agreements for these sites in place but they are few and far between, and only last five years.

Agriculture comes under The Scottish Executive Environment & Rural Affairs Department, or SEERAD, as it is better know. SEERAD started the first agri-environment scheme in c1987 with the Environmentally Sensitive Areas, or ESAs as they were better known. This Scheme was proposed to assist farmers in poorer

agricultural land, or less-favoured areas, in some of the glens of Scotland, covering about 19% of Scotland. For the first time we had the unusual situation of Officers from SEERAD meeting archaeologists and having training days to try to understand and recognise archaeological features. This was a task on its own, as they can be as mercenary as farmers! Taking account of archaeology in farming was a totally new concept. However, this scheme had standard protection of archaeological sites for all participants, and there were high levels of take-up (ca 90% in some areas).

In 1997 a new Scheme started up for those parts of the country not covered by the ESA's. This was called the Countryside Premium Scheme, where farmers had to start taking more account of their environment and were paid different rates depending on what they did. Although Archaeology was mentioned and an audit was required for participating farms, there was no particular protection for sites and no significant payment. All farmers entering the Scheme had to be made aware of what archaeology lay on their land, so aerial photography played a major part in the recording of new sites, especially in upland areas and arable areas (figs. 3 and 4). Unfortunately archaeology did not gain many points in the scoring system. Land containing a site of archaeological or historic interest was eligible for payment at a rate of £80 (116 euro) per 0.25 hectares or part thereof, up to1.5 hectares, and after that the rate dropped to £20 (29 euro) per 0.25 hectare.

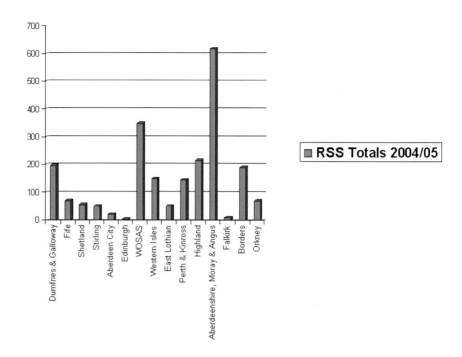

	Dumfr ies & Gallo	F if e	Shetla nd	Stirli ng	Aberd een City	Edinbur gh	WOS AS	West em Isles	East Loth ian	Pert h & Kinr	Highla nd	Aberdeensh ire, Moray & Angus	Falk irk	Bord ers	Or kn ey
Tot als 04/ 05	196	6 9	55	49	20	3	349	150	50	145	214	619	8	190	69

Fig. 5: Graph of number of agri-environment schemes dealt with in all Council areas in Scotland in 2004.

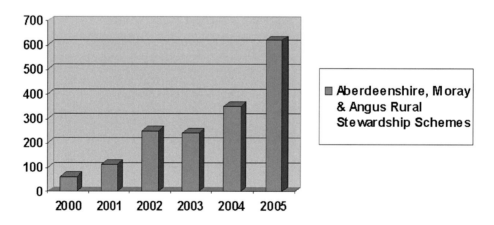

*Fig. 6: Graph showing increase in number of schemes handled
by Aberdeenshire Council Archaeology Service over 5 years.*

There was no management option for crop mark sites. Archaeology was competing with increased grass margins and the creation of beetlebanks, which received £184 (268 euro) per 0.25 hectares. So you can guess which one was chosen first ! There was also no particular ceiling for a single scheme, so the big estates tended to be the winners, with small farms loosing out. Due to shortage of funds entry was competitive with applications being selected on the basis of locally defined conservation priorities.

It wasn't until the latest Agri-environment Scheme, called the Rural Stewardship Scheme (RSS), started in 2001, and still current, that Archaeology started to come into its own. Entry for this is competitive, with applicants being selected by a ranking system. Though it is biodiversity-driven, the management of archaeological sites does now score relatively high-ranking points, so this has led to many applicants selecting a site for management. Payment for the scheme has been capped at £20,000 (29,154 euro), giving every farmer a better chance.

Fig. 7: Cunninghar, Aberdeenshire: this motte is showing evidence of severe erosion by rabbits.

Fig. 8: Cunninghar, Aberdeenshire: the same site taken on the ground in 2005
shows there is still a major problem with rabbits. A fence has also been erected across the motte.

Fig. 9: Barflat, Aberdeenshire: crop mark of a multi-vallate enclosure with a Pictish symbol stone standing within it.

A farmer can choose to manage an archaeological site and get paid for it! For some strange reason we suddenly saw an increase in interest – from not wanting an archaeological feature on their land we have the situation of farmers wanting archaeology on their land, and being disappointed if there is nothing there. With the higher payments we have seen a rapid rise in numbers since the introduction of RSS's (figs. 5 and 6), so much so that this year we had to take on temporary staff to help us enter new data.

However, before getting carried away with our success, when some agricultural advisers were asked how many archaeological sites they would include for management if there was no ranking system, they overwhelming answered 'none' !

We can suggest that active management would be best for a specific site, but this is not necessarily taken up by the farmer or his agricultural adviser, especially if he has already enough points and nearing his limit of £20,000 from other environmental aspects of the scheme other than archaeology. Sites being selected for management are often not the most significant, or most in need of management. In some cases there are more important sites not being selected because of their location (eg in the centre of a cultivated field), or because only a token site or sites have been selected for management, leaving others to decline. Many sites are crying out to be managed better, and a considerable number of these are Scheduled Ancient Monuments (figs. 7, 8, 9 and 10).

Farmers often tend to choose the easy option to manage, such as the remains of 19th century buildings, with its smaller buffer zone, rather than a larger area of a prehistoric field system, or even a stone circle.

Features surviving as crop marks can be managed by taking out of arable and put into grass, with a payment of £320 (466 euro) per 0.25 hectare. With the drop in prices for grain, managing an archaeological site has become a little more attractive. Without the help of aerial photography it is extremely difficult to explain what a crop mark site is to some farmers. If they can't see it they think it is not there. Combining a photo with an excavation shot brings it more to life, and with a ground photo of a site eroded by ploughing can also help (figs. 11, 12 and 13).

Aerial photography has started to take a new path as a useful tool towards managing archaeology in the agricultural landscape. Showing a farmer an aerial photograph of a site that has survived because no ploughing has taken place compared to the surrounding area, which has been eroded by agriculture, is useful (fig. 14). Photos can also show a feature which has been damaged by his agricultural practice, and this can really bring it home to him, as he is able to see a site as a whole rather than only partially on the ground (fig. 15). In some cases until they have seen a photo they have not realised there was a site on their land.

The types of sites I do have problems with being accepted as archaeology are World War II features, such as radar

*Fig. 10: Barflat, Aberdeenshire: the same site on the ground in 2005,
showing erosion around the stone caused by cattle and sheep.*

Fig. 11: Balbridie, Aberdeenshire: crop mark of a Neolithic timber hall.

Fig. 12: Warren Field, Crathes, Aberdeenshire: a Neolithic timber hall near Crathes under excavation 2005.

stations, airfields or pill-boxes because they were built within living memory.

Buffer zones around a site can also cause problems. SEERAD can be, or have been, over-zealous in insisting on a 10m buffer for every type of site, until I brought a case to their attention in which a 10m buffer was being asked for around a boundary stone sitting on a fence line. I felt this extreme, as I also feel a 10m buffer for 19th century building remains is. Now they are leaving it to the discretion of the archaeologists giving the management advice.

You do get the few exceptions where a 10m buffer is taken on board no problem, rather than 'Oh that's an awfy lot o' land to loose' (fig. 16). In the case of some stone circles some farmers think that as long as they stop ploughing through the middle they are protecting it and don't see the need for a big buffer (fig. 17).

At present we are in the ridiculous situation of not knowing what archaeological sites are actually being managed under the Scheme. Even Historic Scotland doesn't know which Scheduled Ancient Monuments have been accepted for management. We have asked SEERAD for this information several times but they kept saying this was confidential information, but, with the new Access to Information Act now in place we are hopeful this will be rectified before the end of this year. When flying over the area I can, of course, see a few sites that

are being actively managed and some that are obviously not, many again of which are Scheduled Ancient Monuments (figs. 18 and 19).

In my area SEERAD appear to have started to change their way of thinking. I have heard that SEERAD will even consider stopping payment if a farmer knows he has a site on his land that we don't have recorded, and he doesn't report it to us! However there is still an uphill battle.

We have only got to where we are now, mainly due to one person, called Jonathan Wordsworth, whose post as Rural Land Use Adviser is jointly funded by Historic Scotland and the Council for Scottish Archaeology. Jonathan has never ceased in his fight for archaeology to be included in agri-environment schemes by lobbying Members of the Scottish Parliament and SEERAD.

Now we are changing again with new legislation. Existing protection is offered through Good Agricultural and Environmental Conditions (GAEC) that form part of the Single Farm Payments and is primarily limited to sites already legally protected as Scheduled Ancient, Monuments and Listed Buildings. Protection is also offered to Designed Landscapes of historic importance. The new Land Management Contract (LMC) process, which started this year with a Tier 1 and Tier 2 system, is a scheme, which will provide flexibility and choice for land managers and is available on a non-competitive basis.

Fig. 13: Kintore, Aberdeenshire: remains of a souterrain lying immediately under the topsoil, recorded during an archaeological evaluation.

Fig. 14: Ardlair, Aberdeenshire: this area rig & furrow survived only because it was under forestry. None survive in the surrounding fields as they have been ploughed out.

Fig. 15: Tulloch, Aberdeenshire: remains of a late medieval settlement with farm track cutting across it.

Buffer zones are part of this. By 2007 Tier 3 will come in and be available on a competitive basis. Money will be available for actively managing the environment, and Scheduled Ancient Monuments will have to be included in any management plan for LMC's, although these only cover ca 10% of archaeological sites in Aberdeenshire. Managing other archaeological sites can however also be included in this. Tier 3 although similar to the present Rural Stewardship Scheme, will go further. It will enable activities to be carried out at the appropriate spatial scale, where some priority issue may be greater than an individual holding.

I now even get calls from farmers worried that their Single Farm Payment may be stopped because SEERAD have said they shouldn't be planting potatoes in a field with a crop mark site, unless the archaeologist says they can. They can't understand why they have to stop, when they have been planting potatoes in the same field for years. When you do get a farmer or landowner more than willing to manage a site simply because he wants to protect it, and is genuinely interested in archaeology, it is a bonus.

One thing is obvious, we cannot sustain the continuous rise in numbers of schemes we are being asked to check. Agri-environment schemes are now taking up nearly 75% of our time, so other work suffers. Sites & Monuments Records are not statutory in Scotland, although we have statutory duties in Planning. With every farm in Scotland

having to have an LMC in the future this will have a major impact on our workload. In Scotland there are 15 SMR's or HER's in Local Government areas, all at different stages of development. Few, apart from ourselves in Aberdeenshire, Moray & Angus are polygonised to show the extent of a site with its buffer zone. To help alleviate the impact of LMC's there are now proposals to have all, at present, unrecorded sites taken from old maps and vertical aerial photographs entered in to all SMR's or HER's, and the National Monument Record of Scotland at the Royal Commission of the Ancient & Historic Monuments of Scotland, clean out and tidy up all the records and have all sites polygonised and made available on-line by 2007, although more realistically by 2008.

There is a concerted effort to obtain funding from The Scottish Executive, through Historic Scotland and SEERAD, for this massive project for extra staff & equipment. A report has already been drawn up regarding the present state of play and recently presented to both departments. If approved this will help cut down our workload significantly for the Tier 1 and 2, and we can then concentrate on management advice for Tier 3. Working in conjunction with Historic Scotland and the Royal Commission on the Ancient and Historic Monuments of Scotland the aim is to have this information available on-line in the Historic Scotland web site called Pastmap2. Farmers and landowners will then be able to directly access the information from the

Fig. 16: Dunecht, Aberdeenshire: remains of a stone circle being managed well, with a large buffer zone to protect it.

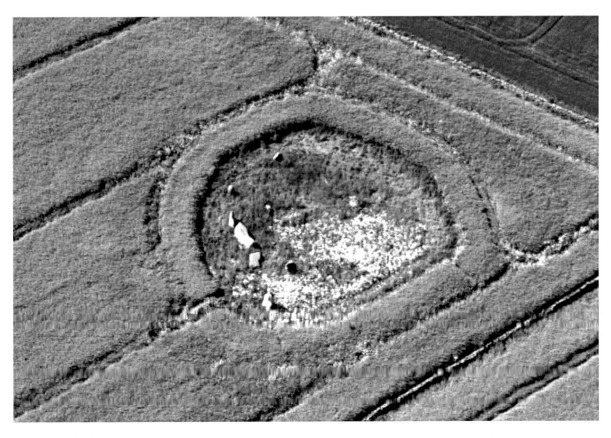

Fig. 17: Balquhain, Aberdeenshire: recumbent stone circle with outlier beside it. Although there is a small buffer it is not sufficient to protect the stones or any outlying buried features from further damage.

Fig. 18: Candle Stane, Aberdeenshire: remains of a stone circle being damaged by ploughing across it.

Fig. 19: Turin Hill, Angus: hill fort dissected by 18th-19th century wall,
with modern farm track cutting across the ditches and ramparts of the fort.

internet instead of coming to the SMR's for the initial site check, freeing us up for more site visits for management advice.

I leave you with this thought – perhaps we could be in danger of becoming too successful. What if all crop marks sites were managed by taking out of arable and put into grass ?

Moira GREIG
Archaeology Service
Aberdeenshire Council
Woodhill House
Westburn Road
ABERDEEN AB16 5GB
United Kingdom

Apologies

This article was written by the author in 2005-06 but due to various difficulties it was only published in 2011, for which I want to apologise sincerely – Marc Lodewijckx (editor).

Postscript

Since writing the article in 2005 a number of changes have happened. SEERAD is now called Scottish Government Rural Payments and Inspections Directorate or SGRPID. The Rural Stewardship Scheme, which significantly raised the profile of archaeology came to an end and the Scotland Rural Development Programme (SRDP) started in 2007. Archaeology Services are no longer automatically consulted as part of the process, nor are they provided with a farm map to be able to supply details of all archaeology within the area and suggest management to farmers. Applicants are now expected to check what is on their land through government websites. Forestry has now come under the wing of SRDP and now it is mainly Forestry issues that archaeologists are consulted on with very little through agriculture. One thing has not changed – we still cannot get a response from SGRPID as to what sites are being actively managed. The Scottish HER/SMR polygonisation programme has taken a step forward since 2005 but it is still on going and will not be completed for several years yet.

AERIAL PROSPECTION IN THE DANUBE REGION ON THE TERRITORY OF SLOVAKIA

IVAN KUZMA

Introduction

Danube, the second longest river in Europe, touches the territory of Slovakia by its middle part: from the Ipeľ estuary at km 1708,2 down to the Morava estuary at km 1880,2 (measured from the Danube estuary to the Black Sea). In spite of its relatively short flow (172 km) at the territory of Slovakia, it is the country's main river artery. It drains almost its entire territory, directly or by the river Tisa. After its enter through the Devin Gate to the Danubian lowland it flows on its own extensive silt cone with its borders armed with two biggest Danubian branches, the Little Danube (128 km long), which bounds the Veľký Žitný ostrov area (Grosse Schüttinsel, Csallóköz) on the Slovak side, and the Mošonský Danube, which bounds the Malý Žitný ostrov area (Kleine Schüttinsel, Szigetköz) on the Hungarian side.

Beside its dominant hydrographic position, the Danube had a great cultural and economic importance already in the prehistoric times, when prehistoric and protohistoric settlements were concentrated on both of its banks. Based on the landscape relief and type, three regions can be defined at this section: that of Bratislava, that of the Veľký Žitný ostrov and that which goes from the confluence of the Danube and Váh to the Danube's meeting with Ipeľ (fig. 1).

The region of Bratislava played an important role mainly in the prehistoric times as it was mediating impulses and contacts from the more advanced cultural centres of southern and south-eastern Europe. It represented the crossing point of two distant ways: the trans-European north-south, so called Amber Way, and the trans-continental Danubian-Rhinish way, which connected the East to the West. This relevant geographic position was the reason of a dense settlement of the Bratislava territory as early as in the prehistory. Here lies the only part of Slovakia situated on the right bank of the Danube, and includes Petržalka, Rusovce (ancient Gerulata), Jarovce and Čuňovo. In the Roman period this area was part of province Pannonia. Archaeological sites at the area of Bratislava have been completely elaborated in two books, which summarize the present state of the research in this region. In 'Archeologická topografia Bratislavy' (Archaeological topography of Bratislava; POLLA-VALLAŠEK 1991) about 100 sites are mentioned and in 'Najstaršie dejiny Bratislavy' (The oldest history of Bratislava; ŠTEFANOVIČOVÁ *et alii* 1993) as many as 252. However, their number is now undoubtedly higher.

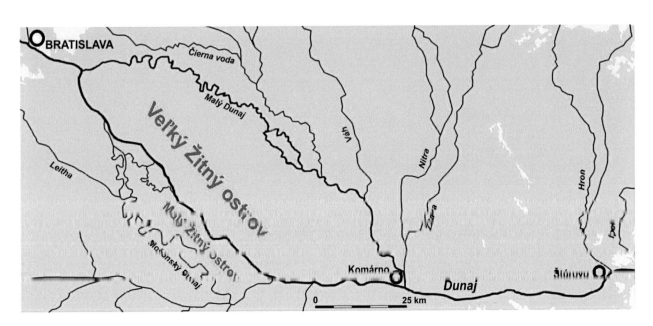

Fig. 1: Map of the Danube region.

Fig. 2: Chotín, polycultural site (02.06.1990).

Fig. 3: Orechová Potôň, ditch structure with rounded corners, dimensions approximately 40x60 m (09.07.1998).

The second significant region is the area of Veľký Žitný ostrov. Its importance for the settlement history and development of the relevant part of southern Slovakia has not yet been adequately appreciated. Already K. Willvonseder (BARTA-WILLVONSEDER 1934: 2) stated that there did not exist any work dealing with the settlement of this region. In those days only several sites were known and six of these are mentioned by J. Eisner (EISNER 1933), plus some references in older Hungarian literature, mostly in Archeológiai Értesítö. K. Willvonseder sees the reason of this lack of interest in the Žitný ostrov area first of all in the fact that the territory was often inundated and swampy in the past and therefore considered unsettled. Not even after 70 years of research, the present state of our knowledge concerning the settlement of Veľký Žitný ostrov area is not sufficient and summarizing work is still missing. This can be considered a remarkable handicap as it concerns a large territory with the area of 1855 km².

Although, due to various research activities, the Žitný ostrov is no longer considered an unsettled area in the past, the little interest in more consistent explorations has its origin in the fact that their results are relatively limited.

Fig. 4: Bratislava-Jarovce, Roman road from Gerulata to Carnuntum (08 06 2000)

The exact number of archaeological sites on the territory of Žitný ostrov cannot be fixed without a more detailed data elaboration. Wider information on the settlement, however, has been obtained by elaboration of private collections. One of the latest published and completing the picture of the Žitný ostrov settlement is the collection

of Antal Khín, which became the basis of archaeological collections deposited in the Žitnoostrovské Museum in Dunajská Streda (PICHLEROVÁ-TOMČÍKOVÁ 2001: 111). The collection includes archaeological finds from field surveys on 22 sites, mostly from the regions of Šamorín and Dunajská Streda (PICHLEROVÁ-TOMČÍKOVÁ 2001: 112). In general we can say that more than 100 sites dated to various historical periods have been found recently and documented by typical methods. Based on existing information we can state that the settlement of Žitný ostrov was relatively intensive in almost all historical periods from the prehistory up to the Middle Ages.

The third of the regions mentioned above is the area between the confluence of the Danube and Váh (km 1766) up to its confluence with Ipeľ (km 1880,2). Within this area places where archaeological sites are situated, can be relatively well determined already according to the above-sea-level height (which is not always possible in the Žitný ostrov region). Settlement in this area can be presupposed from 108-109 m a.s.l., which has been also documented by surface explorations. Archaeological sites in the area between Komárno and Chľaba were found directly on the Danube bank in Iža, Patince, Kravany nad Dunajom, Moča, Mužla-Čenkov, Štúrovo and in Chľaba. Besides, traces of settlement were found also under silts of the Danube, and on the Žitný ostrov area, e.g. in Komárno-Veľký Harčáš, where the Roman settlement appeared rather deeply under the recent surface and was covered with 1-1,4 m high silts (RAJTÁR-ROTH 1982: 231).

The most complex research up to now, which was oriented first of all on the immediate region of the Danube flow, approximately to the distance of 3-6 km, was done in the years 1977-1981 by the Archaeological Institute of the Slovak Academy of Sciences in Nitra. The Institute was in charge of protecting archaeological monuments and sites in the area between Gabčíkovo and Nagymaros where the System of Danube water works was constructed. The section from Bratislava to the Ipeľ estuary was therefore explored systematically; almost 200 sites were determined where archaeological finds were anticipated. The most significant of them have been selected for rescue archaeological excavations.

Aerial Prospection

In last year's the aerial photography has contributed remarkably to widening the knowledge on the settlement of Danube and Žitný ostrov areas. The first prospection flight aimed at search for archaeological sites was carried out in 1977 in connection with explorations in the region of Gabčíkovo-Nagymaros, but it did not bring any specific results. The situation started to change after 1987 when the Archaeological Institute in Nitra started with a systematic aerial prospection.

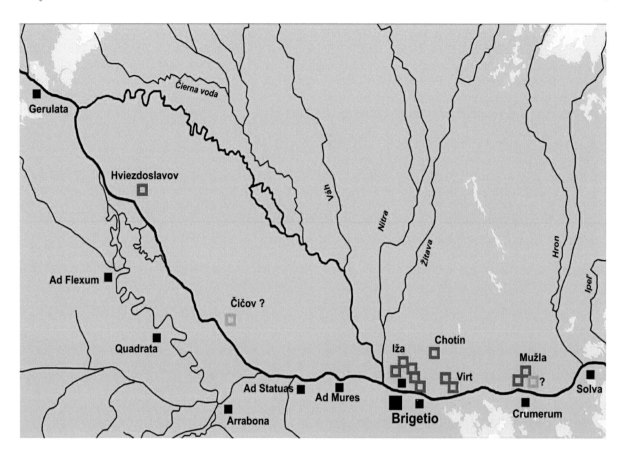

Fig. 5: Map of the Roman temporary camps on the Danube.

Talking about the aerial reconnaissance on the Danube, we have to say that it is not limited only to a narrow strip of the bank along the river, but it involves the territory of approximately 10-15 km. Such a distance is generally accepted when searching of accessibility areas (10 km means approximately 2 walking hours).

The main question was how the aerial prospection could be applied on the area with such complicated hydro-geographical conditions as those in the region of Žitný ostrov. The reason for this question was first of all experience from the surface surveys. Especially prehistoric sites are situated rather deep because of multiplied inundations, so their determining by typical archaeological methods, such as the surface survey, is often impossible. We could verify this also during field walking in 1980 and 1981, when we found traces after a Neolithic settlement in a sand pit profile north of Čičov. The objects in question were covered with an almost 1 m thick inundation layer, and finds on surface were completely missing (CHEBEN-KUZMA-RAJTÁR 1982: 98).

As it became clear later, however, our apprehensions were not legitimate. Effectiveness of the aerial prospection was fully vindicated also in this region. Bigger difference in comparison with other areas can perhaps be in the fact that here favourable conditions, which last for a very short time, have to be perceived

much more accurately. In several cases they lasted only a few days. A similar situation is typical of the territory north of the Žitný ostrov area, between the Little Danube and Čierna voda, Dudváh a and Váh. These regions are situated in the belt of a black soil on inundated clays with gravel bottom layer. Very favourable conditions were in the extraordinarily dry year 2000. During several flights we photographed there more than 50 new sites. Majority of them are situated in the vicinity of recent meanders of the Little Danube and north parts of Čierna voda. In several cases archaeological objects were situated along disappeared meanders or directly in them.

Until 2005 we have found and documented about 200 sites in the Žitný ostrov region; others were located in the area between Komárno and Štúrovo. Majority of newly found sites is settlement sites, mostly multi-cultural (fig. 2), various independent line or circular formations, ground plans of buildings, fortifications, burial mounds, burial grounds, temporary Roman camps, different ground plans of recently unknown function and dating, e.g. that in Orechová Potôň (fig. 3), ground plans of houses, etc.

Of course, not all of the regions have been covered with flights equally. A relatively smaller number of sites has been registered in Bratislava surroundings, what is a consequence of rather limited free agricultural areas.

Fig. 6: Iža, ground plans of Roman temporary camps 2, 3 a 4 (31.05.1990).

Some findings were attained on the Danube right bank around Bratislava-Jarovce and Rusovce. In 2000 we photographed a Roman way from Gerulata to Carnuntum (fig. 4). We also found some ground plans of buildings that could belong to the Roman period.

Up to now only a construction in Bratislava-Rusovce, in position of Horné pole discovered in 1993 (HANZEL-YOVÁ-KUZMA-RAJTÁR 1995: 54) has been verified and documented. The oblong building with a stone basement and dimensions of 11x7,2 m can be dated to the 3rd or beginning of the 4th century (VARSIK-KOVÁČIKOVÁ-IVAN 1999: 161). In Bratislava-Rusovce, position of Pieskový hon (KUZMA 2005: 57, Tab. 4: 2), a significant burial ground from the Migration period was found in 1996 (fig. 26: 1). The site was excavated and rescued in the years 2002-2003 (fig. 26: 2) before family houses were built there (SCHMIDTOVÁ-WEBEROVÁ 2004: 169)

Temporary Roman camps

Noticeable contribution of the aerial photography is expressed first of all in attaining a totally new evidence and knowledge about the Roman military stay on the territory of south-western Slovakia. For a long time only one Roman castellum was known north of the Danube in Iža near Komárno. Although the occurrence of short-term Roman military camps has been presupposed here, they were not discovered until the aerial prospection was carried out.

In the present 12 reliably identified Roman temporary camps in the Danube region are recorded in Iža – 5; Radvaň nad Dunajom – 2; Mužla – 3; Chotín – 1 and the only one up to now at the Žitný ostrov in Hviezdoslavovo (fig. 5). Besides these confirmed ones we might think about existence of others in Čičov, Chotín and in some locations that have to be confirmed and verified.

IŽA, district of Komárno

Five of these camps were discovered close to the known stone castellum in Iža by a survey flight in spring 1990. All of them were recognized as negative crop marks situated next to each other, but not overlying in any case (fig. 6). Oblong, slightly oblique ground plans with rounded corners were oriented with their longitudinal axes approximately in the W-E direction. According to the original detection all the camps were fortified only with one ditch. In 2005, however, we found what is probably a double ditch of the NE front in the camp 5

Fig. 7: Iža, temporary camp 5 (10.06.2004).

Fig. 8: Iža, temporary camp 2 (31.05.1990).

Fig. 9: Virt, Roman temporary camps 1 (03.06.1993) and 2 (04.05.1994), rounded corner of camp 2.

(fig. 7). Entrances on shorter sides were always situated in the middle, those on longer sides in two thirds of their length, set forward to the East. They reached the size of 130x90 m up to 210x150 m. Northern front of the biggest camp was approximately 330 m long and an advance short section of a ditch – *titulum* (fig. 8) – can be distinguished in front of its entrance.

Ditches of all five camps were examined on several areas by cuts. They had identical V shaped forms, widths of 2-2,5 m and depths of 150-170 cm. Besides small pottery fragments, a denarius of Emperor Commodus coined for Crispina in the years 178-182 or 180-183 was revealed in the filling of one ditch, proving the presupposed dating of the camps to the period of the Marcommanic Wars (HÜSSEN-RAJTÁR 1994: 219).

VIRT, district of Komárno

Other two camps were detected several kilometres east of Iža in the Hadvaň nad Dunajom cadastre, situated on the river Žitava terrace above its original estuary to the Danube. The camp no. 1 was discovered in 1993 as a crop mark, when a part of its SE front ditch and a rounded NE corner were clearly outlined in an uninterrupted length of approximately 270 m (fig. 9). A small excavation trench in the same year revealed a V shaped ditch as much as 280 cm deep and 4.5 m wide.

Within the years 1993 and 1994 a geophysical survey by a proton magnetometer was carried out here. We succeeded in observing the NE front line of the camp – a ditch – in the length of more than 800 m, with its course interrupted in two sections. A detailed measurement proved the camp entrances, both of them protected by an advance ditch section (*titulum*). At the same time the NW corner was located, length of the NE front was approximately 830 m, the presupposed width around 600 m. According to this, the camp area was almost 50 ha (RAJTÁR-TIRPÁK 1996: 143). Continuation of the SE front ditch was recognized by aerial prospection in 1996 (BLAŽOVÁ-KUZMA-RAJTÁR 1998: 35).

The camp no. 2 was located in 1994 in the close vicinity of the camp no. 1 (fig. 9). The distinguishable part of its eastern front with rounded corner has the length of approximately 340 m, a part of the northern front was 440 m long. The course of the northern front ditch of the camp 2 indicates that it crosses the SE front ditch of the camp 1, as the both camps are partially overlapping themselves and they were built at a certain time interval. A trench revealed a V shaped ditch, with its bottom 130 cm deep from the recent surface and its width reaching 1,6 m. Filling of the ditches did not contain any datable finds, but they can be dated, like in Iža, to the period of the Marcommanic Wars (RAJTÁR-TIRPÍK 1996: 144).

Fig. 10: Mužla, camp 1 (04.05.1994).

Fig. 11: Mužla, camp 3, western ditch (10.06.2004).

Fig. 12: Mužla, camp 3, eastern ditch (28.05.1994).

MUŽLA, settlement of Jurský Chlm, district of Nové Zámky

Three Roman camps were revealed in the village Mužla cadastre. The camp no. 1 was recognized during a prospection flight in May 1994 as a crop mark on the border of a loess terrace (fig. 10). Geophysical measurements by a proton magnetometer précised the camp ground plan and located the both corners of its northern front in a distance of approximately 135 m from each other; the southern front of the camp cannot be observed in the present because of terrace erosion. Three excavation trenches fully proved results of the aerial prospection as well as those of geophysical measurements. In three cuts a ditch with a width of 2-2,2 m was revealed, and was 125-130 cm deep. The ditch filling did not contain any datable finds.

The camp no. 2, situated under the terrace in close vicinity to the camp no. 1, was recognized as a crop mark by aerial prospection as early as in July 1988. In 1994 also geophysical measurements were realised here by a proton magnetometer; but unlike the camp no. 1 the ditch course was not recognized. Three trenches revealed a ditch with a width of 1,9 2 m and depth of 95 125 cm. In one of them the ditch partially overlapped a filling of a Germanic hut, which can be dated by finds to the second half of the 2nd century. We assume that both of the

temporary Roman camps were constructed in the period of the Marcommanic Wars (KUZMA-RAJTÁR-TIRPÁK 1996: 116).

The camp no. 3 was probably recognized on aerial photographs as late as in 2004 (fig. 11). Its eastern front was photographed in 1994 already as a straight line 180 m long. However, we supposed it is a ditch separating and protecting the Danube terrace promontory (fig. 12). But on photographs from the year 2004 we clearly identified the SW corner of the camp; the SE corner cannot be observed in the present because of terrace erosion.

CHOTÍN, district of Komárno

The camp in Chotín was recognized in the village cadastre, approximately 6 km from the Danube, in 1993 as a crop mark with dimensions of 110x100 m (fig. 13). An excavation trench in 1994 revealed a ditch 3 m wide and 130 cm deep, without any finds. Several repeated surface collections provided us with finds that correspond to those from Iža and so they can be dated to the same period. We found also another line with a rather unclear rounded corner, in the length of about 400-430 m. In 1994 we cut also this line and revealed a huge pointed ditch 4 m wide and 2,7 m deep, which could correspond with a ditches of a temporary Roman camps. This interpretation, however, seems to be premature now.

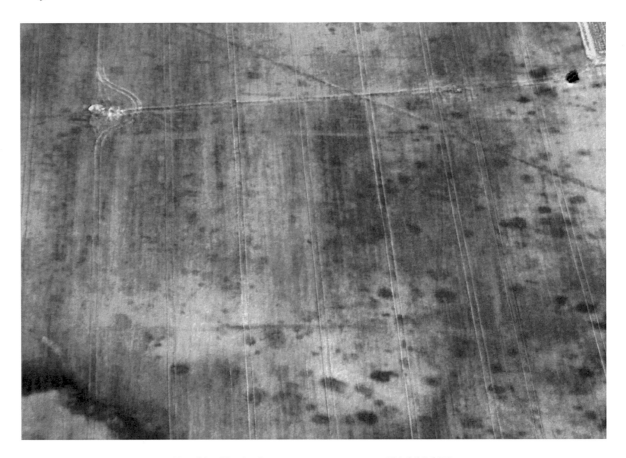

Fig. 13: Chotín, Roman temporary camp (21.06.2005).

Fig. 14: Hviezdoslavov, Roman temporary camp (08.06.2000).

Fig. 15: Čičov, Roman temporary camp ? (24.05. 2000).

Fig. 16: Patince, ditch fortification, the Middle Ages ? (04.05.1994).

HVIEZDOSLAVOV, district of Dunajská Streda

In 2000 we recognized a ditch observable from the camp corner in the length of maybe 250 and 800 m (KUZMA *et alii* 2001) in the distance of approximately 6 km from the Danube in Hviezdoslavov (fig. 14). This is a first camp on the territory of Žitný ostrov, in the area between Bratislava and Komárno. Although it has not been confirmed yet, we suppose it can be dated to the Marcommanic Wars like the other camps.

ČIČOV, district of Dunajská Streda

A ditch-like rectangular ground plan with rounded corners (fig. 15) was recognized in 2005 in Čičov (originally incorrectly determined as Veľký Meder), in the distance of perhaps 7 km from the Danube (KUZMA *et alii* 2001). In the year 2003 a survey was carried out here (VARSIK 2004: 192), but the existence of the camp has not been proved yet; in one probing cut a shallow ditch with a flat bottom was recognized. Survey collection contains also a Roman coin from the 4th century, and therefore its dating to the Roman period cannot be excluded.

Temporary Roman camps found so far are prevailingly situated on the left bank of the Danube directly or in its vicinity. All of them lay opposite camps on the Hungarian bank of the Danube (fig. 5). Five such camps in Iža were concentrated directly opposite the legionary camp in Brigetio. It is obvious that Roman troops crossing the Danube used the shelter of Brigetio for several times. Similarly, camps in Virt, only 9 km down the river Danube, could be built by troops from Brigetio. Three camps in Mužla are more distant from the Danube (6 km),

but still in the close clearway, opposite the camp Crumerum (today's Nyergesújfalu).

They probably worked as guarding or strategic points or as supplying camps on the important join line that led along this remarkable terrace towards the Hron estuary. The camp in Hviezdoslavov lies opposite the Roman castellum Ad Flexum near Mosonmagyarovár; until now unproved camp in Čičov lies within 15 km approximately in the same distance from the *castella* Quadrata, Arrabona and Ad Statuas. Hence in future we have to concentrate on areas that lie opposite the Pannonian *castella* and try to widen the number of temporary camps on the territory of Slovakia.

Other ditch-like formations

Besides the Roman temporary camps we recognized also some extensive and geometric ditch-like formations by our prospection flights, but according to our recent results they cannot be unambiguously classified among the Roman fortifications. We also discovered smaller square ditch-like formations (ground plans) with rectangular or rounded corners and an entrance. They were found at the sites in Chotín, Komárno Mužla, etc.

Two such objects (fig. 8) in Komárno-Veľký Harčáš were verified by excavations. They were shallow ditches or gutters with oblique walls and flat or rounded bottom, which surrounded small areas with dimensions of 11x11 m and 12x15 m. Filling of the ditches contains sparse pottery fragments that can be dated to the 11th-12th century.

 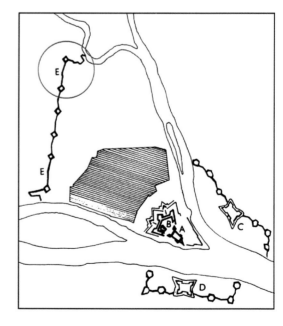

Fig. 17: Komárno, Palatín line (02.05.2005) and plan of Komárno fortress (GRÁFEĽ 1986).

Fig. 18: Štúrovo, 1, 2. hexagonal redoubt and a line with several lunettes in regular intervals (13.06.2000);
3. sector from the map of Ostrihom district, 4. sector from the map of Ordnance survey the first;
5. western end of fortification (02.05.2005).

Fig. 19: Bajtava, circular enclosure, Lengyel culture (10.06.2004).

PATINCE, district of Komárno

In the village cadastre two ditch-like formations were discovered. In the first case only a remarkable rectangular corner was preserved; the remaining part of the fortification was interrupted by a contemporary channel and the village buildings. A trench revealed a V shaped ditch 2 m wide and 140 cm deep. The ditch filling did not include any archaeological material.

Another spacious ditch-like formation with an annex (?) was recognized on the eastern border of the village not far from the original Žitava estuary to the Danube (fig. 16). In two cuts a V shaped ditch 3 m wide and 130 cm deep was found. Datable archaeological material was not revealed.

KOMÁRNO, district of Komárno

Besides documenting the present state of the Komárno fortification, we have photographed the course and the last two out of six redoubts of the so-called Palatín line built in 1809 (GRÁFEL 1986: 22), which have remained undistorted by building of town (fig. 17).

ŠTÚROVO, district of Nové Zámky

In the position 'Valy pod vŕškom' the course of a medieval earthen fortification was recognized as positive crop mark in 2000, and it was observable in the length of 2200-2500 m. It consisted of a straight line with several lunettes arranged in regular intervals, with joined advance redoubt with two lunettes and with an advance hexagonal redoubt having four visible bastions on its western border (fig. 18: 1, 2).

In 2005 we succeeded in photographing also its ending on the eastern side (fig. 18: 5). In maps from first ordnance survey (1782-1785), however, the fortification did not occur (fig. 18: 4). In Budapest Orszáogs Széchenyi Könyvtár we fortunately found a map of the Esztergom district made around 1740, on which the fortification exists and fully corresponds with our findings (fig. 18: 3). It is interesting that on maps only 40 years younger the fortification did not occur, although it has to be a rather huge construction (the position name is interesting, too: Valy pod vŕškom, i.e. mounds under the hill).

What we succeeded to recognize is the outer line of the fortification; the inner one has been completely destroyed by a pulp mill and town housing. There is only a small area, on which the inner line could be discovered. Although dating of the fortification has not been proved up to now, we expected it to be a part of the fortification system built for Esztergom protection during the Turkish wars.

Fig. 20: Svodín, circular enclosure Svodín 3 ? (02.05.2005).

Circular ditch formations

Several ditch-like formations of various kinds were found also in the Danube region. Most of them are not roundels, but circular ditches of different functions. The Lengyel-culture circular enclosure was discovered only in Bajtava (fig. 19) in 1994. The site is situated near the Kováčov hills on the elongated ridge with SW exposition, 216 m a.s.l. In 2004 geophysical measurements were carried out here, which proved two ditches with dimensions of 188x130 m and 150x115 m. This is a non-standard type of circular enclosure, where the outer ditch is rather oblong than circular or oval (KUZMA-TIRPÁK 2005: 13).

A circular ditch that could be possible classified as a roundel was detected in the Svodín cadastre (Svodín 3) in the distance of perhaps 6 km from the enclosures in Svodín 1 and Svodín 2. It was recognized as a soil mark with the diameter of approximately 100 m (fig. 20). It has not been proved yet by geophysical measurements; the surface survey did not contribute to its dating.

Other discovered circular formations reach dimensions from 6 to 30 m; mainly circles with the diameter of perhaps 6 m are quite frequent. Those, which are bigger – from 30 to 40 m – are circles in Mad (fig. 21) and Mostová (fig. 22); their dating as well as their function are unclear so far.

Burial mound complexes and burial grounds

In western part of Žitný ostrov, in the circle of around 20 km from Bratislava, several burial mound complexes from the Hallstatt period were revealed, some of them also excavated in the recent past. Exact number of burial complexes is not known, as majority of them has not been observable on the earth surface. At the burial mound complex from the Hallstatt period in Dolné Janíky together with three already known preserved burial mounds also traces of other 40-50 were found, which were destroyed by ploughing (fig. 23), and which followed the old riverbed. Further burial grounds were documented in Veľká Paka-Čukárska Paka (fig. 24), Dunajská Lužná, Reca (fig. 25) and in Pusté Úľany.

Very important are discoveries of flat burial grounds, a very good example can be Bratislava-Rusovce (fig. 26). The micro-region, within which the greatest number of burial grounds found out by aerial prospection has been recognized up to now, is the neighbourhood of Mužla and Štúrovo, where seven burial grounds have been documented. At the same time the region of Mužla is 'the best flown-out'. We know 47 sites in its surroundings, of which 32 were revealed by aerial photography. Newly found cemeteries from the Avarian Khaganate period are relevant first of all. Two of them (Mužla-Jurský Chlm 2 and Štúrovo-Obidská pusta) were proved by excavations, too, and they have completed the recent knowledge on

Fig. 21: Mad, circular enclosure, barrow ? (21.06.2005).

Fig. 22: Mostová, circular enclosure (09.06.2000).

settlement similar to that in Komárno, where seven burial grounds from this period have been revealed recently.

Fig. 23: Dolné Janíky, barrows of the Hallstatt culture (03.12.1987).

their occurrence in the wider area of Štúrovo, where their number increased to five (Štúrovo-Vojenské cvičisko; Štúrovo-Obid; Štúrovo-Obidská pustatina; Mužla-Jurský Chlm 2 and 3). We do not exclude that the burial grounds in Mužla-Jurský Chlm 1 and Mužla 5 or even the burial ground in Štúrovo-Obid, can belong to them, too. The region of Štúrovo seems to be another centre of Avarian

Fig. 24: Veľká Paka-Čukárska Paka, barrows of the Hallstatt culture (21.06.2005).

Fig. 25: Reca, barrows of the Hallstatt culture (21.06.2005).

Fig. 26: Bratislava-Rusovce, cemetery from the Migration period (30.05.1996); a (17.05.2003).

MUŽLA-JURSKÝ CHLM 1, district of Nové Zámky

A burial ground (fig. 27) was found out by aerial prospection in 1994 and then proved by small excavation. Four inhumation graves were recognized here. Although all graves were without accompanying finds, they probably can be dated to the second half of the 10th or first half of the 11th century; their earlier dating, however, cannot be excluded (KUZMA-RAJTÁR-TIRPÁK 1996).

MUŽLA-JURSKÝ CHLM 2, district of Nové Zámky

A necropolis in the position Jurský hon (fig. 28) was discovered by aerial prospection in 1993. It occupies an oblong area of approximately 150x100 m; we estimate the number of graves at more than 150. Three graves were excavated here that can be dated to the Avarian Khaganate period, terminating 7th up to the incipient 8th centuries (HANZELYOVÁ-KUZMA-RAJTÁR 1995: 56).

ŠTÚROVO-OBIDSKÁ PUSTATINA, district of Nové Zámky

In 1994 a burial ground with the irregular area of perhaps 130x60 m (fig. 29) was detected here. Estimated number

of burials reaches 150. We supposed it to be the necropolis from the Avarian khaganate period. Following excavations with finds (bronze golden earrings, bronze cast bracelet with elaborately moulded terminals, a small bucket, etc.) proved it's dating to the 8th century.

Besides the cemetery, also several darker lines of various widths were recognized. Apart from two straight ones, which belonged unambiguously to irrigation pipes, also three circular lines were distinguishable. Considering their length of approximately 700 cm we suppose they are recent, too. As it occurred later, one of them was a ditch 350 cm wide and 175 cm deep, dated probably to the Bronze Age; the origin of the other two is still unclear (KUZMA 1996).

ŠTÚROVO-OBID, district of Nové Zámky

In the vicinity of maybe 500 m north-west of the village we found a burial ground with symmetric oblong area (fig. 30) by aerial prospection in 1994. Graves here are of the E-W orientation; their number is estimated at more than 200. A small excavation revealed two graves with finds dating them to the terminating 7th up to the incipient 8th centuries (KUZMA 1997: 116).

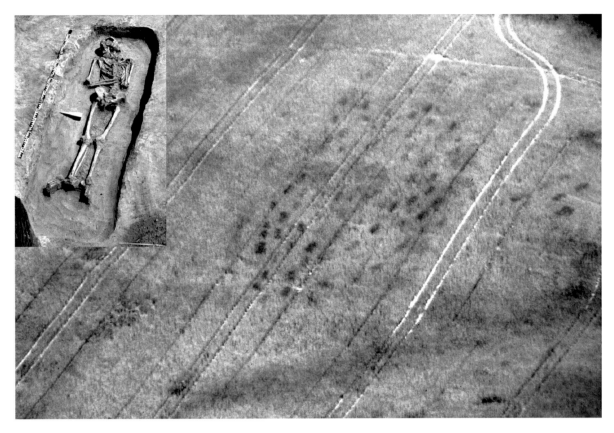

Fig. 27: Mužla-Jurský Chlm, cemetery 1, 10th-11th century (25.05.1993).

Fig. 28: Mužla-Jurský Chlm, cemetery 2, (photo O. Braasch 1994).

Fig. 29: Štúrovo-Obidská pusta, cemetery from the Avarian period (04.05.1994).

Fig. 30: Obid 'Bánom', cemetery from the Avarian period ? (28.05.1994).

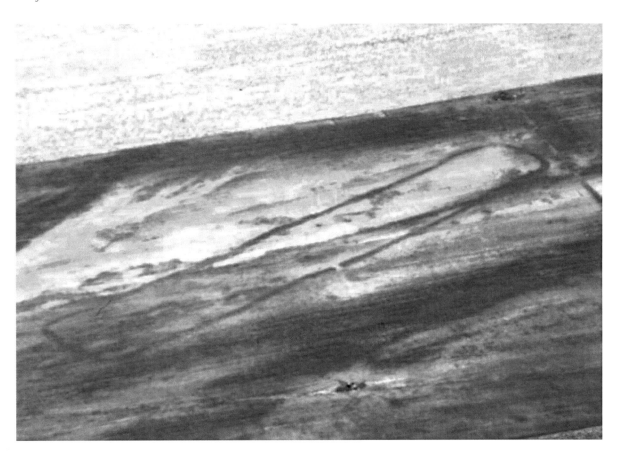

Fig. 31: Zlaté Klasy, ground plan of a long house (08.06.2000).

Fig. 32: Čierna Voda, ground plans of houses (07.06.1999).

Fig. 33: Tomášov, ground plans of houses (06.05.2001).

Fig. 34: Tomášikovo, ground plans of houses (07.06.1999).

Fig. 35: Jelka, ground plans of houses and circular ditches (17.05.2003).

Houses

One of the most significant new findings in recent years is a big group of sites, on which various formations of objects with oblong ground plans and rounded corners, having the width of 5-7 m and length up to 40 m, are situated. In some cases we can observe their division into two spaces. They are situated on dunes or elevations first of all in the surroundings of the Little Danube and its tributary Čierna voda, but generally on the whole area of Žitný ostrov.

In the present we register more than 30 places of such ground plans in Veľké Blahovo, Horné Saliby, Zlaté Klasy (fig. 31), Čierna Voda (fig. 32), Tomášov (fig. 33), Tomášikovo (fig. 34), Jelka (fig. 35), Jahodná, Orechová Potôň (fig. 36), etc. In several cases they are relatively dense agglomerations of ground plans, e.g. in Komárno-Nová Stráž (fig. 37), etc.

First, and so far the northernmost ground plans of this type we recognized in 1994 in Komjatice, where approximately 20 of them are situated on sand dunes. As their dating was unclear, the excavations were carried out in 2000, with the goal to confirm the dating of these objects and thus contribute to their interpretation (fig. 38: 4). Considering a small number and unremarkable character of excavated finds, the objects were dated only

generally to the prehistory and their interpretation is still open (KUZMA 2002).

Fig. 36: Orechová Potôň, ground plans of houses and circular ditches (09.06.2000).

Fig. 37: Komárno-Nová Stráž, cluster of house ground plans (20.07.2004).

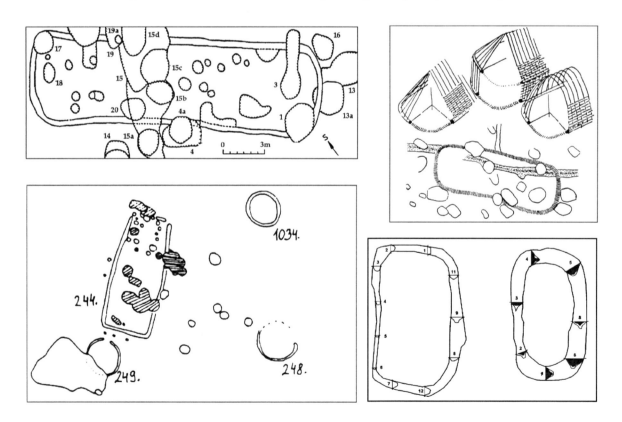

Fig. 38: Ground plans of excavated houses 1. Dvory nad Žitavou (PAVÚK 2002),
2. Hurbanovo (NOVOTNÝ 1958), 3. Lebény (NÉMETH 1994), 4. Komjatice (KUZMA 2002).

In spite of this, analogies give us the right to suppose they could belong to the Neolithic and thus represent a new type of houses. From the 1950s already two ground plans of oval houses with circular ditches are known from Hurbanovo (fig. 38: 2), together with a part of similar hut excavated in Šarovce (NOVOTNÝ 1958). In both cases they are dated to the Young Linear Pottery culture. On more sites revealed by aerial prospection such ground plans occur together with circular ditches with the diameter of 5-6 m (fig. 38). Three houses of oblong ground plan with rounded corners (fig. 38: 1) were discovered also during excavations in Dvory nad Žitavou (PAVÚK 2002) and were dated to the Želiezovce group period. Huts of similar shape in the vicinity of circular objects were excavated also in Lébény near Györ (fig. 38: 3) and were dated to the Balaton-Lasinja period (NÉMETH 1994). We cannot exclude existence of more similar cases, which have not been published yet because their shape and appearance that do not correspond with the common scheme of the Neolithic house typology.

Although all new findings cannot be mentioned in this paper, selected examples refer to the possibilities of filling up the white places on the map of archaeological sites with the help of aerial photography also in the regions with unfavourable geological conditions.

Ivan KUZMA
Archeologický ústav SAV
Akademická 2
SK – 949 21 NITRA
Slovakia
ivan.kuzma@savba.sk

Apologies

This article was written by the author in 2005-06 but due to various difficulties it was only published in 2011, for which I want to apologise sincerely – Marc Lodewijckx (editor).

Bibliography

BARTA H. and K. WILLVONSEDER 1934. Zur ur- und frühgeschichtlichen Besiedlung der Grossen Schütt, *Sudeta* 19, Reichenberg: 1-22.

BLAŽOVÁ E., I. KUZMA and J. RAJTÁR 1998. Letecká prospekcia na Slovensku, *Archeologické výskumy a nálezy na Slovensku (AVANS) 1997*: 32-35.

CHEBEN I., I. KUZMA and J. RAJTÁR 1982. Výsledky prieskumu v oblasti sústavy vodných diel na Dunaji, *Archeologické výskumy a nálezy na Slovensku (AVANS) 1981*: 98-103.

EISNER J. 1933. Slovensko v pravěku, *Práce Učené společnosti Šafaříkovy v Bratislave* 13, Bratislava.

GRÁFEL Ľ. 1986. *Pevnostný systém Komárna*, Bratislava.

HANZELYOVÁ E., I. KUZMA and J. RAJTÁR 1995. Letecká prospekcia na juhozápadnom Slovensku, *Archeologické výskumy a nálezy na Slovensku (AVANS) 1993*: 54-58.

HANZELYOVÁ E., I. KUZMA and J. RAJTÁR 1996. Letecká prospekcia na Slovensku, *Archeologické výskumy a nálezy na Slovensku (AVANS) 1994*: 81-88.

HÜSSEN C.M. and J. RAJTÁR 1994. Zur Frage archäologischer Zeugnisse der Markomannenkriege in der Slowakei. In H. FRIESINGER, J. TEJRAL and A. STUPPNER (Eds.), *Markomannenkriege – Ursachen und Wirkungen*, Brno: 217-232.

KOPECKÝ M., I. KUZMA and J. RAJTÁR 1990. Výsledky leteckej prospekcie, *Archeologické výskumy a nálezy na Slovensku (AVANS) 1988*: 100-102.

KUZMA I. 1992. Výsledky leteckej prospekcie na juhozápadnom Slovensku, *Archeologické výskumy a nálezy na Slovensku (AVANS) 1990*: 62-64.

KUZMA I. 1996. Pohrebisko z obdobia avarského kaganátu v Štúrove – Obidskej pustatine, *Archeologické výskumy a nálezy na Slovensku (AVANS) 1994*: 114-115.

KUZMA I. 1997. Pohrebisko v Štúrove-Obide, *Archeologické výskumy a nálezy na Slovensku (AVANS) 1995*: 115-117.

KUZMA I. 2002. Výskum v Komjaticiach, *Archeologické výskumy a nálezy na Slovensku (AVANS) 2001*: 92-95.

KUZMA I. 2005. Letecká archeológia na Slovensku. In *Ve službách archeologie VI*, Brno: 49-64.

KUZMA I., E. BLAŽOVÁ, M. BARTÍK and J. RAJTÁR 2001. Letecká prospekcia na Slovensku, *Archeologické výskumy a nálezy na Slovensku (AVANS) 2000*: 112-138.

KUZMA I., J. RAJTÁR and J. TIRPÁK 1996. Zisťovací výskum v Mužli – Jurskom Chlme, *Archeologické výskumy a nálezy na Slovensku (AVANS) 1994*: 118-119.

KUZMA I. and J. TIRPÁK 2005. New Neolithic Enclosures from Slovakia, *Proceedings of the 6th International Conference on Archaeological Prospection, Extended Abstracts*, Roma. 13-16.

NÉMETH G.T. 1994. Vorbericht über spätneolithische und frühkupferzeitliche Siedlungsspuren bei Lébény

(Westungarn), *A nyíregyházi Jósa András Múzeum Évkönyve* 36: 241-61.

NOVOTNÝ B. 1958. *Počiatky výtvarného prejavu na Slovensku*, Bratislava.

PAVÚK J. 2002. Die Apsidenbauten mit Fundament-gräbchen der Želiezovce-Gruppe, *Budapest Régiségei* XXXVI: 63-78.

PICHLEROVÁ M. and K. TOMČÍKOVÁ 2001. Archeologické nálezy zo Žitného ostrova, zbierka Antala Khína, *ZSNM* XCV, *Archeológia* 11: 111-134.

POLLA B. and A. VALLAŠEK (Eds.) 1991. *Archeologická topografia Bratislavy*, Bratislava.

RAJTÁR J. and P. ROTH 1982. Zisťovací výskum v Komárne-Veľkom Harčáši, *Archeologické výskumy a nálezy na Slovensku (AVANS) 1981*: 227-233.

RAJTÁR J. and J. TIRPÁK 1996. Rímske poľné tábory v Radvani nad Dunajom, *Archeologické výskumy a nálezy na Slovensku (AVANS) 1994*: 143-147.

SCHMIDTOVÁ J. and B. WEBEROVÁ 2004. Pokračovanie výskumu na pohrebisku z doby sťahovania národov v Bratislave-Rusovciach, *Archeologické výskumy a nálezy na Slovensku (AVANS) 2003*: 169-170.

ŠTEFANOVIČOVÁ T. *et alii* 1993. *Najstaršie dejiny Bratislavy*, Bratislava.

VARSIK V. 2004. Doplňovací výskum vo Veľkom Mederi a zisťovací výskum v Číčove, *Archeologické výskumy a nálezy na Slovensku (AVANS) 2003*: 192-193.

VARSIK V., J. KOVÁČIKOVÁ and P. IVAN 1999. Ukončenie záchranného výskumu na trase diaľnice D2 v Bratislave-Rusovciach, *Archeologické výskumy a nálezy na Slovensku (AVANS) 1997*: 161-162.

SPATIAL CHARACTERIZATION OF BURIED ARCHAEOLOGICAL REMAINS USING SATELLITE QUICKBIRD IMAGERY

ROSA LASAPONARA – NICOLA MASINI

Abstract

This paper focused on the assessment of the capability of VHR satellite images to provide useful information that can facilitate exploration of archaeological sites and permit the detection of buried remains. The capability of satellite QuickBird imagery for the identification of surface anomalies linked to the presence of archaeological buried remains is here discussed for four archaeological sites located in the South of Italy. The considered test sites present complex topographical and morphological features which make archaeological prospection with any remote sensing technologies difficult.

Results from the performed investigations showed that the satellite QuickBird imagery can be a valuable data source for reconstructing the urban shape of buried settlements up to single building scale. Such analyses can be useful for detecting locations and extracting features of archaeological sites especially prior to any excavation work and for increasing the cultural value of historical sites.

1. Introduction

During the last century both oblique and vertical aerial photography have been widely used to date for the identification of archaeological structures delineated by typical shadow, soil and crop marks (CRAWFORD 1929), namely surface anomalies linked to the presence of archaeological remains. Such marks can be usually seen on conventional air photography at appropriate scales and viewing angles. The ability to correctly identify archaeological remains by remote sensing is largely determined by the image spatial resolution. Although, crop and soil marks are more difficult to detect with certainty compared to shadow marks because their visibility often depends on vegetation/soil type and conditions, sun-sensor geometry and film sensitivity. For these reasons the detection of archaeological remains using aerial photos can be very difficult and expensive because many surveys in different time of the year can be required.

Satellite multispectral imagery may cope with some of these restrictions because they are providing information for a wide range of different wavelengths, many of which are more sensitive to vegetation/soil status and compositions. Moreover, satellite data acquisitions are assured on a regular time basis at a relatively low-cost even for remote areas. Currently spatial, spectral, radiometric and even temporal resolutions of Very High Resolution (VHR) satellite imagery, such as IKONOS (1999) and QuickBird (2001), have developed to such an extent that satellite imagery shares many of the physical characteristics of aerial imagery.

For these reasons, it is expected that archaeological applications involving satellite imagery will be increasing (LASAPONARA-MASINI 2005). VHR satellite may provide a valuable data source for archaeological investigations ranging from synoptic view (i.e. identification of high probability locations of ancient buried sites) to small details (i.e. single subsurface building); thus, overcoming the drawbacks linked to the low spatial resolution of early satellite sensors, such as Landsat Temathic Mapper (multispectral data at 30 m) or Spot (pancromathic at 10 m). The early satellite sensors were undoubtedly suitable for paleogeographic environment studies (PARRY 1992; DRAKE 1997; WHITE-ASMAR 1999), human ecology and landscape archaeology investigations (SHEETS-SEVER 1988; CLARK *et alii* 1998; SEVER 1998), but could not be adequate for the identifications and spatial characterization of buried structures (LASAPONARA-MASINI 2005). The availability of high spatial and spectral resolution of QuickBird satellite data can open new perspectives in the field of archaeological prospections.

The present paper discusses the results obtained from the processing of satellite QuickBird imagery performed for four archaeological sites characterized by different features from the geological, pedological and land-use point of view.

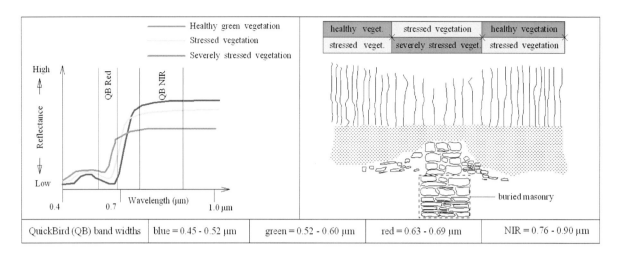

Spectral reflectance observed for different status of a
given vegetation type.

A detail of the typical crop marks caused by the presence
of buried structures.

Fig. 1: Crop-marks: phenological and spectral characteristics.

2. QuickBird satellite data description

QuickBird satellite has panchromatic and multispectral sensors with resolutions of 61-72 cm and 2.44-2.88 m, respectively, depending upon the off-nadir viewing angle (0-25 degrees). It provides a good stereo geometry and a high revisit frequency of 1-3.5 days depending on latitude. The reader is referred to technical notes available on line at the website http://www.digitalglobe.com/product/product_docs.shtml.

The panchromatic sensor collects information at the visible and near infrared wavelengths and has a bandwidth of 450-900 nm. The multispectral sensor acquires data in four spectral bands from blue to near infrared (NIR). Both panchromatic and multispectral sensors offer 11 bit (2,048 grey levels) resolution. The QuickBird imagery products are available at different processing levels (basic, standard, ortho) serving the needs of different users.

3. QuickBird-based spectral characterization of archaeological marks

The different kinds of marks, such as, soil, shadow and crop marks, that are generally associated with the presence of buried archaeological remains, could be detected using satellite data acquired in different spectral bands. This is because the characteristics and visibility of the spatial patterns linked to the presence of subsurface archaeological remains strongly depend on the type of surface anomalies that can be detectable on the vegetation cover and/or soil conditions. As an example, soil-marks can appear as changes of colour or texture in freshly ploughed fields before the germinating crops mask the surface of the soil. The main difficult in recording them is

getting over the fields at the right time, when the soil is damp. Shadow marks can be seen in the presence of micro-topographic relief variations that can be more visible in early morning or late evening.

Crop-marks are an indirect effect of buried archaeological deposits, that can be pits and ditches or walls. In the first case, the re-fillments of archaeological features store more water and nutrient. For this reason, the plants over them will grow higher ('positive marks'), stay green for a longer period and will have a darker green than the plants around. Thus, producing a tonal contrast. The opposite will take place with plants over buried walls.

On the basis of remotely sensed multispectral data, the different marks linked to the presence of archaeological remains should be detected by using specific spectral channels and/or their spectral combinations. Recently, some evaluations concerning the different sensitiveness of the QuickBird spectral channels were performed by Lasaponara and Masini (LASAPONARA-MASINI 2005 and 2006) for two different archaeological test sites characterized by different marks and surface conditions. In particular, results from these investigations performed for a test site buried under a bare surface showed that the processing of red channel allowed to better enhance shadow and soil marks (LASAPONARA-MASINI 2005). This is because, in this case, the presence of archaeological deposits influences the soil constituents and especially moisture content.

Crop-marks can be suitably enhanced by QuickBird NIR channel (LASAPONARA-MASINI 2006). This is due to the fact that green and healthy plants tend to exhibit high NIR reflectance values; whereas, vegetation under stress, due to lack of water or nutrient deficiencies, is characterized by low NIR reflectance values depending

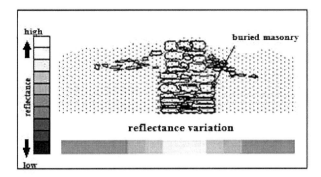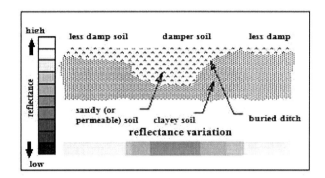

Fig. 2: Spectral characteristics of soil-marks related to buried structures (positive presences) and ditches (negative presences).

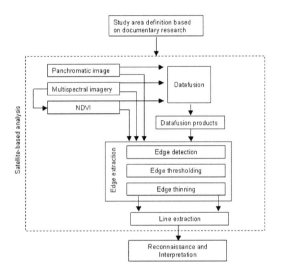

Fig. 3: Flow-chart of the methodology adopted for the processing of satellite data.

by vegetation. High (low) values of the vegetation index identify pixels covered by substantial proportions of healthy (disease or stressed) vegetation. It is expected that crop-marks created by vegetation patterns should be emphasized by using NDVI.

4. Method

The methodological approach adopted for the identification of archaeological features is mainly based on the use of data fusion and edge detection (see figure 3). The data fusion is performed to integrate the spatial details of a panchromatic image with the spectral property of multispectral channels. In such a way, improved capabilities, not available using solely the individual dataset can be achieved. The edge detection is performed, as in a previous study by Lasaponara and Masini (LASAPONARA-MASINI 2005 and 2007), to enhance spatial anomalies linked to the presence of archaeological marks. Additionally, the satellite data analysis is herein enriched by edge thresholding and thinning for improving the pattern recognition step.

The feature detection framework based on edge detection and pattern recognition has several potential advantages over other feature-detection methods, which can be prone to failure in the presence of blurring. Actually, the satellite-based detection of archaeological marks faces several challenges because the presence of underlying structures produces weak signals that can be easily covered by noise. Responses from true features and those from noise can not be distinguishable. This kind of problem could be reduced using edge detection, for a global segmentation, and pattern recognition for a local/contextual analysis. Contextual analysis can be more successful at isolating individual objects, also in a noisy data set, mainly because it allows the elimination of a great amount of redundant information which can hide the relevant details. It is expected that, in the thinned image, weak edges could be preserved and small gaps will be filled in; thus, making thinned objects easier to trace and recognize.

on the level of disease. Additionally, on the basis of remotely sensed data, crop marks may be suitably identified by exploiting vegetation indices that are spectral combinations of different bands. Such indices are quantitative measures, based on vegetation spectral properties that attempt to measure biomass or vegetative vigour. Vegetation indices mainly derived from reflectance data from the Red and near-infrared (NIR) bands. They operate by contrasting intense chlorophyll pigment absorption in the red against the high reflectance of leaf mesophyll in the near infrared. The simplest form of vegetation index is the ratio between two digital values from the red and near infrared spectral bands. The most widely used index (is the well-known Normalized Difference Vegetation index (NDVI) obtained by using the following formula: NDVI = [NIR-Red]/[NIR+Red].

The normalization of the NDVI reduces the effects of variations caused by atmospheric contaminations. NDVI is indicative of plant photosynthetic activity and has been found to be related to the green leaf area index and the fraction of photosynthetically active radiation absorbed

Each step of the data processing chain is detailed in the following sections:

1) Data fusion

Image fusion refers to the process of combining multiple images of a scene to obtain a single composite image. The different images to be fused can come from different sensors of the same basic type or they may come from different types of sensors. The composite image should contain a more useful description of the scene than provided by any of the individual source images. In the current cases under investigation, the QuickBird panchromatic and multispectral images were fused by using a data fusion algorithm that was specifically developed for VHR satellite images (ZHANG 2004). This algorithm exploits a method based on least squares for founding the best approximation between the fused image bands and the original data. This obtains the maximum increase in detail coupled with a minimum distortion. This algorithm has been adopted by Digital Globe and it is also available in a PCI-Geomatica routine.

2) Edge detection

In order to emphasize the marks arising from the presence of buried structures, an edge detection algorithm was applied to data fusion products. The edge detection was performed by applying a multi-scale approach based on the scale-space theory (LINDEBERG 1998) that uses Gaussian smoothing kernels. The selection of scale was undertaken keeping in mind that, in our case it was necessary to focus on structures having small sizes and signal amplitudes as expected in the case of surface anomalies due to buried walls, buildings and roads.

3) Edge thresholding

In this study, histogram-based thresholding was used to produce a binary image, in that all edge elements have value one. The threshold is not an absolute one, but an upper percentage from the cumulative distribution function of the edge detection filtered image.

4) Edge thinning

Thinning algorithms are used on binary images to generate skeletons that preserve the same connectivity structures as the objects in the original images. Thinning is a pre-processing operation of pattern recognition since a thinned object is easier to trace and hence is easier to recognize. Generally, a thinning algorithm is used to erode an object, layer by layer until only a unit-width skeleton is left.

In the present study case, the fast parallel thinning algorithm by Chen and Hsu (CHEN-HSU 1988) was used. Such an algorithm was selected because it preserves the merits of the original, such as the edge noise immunity and good effect in thinning crossed lines. It also overcomes weaknesses such as the serious shrinking and line connectivity problems. A 3 x 3 pixel window size, shown in table is used, as previously, in the edge detection step.

5) Line extraction

Using visual inspection, we only considered regular pattern anomalies because the presence of geometric features, being quite rare in nature, generally provide useful information for the identification of signs indicating ancient human activities.

Finally, the last step of the adopted procedure is the reconnaissance and interpretation of marks. This is a very important task, that is performed also using additional information, such as the traditional cartography and/or field survey etc... This facilitates the elimination or at least reduction of the potential coarse errors linked to the presence of road networks, bridges, pipeline etc. that can also be detected by the edge identification procedure.

5. Satellite data analysis

The investigations were performed for four archaeological sites, dating back to Middle Age, located in the South of Italy (see figure 4). These areas were selected because they are well documented and above all are characterized by different features from the geological, pedological and land-use point of view. These different characteristics allowed the analysis of performance obtained from satellite data for different features and surface characteristics. Figure 5 shows the satellite pictures for the investigated sites.

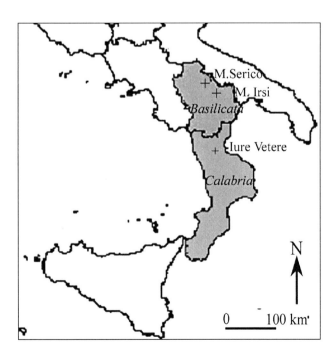

Fig. 4: Locations of the study areas.

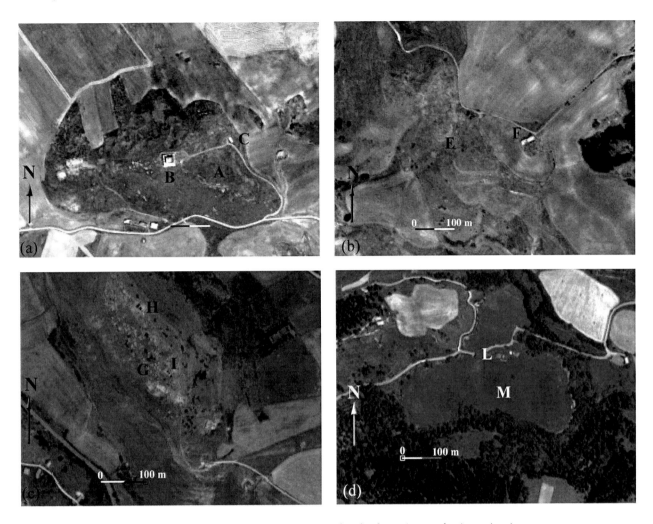

Fig. 5: The satellite Quickbird pictures for the four sites under investigation.

5.1. Iure Vetere

5.1.1. Study area

Iure Vetere is located on the ridge of a hilly plateau in the Sila territory in the Calabria Region (Southern Italy). The historical value of Iure Vetere is due to Gioacchino da Fiore who founded the first monastery of Florense Orden at the end of the 12th century.

The site faces the watershed between the basins of the Arco river and it's affluent and is characterized by the presence of vegetation composed of dense herbaceous plants. From a geological point of view Iure Vetere is within the Monte Gorigliano unit made up of high grade metamorphic rocks, such as granodiorites and magmatites. The soils are mainly composed siliceous sands, products of the chemical and mechanical alteration of acid igneous rocks, with a minor part of clays made up of kaolins and vermiculites (ROUBIS *et alii* 2003).

Before starting archaeological excavations (2002-2004) preliminary investigations based on aerial photos (1998-1999) and geophysical surveys were performed in order to identify the location of buried settlements. Results

obtained from both aerial photos and geophysical surveys allowed to identify the highest probable location of ancient buried remains. Such results were confirmed by the excavation campaigns that unearthed a large structure related to the church of the monastery. Actually, the location of the rest of the medieval monastery is still unknown. For this reason, the archaeologists enlarged the study area to the whole plateau. The enlargement of the study area and its physical characteristics suggested the integration of the remote sensing data set with satellite QuickBird imagery.

5.1.2. Satellite data analysis

Figure 6 shows the QuickBird panchromatic, red, NIR and NDVI data for the study area. A visual inspection of these figures puts in evidence the presence of potential anomalies in the south part of the excavated area. Such anomalies are more visible in the NIR and NDVI than panchromatic and red images. Blue and green spectral channels were not shown because they did not exhibit any visible marks.

Nevertheless, a multi-spectral edge extraction procedure is highly recommended for each case to be investigated in

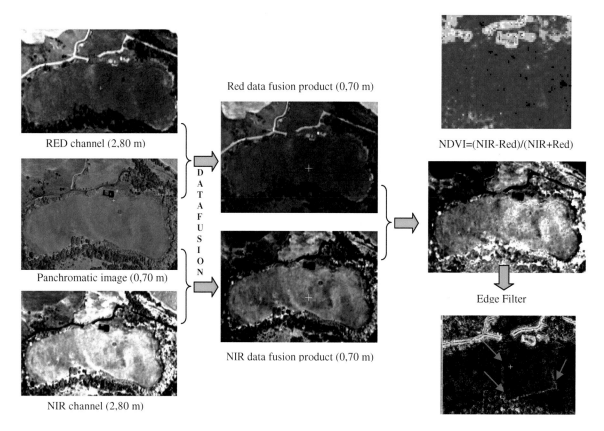

RED channel (2,80 m)

Panchromatic image (0,70 m)

NIR channel (2,80 m)

Red data fusion product (0,70 m)

NIR data fusion product (0,70 m)

NDVI=(NIR-Red)/(NIR+Red)

Edge Filter

Figure 6: The Iure Vetere Study case

order to combine the different information that should be extracted from the different QuickBird spectral data sources. This can suitably reveal the presence of anomalies veiled on a visual inspection. For this reason all the QuickBird spectral channels and the NDVI map were analyzed according to the flowchart shown in figure 3.

Results obtained from the QuickBird NDVI and spectral channels processed at their own spatial resolution (2.8 m) were the follows. The most interesting outputs were obtained from the NDVI; whereas, the processing of panchromatic as well as multispectral channels did not provide additional significant information. In particular, the processing of NDVI map put in evidence the presence of crop-marks having a rectilinear morphology. The edge thresholding was performed by setting at 3,5% the histogram threshold. Lower values selected a number of pixels not enough to detect rectilinear marks; whereas, higher threshold values tended to emphasize the noise.

The application of the edge thinning step allowed a detailed spatial identification of the rectilinear marks that compose a quadrangular shape of about 45 x100 m. These features could be referable to underlying remains of the monastery as expected by the archaeologists.

The results obtained from the edge detection extraction applied to data fusion products (fig. 6) substantially agree

with those found from the NDVI and spectral channels processed at their own spatial resolution. In this test case the main advantage of using data fusion products was that the increased spatial resolution. This provided a more accurate localization of the marks, that was very helpful during the geophysical prospection campaign (July 2005) which confirmed the anomalies detected by using QuickBird.

The most significant finding of the performed investigations is that the use of QuickBird NDVI provides the most accurate enhancement of crop-marks. Thus, considering that the study area is covered by dense herbaceous plants, it is not surprising. In fact, traditionally, vegetation monitoring by remotely sensed data has been carried out by using NDVI, that is a quantitative measure of biomass and vegetative vigour.

The NDVI operates by contrasting intense chlorophyll pigment absorption in the red against the high reflectance of leaf mesophyll in the near infrared. NDVI is indicative of plant photosynthetic activity and related to the green leaf area index. Therefore, variations in NDVI values become indicative of variations in water and nutrient availability. Thus, explaining the high capability of NDVI to enhance vegetation patterns linked to superficial anomalies created by near-surface archaeological deposit.

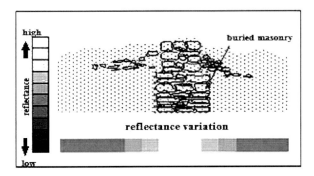 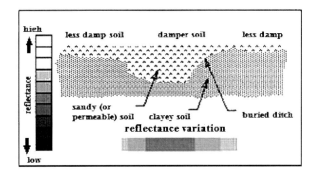

Fig. 7: Monte Serico case study: soil-marks related to buried structures (positive presences) and ditches (negative presences).

Fig. 8: Panoramic view of Monte Serico.

5.2. Monte Serico study area

5.2.1. Study area

The site is found on a hill (520 above sea level) located in Southern Italy, in the North East of the Basilicata Region near the boundary lines of Apulia. From a geological point of view, during the Middle Pliocene Era the area was characterized by strong marine clastic sedimentation. In particular, the stratigraphic sequence is composed of Subappennine Clays, Monte Marano sands and Irsina conglomerates that crop out of the ground. Sporadic hazelnut plants grow over the investigated areas, whereas the hill surroundings are fields of grain crops. After the harvest, the whole area appears completely bare.

Historical sources state that around the 11th century, a castle was built on the hill to guard the surrounding Bradano valley territory. The Monteserico village was founded in the 13th century and it reached significant size as proven by its population which was about 700-1000 and by the presence of four churches (BRUHL 1987).

Between the end of the 14th and the first half of 15th century the Monteserico village was gradually abandoned due to changes in territory exploitations and to the loss of importance from military point of view. Today the only buildings remaining are the castle and a church situated respectively on the western and northeastern sides of the hill. On the southern side of the hill, the presence of earthenware, pottery and crumbling building materials, such as calcarenites, limestones, bricks and tiles, indicates the existence of a buried settlement. The state of preservation of these archaeological evidences is the result of collapsed buildings followed by the washing away of the terrain and the crumbling material, due to the slope of the area. This caused small differences in height level between buried structures and neighbouring areas strongly affected by erosion processes due to the lack of vegetation. Such differences are visible from aerial view, as shown by Masini (MASINI 1995), by the typical indications, generally called shadow-marks and soil-marks according to the archaeological classification (CRAWFORD 1928).

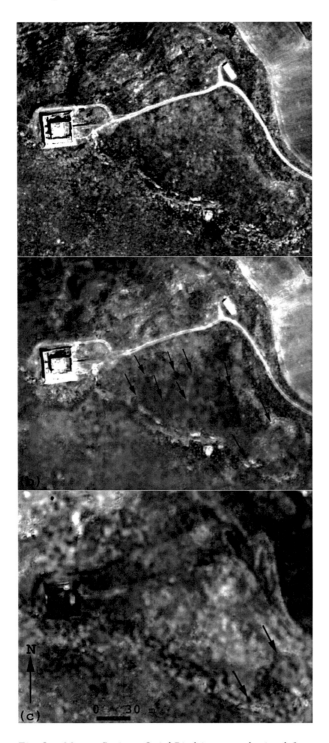

algorithm allows us to emphasize marks having higher or lower reflectance values, among which we only consider those having rectilinear morphology selected by using a visual inspection. Results from single channel processing show that only a small number of anomalies of archaeological interest are visible. In particular, panchromatic image and the blue, green and NIR channels do not show significant marks as well; whereas, the red channel Considering that the study area is sparsely vegetated, it is not surprising that the red channel is capable of better emphasizing the presence of buried structures as found by Shennan and Donoghue (SHENNAN-DONOGHUE 1992). Nevertheless, such marks are not enough to reconstruct the urban plan.

Results from data fusion processing confirm the fact that the best results have been obtained by the panchromatic and red channel data fusion. In particular, rectilinear features are visible on the southern edge of the hill: some of them are characterized by higher reflectances, others by lower ones. Rectilinear marks having higher reflectance values are due to incoherent building material and referable to partially buried walls. Whereas, marks having lower reflectances are the so-called shadow-marks due to difference in level caused by differential erosion, as confirmed, in our case by ground survey. These shadow-marks are referable to roads or spaces located between buildings.

Fig. 10: Monte Serico: reconnaissance of archaeological marks detected in the red data fusion product.

Fig. 9: Monte Serico: QuickBird images obtained from the edge detection procedure applied to panchromatic (a), red channel data fusion product (b) and NIR channel data fusion product (c). The arrows indicate archaeological marks detected in the red and NIR data fusion product.

5.2.2. Satellite data analysis

The reconnaissance of such marks was performed by analysing the results obtained from the edge detection algorithm (LINDEBERG 1998) applied to both single channel and data fusion products. The edge detection

On the whole, more than 30 marks, having a total length about 480 m, have been detected. They compose a grid of lines inscribed into a lengthened quadrangular area, with a size at about 8000 mq. The lengths of the detected rectilinear marks vary in range from 7,1 to 31,3 m, the minimum length of rectilinear anomalies which can be discriminated is about 7 m, that is enough to map the main features of a settlement plan, from an urban block to a single building. In particular, in the Monte Serico case, the minimum size of urban block surveyed is 9,3 x 7,1 m.

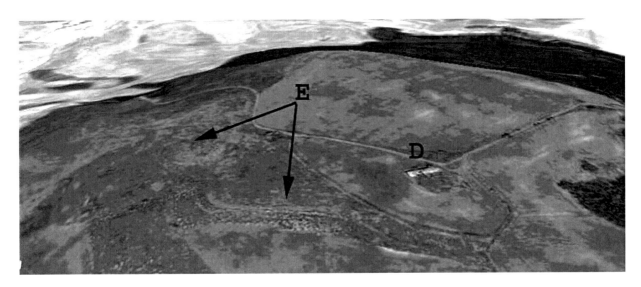

Fig. 11: Panoramic view of Monte Irsi (b). Letters D and E indicate respectively the church and the investigated area.

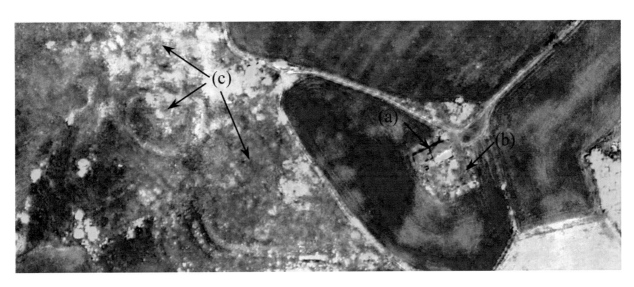

Fig. 12: Monte Irsi QuickBird RGB. Letters a to c denote the location of the church (a), archaeological remains of a roman villa (b), and the medieval settlement (c).

The grid of marks surveyed (se figure 10), shows an urban plan covering a large part of the southern slope of the hill. The reconstruction performed on the basis of satellite QuickBird data analysis agrees with results of independent studies performed on the basis of ground survey and aerial photo interpretation (MASINI 1995 and 1998) and some excavation tests.

5.3. Monte Irsi

5.3.1. Study area

Monte Irsi is a hilly plateau, near the confluence of the Bradano and Basentello rivers, characterized by the presence of vegetation made up of dense herbaceous plants. The strategic location of Monte Irsi favoured a long and intensive human activity from Palaeolithic to

Middle Ages, as testified by archaeological remains (SMALL 1976; SMALL *et alii* 1998). As regards the Middle Ages, documentary sources state the existence of a village (Yrsum) and a monastery (JANORA 1987). The village achieved its maximum expansion between the 12th and 13th centuries and was abandoned in the 15th century, whereas the monastery was destroyed around 1370 (JANORA 1987).

Today the only building preserved is the church of the monastery (archaeological remains near the church and at the highest part of the hill are respectively referable to a roman villa and to a medieval settlement that was built on preexistent structures dating back to the Late Iron Age (SMALL *et alii* 1998). Just the medieval settlement is the object of our investigation.

5.3.2. Satellite data analysis

The reconnaissance of marks referable to buried structures was performed by analyzing the results obtained from the edge detection algorithm applied to both single channel and data fusion products.

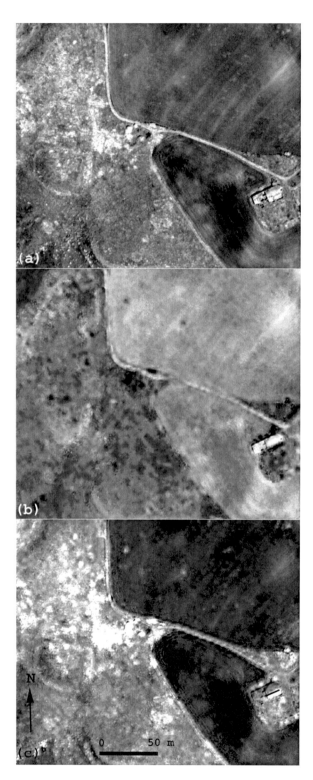

Fig. 13: Monte Irsi: QuickBird images obtained from the edge detection procedure applied to panchromatic (a), Red channel data fusion product (b) and NIR channel data fusion product (c).

Results from single channel processing showed that only a small number of geometric marks are visible from blue, green and red channels. Whereas panchromatic image and the NIR data fusion product provided the best results. The NIR channel is more capable than other spectral bands to better enhance the surface anomalies. This is mainly due to the fact that the NIR is particularly sensitive to different vegetation growing levels that is regarded as a reliable indicator of the presence of buried structures, pits and ditches.

The lengths of the detected rectilinear marks vary in range from 7.1 to 55.6 m. The minimum length of rectilinear anomalies that can be discriminated is about 7 m, which is enough to map the main features of a settlement plan, from an urban block to a single building. On the whole, 36 marks for a total length of 689,4 m have been detected. As shown in table 1, 60,2% of rectilinear marks are visible by using both panchromatic image and NIR data fusion product, 23.1% by only using NIR, and 16,7% by only using panchromatic image.

Ground survey put in evidence that the different responses of the two channels are due to the different surface characteristics. As expected, the NIR provided better results in presence of dense vegetation cover.

Most of the marks surveyed are located on the top of the hill, where a ditch and rectilinear marks referable to foundations and buried walls suggest the existence of a fortified structure. Finally, interesting geometric pattern marks are visible between the top of the hill and the church.

Nevertheless, a multi-spectral edge extraction procedure is highly recommended for each case to be investigated in order to combine the different information that should be extracted from the different QuickBird spectral data sources. This can suitably reveal the presence of anomalies veiled on a visual inspection. For this reason all the QuickBird spectral channels and the NDVI map were analyzed according to the flowchart shown in figure 3.

Results obtained from the QuickBird NDVI and spectral channels processed at their own spatial resolution (2.8 m) were the follows. The most interesting outputs were obtained from the NDVI (fig. 4), whereas the processing of panchromatic as well as multispectral channels did not provide additional significant information. In particular, the processing of NDVI map put in evidence the presence of crop-marks having a rectilinear morphology. The edge thresholding was performed by setting at 3,5% the histogram threshold. Lower values selected a number of pixels not enough to detect rectilinear marks; whereas, higher threshold values tended to emphasize the noise.

The application of the edge thinning step allowed a detailed spatial identification of the rectilinear marks that compose a quadrangular shape of about 45 x 100 m.

Fig. 14: Monte Irsi: reconnaissance of archaeological marks detected in the panchromatic image (a) and red data fusion product (b).

Fig. 15: Satriano village study case: satellite-based detection of shadow marks.

These features could be referable to underlying remains of the monastery as expected by the archaeologists.

The results obtained from the edge detection extraction applied to data fusion products (fig. 5) substantially agree with those found from the NDVI and spectral channels processed at their own spatial resolution. In this test case the main advantage of using data fusion products was that the increased spatial resolution. This provided a more accurate localization of the marks, that was very helpful during the geophysical prospection campaign (July 2005) which confirmed the anomalies detected by using QuickBird.

The most significant finding of the performed investigations is that the use of QuickBird NDVI provides the most accurate enhancement of crop-marks. Thus, considering that the study area is covered by dense herbaceous plants, it is not surprising. In fact, traditionally, vegetation monitoring by remotely sensed data has been carried out by using NDVI, that is a quantitative measure of biomass and vegetative vigour. The NDVI operates by contrasting intense chlorophyll pigment absorption in the red against the high reflectance of leaf mesophyll in the near infrared. NDVI is indicative of plant photosynthetic activity and related to the green leaf area index. Therefore, variations in NDVI values become indicative of variations in water and nutrient availability. Thus, explaining the high capability of NDVI to enhance vegetation patterns linked to superficial anomalies created by near-surface archaeological deposit.

5.4. Satriano

5.4.1. Study area description

The remains of medieval Satriano occupy the acropolis of the Lucanian town (4th century BC), a hilltop site 16 km south-west of Potenza. The earliest records of a medieval settlement at Satriano refer to the 9th century (WHITEHOUSE 1970). Between the 9th and 12th centuries, Satriano was probably the largest settlement within a radius of 15 km. According to a strong tradition, accepted by modern historians, Satriano was destroyed in 1430 and allegedly, it was then abandoned.

The medieval settlement covered the crest of the hill and extended down the slopes on the south-west and south-east sides. Today two buildings, a tower and some walls of the cathedral, survive above ground; whereas, other pieces of masonry are still visible in the form of grass-covered footings.

5.4.2. Results from satellite based analysis

Results from the satellite based analysis performed for Satriano Village showed that the panchromatic image provided the best results. It was more capable than other QuickBird products to better enhance the surface anomalies. This was mainly due to the fact that, in this case the surface anomalies are mainly micro-topographic relieves. Such micro-terrain features are topographic structures remains of ancient buildings, walls, etc that have sizes ranging from 40 cm to 1 m for houses and defence walls respectively. These features are easily apparent in aerial imagery, but they should be missed or confused with other features using QuickBird pan-chromatic imagery since the spatial resolution is 70 cm. Thus, should make reliable detection based on satellite imagery alone problematic. The examination performed for the ruins of Satriano Village showed that the feasibility of QuickBird panchromatic data to detect micro-topographic relieves at the subpixel level. The subpixel anomalies produced a strong signal that allowed the reconstruction of morphology of the ancient village. The grid of marks surveyed, shows an urban plan covering a large part of the hill. A High agreement was found between the urban plan reconstructed on the basis of satellite QuickBird data analysis and the results coming out from previous researches (*Excavations at Satriano* 1970) and independent investigations based on photo interpretation data.

6. Final remarks

Satellite QuickBird imagery were used in order to assess their capability to detect archaeological marks. The analyses were performed for some test cases buried under surfaces characterized by a different status of vegetation (dry/green) when the satellite data were acquired. Results from our investigations showed that the multispectral VHR satellite data provide valuable information for both bare and vegetated areas, where the use of aerial photos can be limited since the visibility of crop marks strongly depends on many factors such as, vegetation type and status, soil conditions, sun-sensor geometry and film sensitivity. So, it is really difficult to obtain photographs taken under optimal conditions. Satellite multispectral data can address some of these problems.

One of the main advantages of VHR satellite is the possibility of combining multispectral and pancromathic data to achieve improved accuracies and better inference about the surface characteristics of the single sensor. In particular, the data fusion allows the enhancement of spatial anomalies linked to the presence of archaeological marks; thus, making their recognition and extraction easier.

Compared to aerial photo the QuickBird imagery can be promptly geo-referenced and offer a very large coverage. This makes them ideal for investigations on regional scale as well as for researches performed in areas where aerial photography is restricted because of military or political reasons.

Nevertheless, there are also some considerable drawbacks. Although, the use of data fusion allowed the identification of features with the spatial detail of pancromathic (0.6 m) instead of multispectral (2.40 m) this spatial resolution is still lower than those obtained from aerial photo. Thus could be a limitation for the identification of small features.

The current cost of archived satellite QuickBird pancromathic plus multispectral images data is 18.20 euro/km², whereas it is 22.75 euro/km² for new data acquisitions. Discounts at around 20% are generally offered for universities and research institutions (the reader is referred to information available on line at the website http://www.digitalglobe.com/product/product_docs.shtml). Currently, the cost of QuickBird imagery is still higher than oblique aerial photos costs, but, it is lower than the aerial photogrammetry.

In conclusion, the main findings of the performed investigation can be summarized as follows:
- the use of data fusion and edge detection procedures improves the identification of crop marks linked to the presence of buried archaeological remains;
- the integration of results obtained from panchromatic and image fusion products provides valuable information for a detailed physical and geometrical characterisation of the archaeological site, as required prior to any excavation work;
- the use of NDVI allowed to better enhance crop marks observed for surfaces covered by green and healthy herbaceous plants;
- the use of NIR channel was able to better enhance crop marks observed for surfaces covered by dry herbaceous plants;
- the red channel suitably allowed to better enhance soil marks, observed for bare surfaces;
- the QuickBird products are still more expensive than oblique aerial photos costs, but they are cheaper than aerial photogrammetric images;
- the spatial resolution of VHR satellite imagery is still lower than those obtained from aerial photo, thus should limit the identification of small features.

Rosa LASAPONARA
Istituto di Metodologie per l'Analisi Ambientale, IMAA-CNR
C. da S. Loja
85050 TITO SC. (PZ)
Italy

Nicola MASINI
Istituto Beni Archeologici e Monumentali, IBAM-CNR
C. da S. Loja
85050 TITO SC. (PZ)
Italy

Apologies

This article was written by the authors in 2005-06 but due to various difficulties it was only published in 2011, for which I want to apologise sincerely – Marc Lodewijckx (editor).

References

BEWLEY R.H. 2003. Aerial Survey for Archaeology, *Photogrammetric Record* 18 (104): 273-292.

BRUHL C.R. 1987. *Rogerii II, Regis diplomata latina*, Bohlau Verlag Köln/Wien.

CHEN Y.S. and W.H. HSU 1988. A Modified Fast Parallel Algorithm for Thinning Digital Patterns, *Pattern Recognit. Lett.* 7/2: 99-106.

CLARK C.D., S.M. GARROD and M. PARKER PEARSON 1998. Landscape Archaeology and Remote Sensing in Southern Madagascar, *International Journal of Remote Sensing* 19/8: 1461-1477.

CRAWFORD O.G.S. 1928. Air Survey and Archaeology, *Ordnance Survey Professional Papers, new series* 7, Southampton.

CRAWFORD O.G.S. 1929. Air Photography for Archaeologists, *Ordnance Survey Professional Papers, new series* 12, Southampton.

DASSIE J. 1978. *Manuel d'archéologie aérienne*, Paris, Éditions Technip.

DRAKE N.A. 1997. Recent Aeolian Origin of Superficial Gypsum Crusts in Southern Tunisia: Geomorphological, Archaeological and Remote Sensing Evidence, *Earth Surface Processes and Landforms* 22: 641-656.

JANORA M. 1987. *Memorie storiche, critiche e diplomatiche della città di Montepeloso (oggi Irsina)*, Matera.

LASAPONARA R. and N. MASINI 2005. QuickBird-Based Analysis for the Spatial Characterization of Archaeological Sites: Case study of the Monte Serico Medieval Village, *Geophysical Research Letter* 32 (12): L12313 10.1029/2005GL022443.

LASAPONARA R. and N. MASINI 2006. On the Potential of QuickBird Data for Archaeological Prospection, *International Journal of Remote Sensing* 27 (15-16): 3607-3614.

LASAPONARA R. and N. MASINI 2007. Detection of Archaeological Crop Marks by Using Satellite QuickBird Multispectral Imagery, *Journal of Archaeological Science* 34: 214-221.

LINDEBERG T. 1998. Feature Detection with Automatic Scale Selection, *Journal of Computer Vision* 30/2: 79-116.

MASINI N. 1995. Note storico-topografiche e fotointerpretazione aerea per la rcostruzione della 'forma urbis' del sito medievale di Monte Serico, *Tarsia* 16: 45-64.

MASINI N. 1998. La fotointerpretazione aerea finalizzata allo studio morfologico dei siti urbani e fortificati medievali della Basilicata, *"Castra ipsa possunt et debent reparari". Indagini conoscitive e metodologie di restauro delle strutture castellane normanno-sveve*, Roma, Edizioni De Luca: 205-250.

PARRY J.T. 1992. The Investigative Role of Landsat TM in the Examination of Pre-Proto-Historic Water Management Sites in Northeast Thailand, *Geocarto Int.*, 4: 5-24.

ROUBIS D., F. SOGLIANI and M. LAZZARI 2003. Ricerche archeologiche a Jure Vetere (S. Giovanni in Fiore): la campagna di scavo del 2002 e le indagini geopedologiche, *Siris, 4, Studi e Ricerche della Scuola di Specializzazione in Archeologia di Matera*: 99-118.

SEVER T.L. 1998. Validating Prehistoric and Current Social Phenomena upon the Landscape of Peten, 'Guatemal'. In D. LIVERMAN, E.F. MORAN, R.R RINFUSS and P.C. STERN (Eds.), *People and Pixels: Linking Remote Sensing and Social Science*, Washington DC, National Academy Press: 145-163.

SHEETS P. and T. SEVER 1988. High Tech Wizardry *Archaeology* 41/6: 28-35.

SHENNAN I. and D.N.M. DONOGHUE 1992. Remote Sensing in Archaeological Research, *Proceedings of the British Academy* 77: 223-232.

SMALL A. 1976. The Iron Age and Roman Site of Monte Irsi. In P.L. SHINNIE, J.H. ROBERTSON and F.J. KENSE (Eds.), *Canadian Archaeology Abroad*, University of Calgary: 23-33.

SMALL A., C. SMALL, I. CAMPBELL, M. MACKINNON, T. PROWSE and C. SIPE 1998. Field Survey in the Basentello Valley on the Basilicata-Puglia Border, *Echos du Monde Classique, Classical Views* 42: 337-371.

WHITE K. and H.M. EL ASMAR 1999. Monitoring Changing Position of Coastlines Using Thematic Mapper Imagery, an Example from the Nile Delta. *Geomorphology* 29: 93-105.

WHITEHOUSE R. 1970. Excavations at Satriano: a Deserted Medieval Settlement in Basilicata, *Paper of the British School at Rome* 38: 188-219.

WILSON D.R. 1982. *Air Photo Interpretation for Archaeologists*, London, St. Martin's Press.

ZHANG Y. 2002. A New Automatic Approach for Effectively Fusing Landsat 7 Images and IKONOS Images, *IEEE/IGARSS'02, 3-24 Jun.*, Toronto, Canada.

ORKNEY FROM THE AIR

PETER J. LEEMING

"The exploration of ancient Scotland from the air has only begun.
It is one of the most promising fields of research anywhere in the world." (CRAWFORD 1939: 290)

For archaeologists, much of the allure of the Orkney archipelago, located off the northern coast of Scotland (fig. 1), is the well-known and impressive concentration of upstanding remains ranging from the Neolithic to the end of the Second World War. However, it is becoming clearer through techniques such as geophysical survey, excavation and surveys of eroding coastlines that an equally impressive concentration of sub-surface remains also exists. Aerial archaeology, a technique used with

considerable and often visually stunning effect in mainland Britain, has, however, had little impact on Orcadian archaeology, apart from being used for illustrating a particular site or excavation in progress (see fig. 3). Why is this so ? There are various reasons which can be proposed, firstly by putting Orkney into the context of flight and archaeological reconnaissance in Scotland and then by considering practical issues of aerial survey.

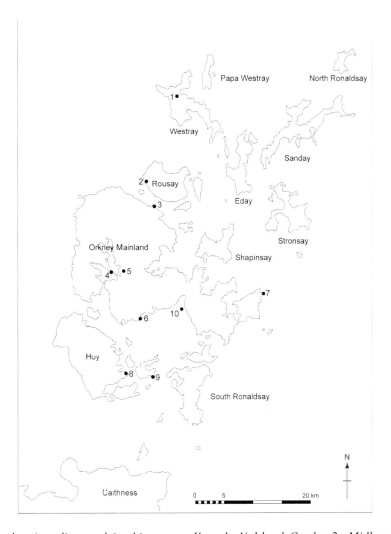

Fig. 1: *Map showing the sites discussed in this paper. Key: 1: Noltland Castle; 2: Midhowe Broch; 3: Broch of Gurness; 4: Ring of Brodgar; 5: Overbigging; 6: Toy Ness; 7: Brough of Deerness; 8: Crockness, Hoy; 9: Stanger Head, Flotta; 10: HMS Royal Oak.*

127

The first encounter with matters aerial in Orkney was on 4th December 1910 when three German aeronauts crashed their balloon near Kirkwall, the capital of the islands, after being swept off course by a storm, having taken off near Munich the previous day. One balloonist was lost during the crash. The earliest powered flight came with the arrival of seaplanes in 1913, based upon HMS Hermes, closely followed by sightings of German airships. During the First World War Orkney was home to seaplanes, airships and balloons and pioneered aspects of aircraft carrier practice, including the first landing on a moving carrier (HEWISON 1985).

Balloons were also attached to cruisers for observation as lookouts, but weather conditions were against this as a frequent practice. From this period is the first record of aerial photographs in the islands, from the memoirs of T. Crowther Gordon, a flying boat pilot, where he records a sortie in 1918 taking in an area between Foula and Westray from which good results, now sadly lost, were obtained (CROWTHER GORDON 1985). Images taken by the balloonists survive, but are military in subject matter. The first 'airfield' was at Smoogro (see fig. 8 for the likely site), where the field's owner, J. Storer Clouston, subsequently used his experiences and tales from the crews in his 'shocker' spy novel *The Man From The Air* (STORER CLOUSTON 1948).

Civilian flying came to Orkney comparatively late. The pioneering work, *Wessex from the Air* (CRAWFORD-KEILLER 1928) had been published for several years when the first civilian plane, piloted by E.E. Fresson, flew to Orkney on Sunday 20th April 1931. Fresson was flying an Avro 504 biplane on 'jolly flights' to test the commercial possibilities of an airline, which later opened in April 1933. There was no network of airfields in Orkney until the Second World War, in contrast with Wessex where there were sufficient ex-military airfields for Crawford and Keiller to conduct wide-ranging surveys (MACGREGOR 2000); Orkney had seaplane bases, such as at Houton, instead. Even today there are some islands with no runway, and if the weather conditions are not right the inter-island aircraft will land the old-fashioned way on a grass field which can be mildly disturbing the first time it happens.

The pioneers of aerial archaeology also had financial backing, such as Keiller or Allen. The chief interested amateur with finance in Orkney was W.G. Grant, who was kept busy with his excavations on Rousay (REYNOLDS-RITCHIE 1985). However, in a sense he did begin aerial archaeology in Orkney because he gave Fresson a letter of introduction which won him the commercial contract to carry newspapers which made his air service viable (FRESSON 1967) and led to the first images of archaeological sites in Orkney.

The highly sensitive military character of the islands for much of the 20th century resulted in restrictions on aerial activity – Scapa Flow was a major naval base and there would have been flying restrictions over certain areas. Certainly during the Second World War the passenger windows on civilian flights were painted opaque (W. INNES, pers. comm.).

The serious archaeological study of aerial photographs in Scotland was begun in the years following the Second World War with the availability of the post-war RAF vertical survey of Britain (STEER 1947) and given impetus by the production of the various Royal Commission Inventory volumes, such as the Roxboroughshire Inventory (RCAHMS 1956) where over a hundred sites are credited as being recognized from the study of aerial photographs. The Orkney Inventory (RCAHMS 1946) was already published before these images were made available, so the only image used in it was of Midhowe Broch on Rousay, as something of a novelty, following the example of photographs of hillforts in the Fife Inventory (RCAHMS 1933).

The number of researchers actively pursuing aerial archaeology has always been small, and often there has been an attitude of 'leave it to the experts', resulting in areas with uneven cover. The pioneers, such as Crawford and St Joseph, had research interests which took them to certain areas. In the Scottish context that meant looking for Roman sites (CRAWFORD 1930 and 1939; ST.JOSEPH 1975; WILSON 1975). Orkney's distinctive archaeology lacks many elements for which aerial archaeology has made great contributions: there are no Roman forts or roads, no hillforts and whilst there are souterrains, they are roofed with stone and clay which do not allow for easy identification from the air as is the case in Angus.

The developing discipline began to be codified after the Second World War, with an emphasis upon the rich pickings to be found on threatened river gravels and disparagement of difficult soils and areas less responsive to the development of cropmarks, which of course directed attention away from Orkney, amongst other areas. As St Joseph commented:

> "The incidence of crop marks in Scotland is naturally greatest in areas where there is the highest preponderance of arable land. Crop marks have of course been recorded in such western counties as Dumfries, Kirkcudbright, Lanark and Ayr, but it is nevertheless the cultivated lands of Berwick, the Lothians, Perthshire and Angus that have yielded most discoveries." (ST.JOSEPH 1976b: 55).

This is the context for the comments of Vaughan (VAUGHAN 1977) whereby the farming economy of Orkney is seen as a hindrance to aerial archaeology with a high percentage of land given over to cattle grazing. However, since Vaughan wrote there has been an increase in arable farming (THOMPSON 2001; CHALMERS 2003), particularly in growing barley, a crop very

Fig. 2: Noltland Castle (Crown copyright Historic Scotland, John Dewar Collection).

responsive to cropmarks, one of the two key areas for aerial archaeology. Also, Vaughan's view fails to take into account that sub-surface features can be detected in grass given the right conditions.

The climate of Orkney is a major factor affecting aerial reconnaissance. Flying in Orkney has always been hazardous and every flier who has written about Orkney discusses the dangers of high wind and fogs (FRESSON 1967; VAUGHAN 1977; CROWTHER GORDON 1985). Fresson and the other pilots of Highland Airways used to fly low above the waves to avoid the difficult conditions higher up, which would reduce the opportunities for photography.

The high number of days with rainfall (CHALMERS 2003) can result in the soils, which are often poorly drained (DRY-SINCLAIR *s.d.*) and in many cases enhanced deep pasture (DAVIDSON-SIMPSON 1994) of over a metre depth, becoming waterlogged. St Joseph has discussed sub surface features becoming visible through a depth of over a foot of dumped soils (ST.JOSEPH 1976b) but it is unlikely that marks will show through this greater depth. The light conditions vary and sometimes are far from ideal. All of these factors make aerial survey challenging.

The method of publication of aerial archaeology has had a great impact, despite its lack of consistency. Most of the publication has been in journals, such as Crawford

Fig. 3: Broch of Gurness (Crown copyright, RCAHMS).

(CRAWFORD 1924) or the series of fifty 'recent results' by St Joseph, where he would choose between one and four photographs per article in *Antiquity* (ST.JOSEPH 1964 and 1980) which, when the holdings of CUCAP are numbered in their thousands, means that not just Orkney suffered lack of coverage. After *Wessex From The Air* Bradford noted in 1957 (BRADFORD 1957), there was a wait of twenty-four years before the next book on the subject, *Monasteries from the Air* (KNOWLES-ST.JOSEPH 1952). Orkney does not feature in this thematic survey as there is no post-conquest Monastic architecture in Orkney. Orkney did not feature in several of the next thematic aerial archaeology books, because of geographical (NORMAN-ST.JOSEPH 1969) or historical reasons, or both (BERESFORD-ST.JOSEPH 1979) until the publication of Muir's *History from the Air* (MUIR 1984) which discussed the sites of Maes Howe, Skara Brae and the Ring of Brodgar, all photographs coming from CUCAP. Publication of aerial photographs of Orkney subsequently has followed the pattern of illustrating specific sites, often during excavation (RITCHIE 1996).

Archaeological aerial survey of Orkney began with CUCAP in 1951 and 1965, where the main aim was illustrative, for a variety of disciplines including archaeology. The Royal Commission on the Ancient and Historical Monuments of Scotland began their own surveys in 1977 (MAXWELL 1983b; BROWN 1999),

but only briefly visited Orkney as part of a specific project to record military sites. Flying in Orkney was undertaken by John Dewar, who was commissioned to photograph monuments for illustrative purposes in the 1960s and 1970s. Other fliers such as Gunnie Moberg have taken aerial images and visiting excavators have usually arranged for their site to be photographed during excavation. There have been various vertical surveys, but the prospective reconnaissance for sites as happens in other parts of the UK has not happened in Orkney. In Scotland this imbalance is shown in the coverage by the RCAHMS illustrated in Cowley & Gilmour (COWLEY-GILMOUR 2005: 56) where clear bias to the south of the country is shown.

The lack of coverage of Orkney is illustrated by the standard textbook for interpretation of aerial photographs (WILSON 2000). In it there are no Orcadian sites discussed and a careless lapse:

"It is true, for example, that Martello towers can be recognised from the air along the coasts of southern Britain and Ireland, and that some of them have fallen into ruins. It is also true that in Scotland the remains of Brochs are often found on coastal sites, as well as elsewhere. But it does not seem necessary to set out criteria for telling them apart, seeing that the distribution of the two types of site are well enough known and do not overlap." (WILSON 2000: 89).

The distribution does overlap in Scotland, particularly in Orkney (see figs. 3 and 10).

To date there have only been three publications, Vaughan (VAUGHAN 1977), Braby (BRABY 1996) and Brophy (BROPHY-COWLEY 2005), which deal specifically with aerial archaeology and Orkney. Vaughan discusses the practicalities of flying in Orkney and Shetland, Braby discusses vertical aerial photographs and is outwith the scope of this present paper and Brophy outlines the problems concerning aerial archaeology, discussed above, as part of the research agenda for the World Heritage Site (WHS), the Heart of Neolithic Orkney, comprising Skara Brae and sites around the Stenness-Brodgar basin.

As noted above, Orkney has many upstanding monuments which have occupied and continue to occupy the attentions of archaeological investigators with excavation as the primary means of investigation. The first Orkney Archaeologist, Raymond Lamb, undertook many walkover surveys in the 1980s (e.g. RCAHMS 1987) as little or no field survey had been attempted in Orkney since the work of the Royal Commission in the 1930s (RCAHMS 1946). Also the technique of fieldwalking was re-introduced by Colin Richards in the 1980s-90s and resulted in the discovery, amongst other sites, of the Neolithic village of Barnhouse (RICHARDS 2005). Geophysical survey has recently had equally impressive results in the survey of the World Heritage Site (GSB PROSPECTION 2003).

Brophy (HISTORIC SCOTLAND 2005) points out that there is only one aircraft available with full insurance cover and documentation for low level flying in the whole of Scotland, based at Edinburgh. To fly this to Orkney requires several stops and it cannot be in the air over Orkney at a moment's notice and a flight of this length will probably require survey of areas in-between to make it cost effective.

The WHS Agenda (HISTORIC SCOTLAND 2005) notes that Orkney has not had aerial coverage to the same extent as other areas in Scotland, such as the north-east (e.g. SHEPHERD-GREIG 1996) and offers some reasons for this and suggests certain projects.

This paper is based upon a dissertation at Orkney College, University of the Highlands and Islands Millennium Institute, as part of the MA in Archaeological Practice. It is a small contribution towards the WHS Agenda Zone Specific project no 85 "Desk-based assessment of the archaeological value of the current aerial records, including both vertical and oblique photographs." The following examples demonstrate the value of the approach of aerial archaeology to the archaeology of Orkney. They are all held in the National Monuments Record of Scotland in Edinburgh. The vertical images were studied as part of the dissertation, but this paper will concentrate on the oblique images.

Noltland Castle, Westray HY 429 487 (fig. 2)

To the south (between the castle and the camera on the photograph) of the remains of Noltland Castle on photographs taken by John Dewar in 1971 (O/3522) several maculae, including one of considerable size, are visible. The smaller maculae probably represent pits, but the presence of an early cemetery detected during clearing operations by the H.M. Office of Works may suggest that the two of these at the south western part of the 18th Century range (to the bottom left of the enclosing wall looking at the photograph) may be additional burials. The larger maculae, to the south of these, could be possibly indicative of settlement, perhaps sunken floored buildings or Grubenhäuser in Anglian influenced regions of southern Scotland (Gates and O'Brien 1988), however, in Orkney it would be more likely that this is an indication of a filled-in stone quarry (D.C. COWLEY, pers. comm.). The two maculae at the south-east are on a north-south alignment and are approximately half the size of the largest macula and may also be small quarries. Noltland Castle is built of local grey flagstone of the Middle Old Red Sandstone. Its construction was haphazard and interrupted and the castle itself was left incomplete after 200 years of use (SIMPSON 1981). Quarrying stone from the vicinity may explain the cropmarks visible on this photograph. There are other faint traces in the crop, but they are too indistinct to interpret.

Midhowe Broch, Rousay HY 371 306 (not illustrated)

The Broch at Midhowe was one of a series of monuments excavated by Walter Gordon Grant on the island of Rousay (REYNOLDS-RITCHIE 1985). It has the distinction of being the first piece of Orcadian archaeology to be illustrated in a book by an aerial photograph, in the Orkney Inventory (RCAHMS 1946). This early photograph, from the 1930s, is attributed to Star Photos of Perth, who is probably Sandy McLaren, and therefore the photograph was taken from one of Fresson's aircraft (FRESSON 1967). Fresson was always willing to take photographers for George Low, the man who arranged the Scotsman contract for carrying newspapers which led to other commercial traffic including the mail, and since it was Grant who gave Fresson a letter of introduction to Low (and therefore in an indirect way Grant did sponsor aerial archaeology in Orkney) an unusual angle of one of Grant's sites may have been a token of gratitude from the aviator. This photograph was not located during the search of the National Monument Record of Scotland (NMRS).

Broch of Gurness, Evie HY 381 268 (fig. 3)

This image (O/4454) of the Broch of Gurness is held in the NMRS, is dated 1935 and the excavations are clearly

Fig. 4: Brodgar Peninsula (Crown copyright Historic Scotland, John Dewar Collection).

progressing which makes the date likely. The northern part of the site, the coastline, is more intact than it is today, making this more than just a historical curiosity; it is a unique record of the site. Given the date on the photograph it is likely that this is (as with the Midhowe Broch photograph) the work of Sandy McLaren of Star Photos, Perth, and that this photograph was taken from one of Fresson's aircraft.

Ring of Brodgar, Stenness HY 294 133 (fig. 4)

This famous monument is on a low-lying peninsula which has poor drainage (RICHARDS 1996). The photograph is

an image from 1977 (O/1568) taken by John Dewar and it shows this monument in an exceptionally dry year. The complex of herringbone patterned land drains visible to the left centre of the photograph, on the shore of the Loch of Harray, are a normal feature of young cereal crops on heavy land, and archaeological marks are not to be expected until these have faded (WILSON 2000: 185).

The chief interest in this photograph is the light coloured field to the bottom centre of the image. There a linear feature which turns at its mid-point is shown. This feature extends northwards (to the left of the photograph) and westwards (towards the camera). A site visit discovered that this westward direction ended in an exceptionally wet small hollow by the shore of the Loch of Stenness.

Fig. 5: Overbigging cropmark with Maes Howe in background (Copyright CUCAP).

There were three stone dumping sites in this hollow. The northernmost linear feature was found to head towards a pond which also has drainage leading to the loch. Little was visible above the surface, but the linear feature seems to emanate from a low mound and both branches travel ılı̣lılı̣ dı̣rrılılı̣ Thı̣ı̣ ı̣ndı̣cuutı̣ı̣ that thı̣ı̣ fııturı̣ ı̣ı̣ ı̣ drainage channel of uncertain date. This field is eaı̣ı̣ıaı̣kı̣d fuı̣ futuı̣ı̣ gı̣ı̣phyı̣ı̣cal suı̣vı̣y aı̣ part of the ongoing survey of the World Heritage Site and its environs which will hopefully enable confirmation of this interpretation. One of the photographs taken by Dewar of the Ring of Brodgar has been published, but the cropmark was not commented upon (CLARKE 1985).

Overbigging, Stenness HY 315 132 (figs. 5 and 6)

None of the early visitors to Orkney who wrote an account of their travels observed and recorded the ı̣hı̣ı̣ı̣ı̣ı̣ı̣ı̣ ı̣ı̣ı̣ ı̣ı̣ı̣ı̣ı̣ı̣ı̣ı̣ Thı̣ı̣ı̣ ı̣ı̣ ı̣ı̣ı̣ Oı̣ı̣ı̣ı̣ı̣ı̣ı̣ı̣ equivalent to the observations of antiquaries like Akerman and Stone at Standlake, Oxfordshire (AKERMAN STONE 1858). The realisation that Orkney produced cropmarks did not come until 1965 with the discovery of a sub-circular enclosure c.70m in diameter with an entrance-like gap in the South-South-East, facing Maes Howe.

Fig. 6: Overbigging enclosure (Copyright CUCAP).

This enclosure is situated across a low ridge. To the west of the putative entrance there is a faint trace of a curving ditch c. 35m in length. The enclosure has been detected as a weak magnetic anomaly, with the gap flanked by two magnetically strong ditch anomalies by Magnetometer survey (GSB PROSPECTION 2003).

Discovered and photographed in 1965 by St Joseph, these were the first definite deliberate photographs of cropmarks taken in Orkney (AMD 1-4). Unfortunately they were never published. As well as the publishing constraints discussed above, at this stage in his career, St Joseph was notoriously secretive about new discoveries. He:

"tended to the view that his own photographs were his own responsibility, and he could prove unhelpful to enquirers. Indeed, he was sometimes known to say of some new discovery that 'it was too important for Scheduling as an Ancient Monument, for that, of course would put it in the public domain. Fortunately, discoveries of this calibre were made sufficiently often to allow older examples to drop off the secret list with only a year or two's delay." (WILSON 1995: 430).

CUCAP never returned to Orkney until after St Joseph's retirement, then their survey focus had changed to commercial vertical survey (WILSON 1990) and their recent sorties have concentrated on surveys of the SSSI areas of Orkney.

Fig. 7: Brough of Deerness (Crown copyright Historic Scotland, John Dewar Collection).

The lack of publication of the 1965 images has resulted in a bias in recent writing about this area of west Mainland. This area, particularly the area around the Brodgar/Stenness isthmuses, where many of the monuments are now inscribed on the list of World Heritage Sites, is exceptionally important for archaeological theory. As an example of how the lack of evidence from subterranean features can affect the results of study, Colin Richards' paper (RICHARDS 1996) concerning henge ditches and water does not mention Overbigging, and yet it is only a short distance from one of the monuments he does discuss, Maes Howe, and within the natural bowl where all of the Orcadian monuments he lists are situated. The enclosure at Overbigging may have been useful to his discussion about ditches in this area (as would the enigmatic Ring of Bookan), even if it is not classed as a henge. This lack of

subterranean information is being addressed with the World Heritage Area being subject to geophysical survey.

Brough of Deerness HY596 087 (fig. 7)

The Brough of Deerness is a stack site on the north east corner of the Deerness peninsula. It has attracted considerable attention due to its dramatic setting and collection of ruins. This image, taken in 1965 by John Dewar (O/3418), shows the site to great effect. There are many plans of the Brough, but the need for an accurate survey resulted in the 1977 survey (Bettess in MORRIS-EMEREY 1986: fiche 2 C3-5) whilst the ruined chapel was being excavated. Plane table survey was deemed a possible liability, so a self reducing tacheometer was used

Fig. 8: Toy Ness (Crown copyright, RCAHMS).

(Bettess C4). The survey was hampered by the weather and the vegetation growth, which had not been grazed for some time. However, this survey was backed up by aerial survey. The results were that the survey in the Inventory (RCAHMS 1946) was found to be incomplete.

The aerial survey images shown in the publication (MORRIS-EMEREY 1986) are also striking images of this site. The earthwork features are shown with astonishing clarity, in a tiny fraction of the time the tacheometer survey took. This fieldwork resulted in the 21 depressions in the south (to the left hand side on the photograph) being reclassified from remains of circular huts as in the Inventory, to being the results of shelling, possibly by land-based artillery from the Burma Road.

Seven additional shell craters were identified. By the time of publication of the historical guide to Orkney (WICKHAM-JONES 1998) this damage was reattributed to the Royal Navy during the Second World War. As an interesting aside this appears to be the case, and one of the ships involved was my father's ship, HMS Mendip. The towed target at which the destroyers were firing was sunk too efficiently and the Brough of Deerness was used as an alternative target (A. LEEMING, pers. comm.).

Toy Ness, Orphir HY 355 044 (fig. 8)

The pier and area of Toy Ness, Orphir were photographed by RCAHMS because they have identified it as the best

Fig. 9: Stanger Head, Flotta (Crown copyright, RCAHMS).

candidate to be the First World War landing ground of Smoogro, as it is the only level piece of ground in the area. The pier is thought to be naval and used for hauling seaplanes out of the water.

This image has been included because the positive cropmarks in the field have previously escaped notice. These take the form of various linear features which probably indicate the course of old field boundaries.

Stanger Head, Flotta ND 375 925 (fig. 9)

On this headland is a derelict naval station from the Second World War, illustrated on the photograph, and gun batteries (not shown). The photograph is again part of the RCAHMS military survey. On the southern shore near this complex (on the left on the photograph) are the remains of a rectangular enclosure with the landward side having rounded corners. This earthwork is superficially similar to a Roman temporary camp, but it has no entrances in any of the three sides extant. It is unclear whether the coast had a fourth bank or whether the cliff provided a natural boundary. A survey by RCAHMS discovered that the northern bank (towards the camera) had two redoubts, each about 20m from the corner. The military character has led to the speculation that this is the emergency gun battery built in August 1914 (HEWISON 1985; D. EASTON, pers. comm.).

137

Fig. 10: Crockness Martello Tower and linear soilmark to the right (Crown copyright, RCAHMS).

Crockness, Hoy ND 324 934 (fig. 10)

To the south-west (to the right on the photograph) of the Martello Tower built to guard the northern entrance to Longhope harbour in 1814 is visible a linear soilmark. This has been interpreted as an old field boundary which is not shown on OS maps. A walkover survey in this area subsequently failed to locate this feature (J. ROBERTSON, pers. comm.). The photograph was taken in 1995 by the RCAHMS.

HMS Royal Oak HY 434 051 (fig. 11)

This photograph was taken by RCAHMS in August 1997 (D16676 CN) as part of their military survey. However, it illustrates well the points that the technique can show in one image a site as large as a battleship (189 metres long), a site which is normally not easily understood at surface level - and that it is only in certain conditions that sub-surface features are visible, in this case, when the sea is calm. This wreck has the best diving conditions and visibility of the military wrecks in deeper water within Scapa Flow (WOOD 2000).

The first sub-surface features recorded as observed from the air were sunken ships (probably from the scuttled German fleet) in Scapa Flow, spotted by Fresson on his maiden flight to Orkney in 1931 (FRESSON 1967).

The Royal Oak was torpedoed on the night of 13th-14th October 1939 with the loss of 833 crew out of a

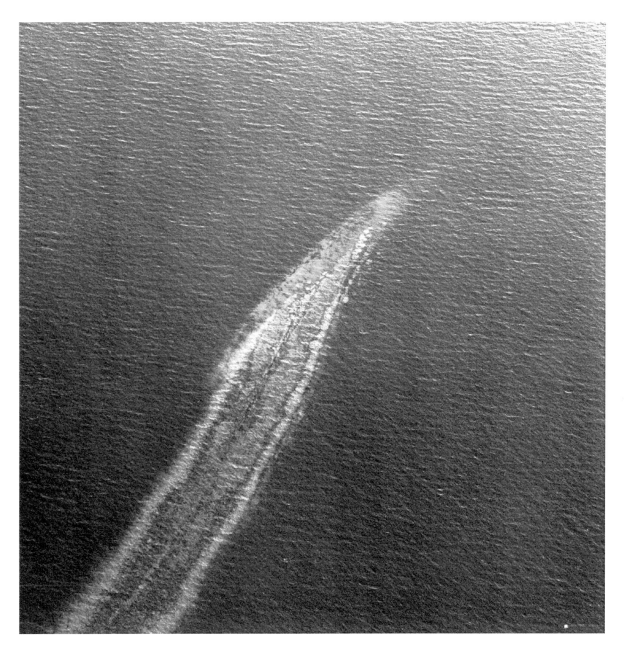

Fig. 11: HMS Royal Oak (Crown copyright, RCAHMS).

complement of 1234. She lies in the north-east corner of Scapa Flow. The Royal Oak was fully fuelled when she was sunk and still leaks oil into the Flow, despite pumping operations recently, over seventy years after being sunk. There are some Orcadians who regard it as fitting that the ship still bleeds as a memorial. The site is a designated war grave (OXLEY 2002; WOOD 2000).

Discussion

This study has presented evidence that interpretation of the existing resource of aerial photographs of Orkney can produce evidence of unknown sites and illuminate even well-known sites. The processes which produce crop-marks, although not ideal in Orkney, have produced evidence of sub-surface sites on a larger scale than the few examples discussed.

Simply because the area is not as responsive as some areas, such as the chalk of Wessex or river gravels, is insufficient reason to not attempt aerial survey. The county of Cheshire in north-west England is similarly wet, and has large deposits of clay. Persistent survey has revealed 16 new Roman temporary or practice camps near Chester in recent years (PHILPOTT 1998) and similar findings are becoming more common once aerial survey is begun in previously neglected areas (FEATHER-STONE *et alii* 1999).

In conclusion, Orkney is one of the areas where Crawford's summary of his early reconnaissance rings true even over sixty-five years later: "The exploration of ancient Scotland from the air has only begun." (CRAWFORD 1939: 290).

Peter J. LEEMING
Greater Manchester Archaeological Unit
3.22 Mansfield Cooper
University of Manchester
Oxford Road
MANCHESTER M13 9PL
United Kingdom

Acknowledgements

Thanks are due to the staff at Orkney College, the Orkney Archaeological Trust, RCAHMS and the Orkney Library. Especial thanks go to the staff at Aberdeenshire Archaeology Service, the late Ian Shepherd, Moira Greig and Bruce Mann. I am grateful to the late Judith Robertson for advice and the map of the islands, to Morag Lawrence for assistance with graphics and to Caroline Ingle and Lesley Mitchell for reading and commenting on a draft of this paper. I wish to thank those at the Leuven AARG conference for their helpful discussion of issues raised by this paper. Any faults which remain are, of course, my own.

Postscript

This paper was written during 2005-6, since that time the RCAHMS have undertaken aerial survey in Orkney and have found sites through cropmarks (COWLEY 2010). Also since this paper was written three dear colleagues from my time in northern Scotland have died, Judith Robertson, Ian Shepherd and Anne Brundle. This paper is respectfully dedicated to their memory.

Apologizes

This article was written by the author in 2005-6 but due to various difficulties it was only published in 2011, for which I want to apologize sincerely – Marc Lodewijckx (editor).

References

AKERMAN J.Y. and S. STONE 1857. An Account of Some Remarkable Circular Trenches and the Discovery of an Ancient British Cemetery at Stanlake, Oxon., *Archaeologia* 37: 363-370.

BERESFORD M.W. and J.K.S. ST.JOSEPH 1979. *Medieval England: an Aerial Survey*, Cambridge Aerial Surveys, Cambridge University Press.

BRABY A.R. 1996. Geramount, Sanday (Lady Parish), Cropmark, *Discovery Excav Scot*: 80.

BRADFORD J. 1957. *Ancient Landscapes. Studies in Field Archaeology*, G. Bell & Sons, London.

BROPHY K. and D.C. COWLEY 2005. *From the Air. Understanding Aerial Archaeology*, Tempus, Stroud.

BROWN M.M. 1999. Aerial Reconnaissance and the Development of the Archaeological Landscape in Scotland, *Revue archéologique de Picardie*, No spécial 17: 231-243.

CHALMERS J. 2003. Agriculture in Orkney Today. In D. OMAND (Ed.), *The Orkney Book*, Birlinn Ltd, Edinburgh: 127-143.

CLARKE D.V. 1985. *Symbols of Power at the Time of Stonehenge*, National Museum of Antiquities of Scotland, H.M.S.O. Edition.

COWLEY D.C. and S.M. GILMOUR 2005. Some Observations on the Nature of Aerial Survey. In K. BROPHY and D.C. COWLEY 2005: 50-63.

COWLEY D.C. 2010. Ultima Thule – Recent Aerial Survey of Orkney, Scotland, *AARGnews* 40: 25-35.

CRAWFORD O.G.S. 1924. The Stonehenge Avenue, *Antiquaries Journal* 4: 57-59.

CRAWFORD O.G.S. 1930. Editorial Notes, *Antiquity* 4: 273-277.

CRAWFORD O.G.S. 1939. Air Reconnaissance of Roman Scotland, *Antiquity* 13: 280-292.

CRAWFORD O.G.S. and A. KEILLER 1928. *Wessex from the Air*, Oxford University Press, Oxford.

CROWTHER GORDON T. 1985. Early Flying in Orkney, *The Orcadian*.

DAVIDSON D.A. and I.A. SIMPSON 1994. *Soils and Landscape History: Case Studies from the Northern Isles of Scotland*. In S. FOSTER and T.C. SMOUT (Eds.) 1994: 66-74.

DRY F.T. and A.H. SINCLAIR *s.d.* The Soils of Orkney, *Soil Survey of Scotland Report* 2, Macauley Land Use Research Unit, Aberdeen.

FEATHERSTONE R., P. HORNE, D. MACLEOD and R. BEWLEY 1999. Aerial Reconnaissance over England in Summer 1996, *Archaeological Prospect* 6: 47-62.

FOSTER S. and T.C. SMOUT (Eds.) 1994. *The History of Soils and Field Systems*, Scottish Cultural Press, Aberdeen.

FRESSON E.E. 1967. *Air Road to the Isles: the Memoirs of Captain E.E. Fresson OBE*, David Rendel Ltd.

GATES T. and C. O'BRIEN 1988. Cropmarks at Milfield and New Bewick, and the Recognition of Grubenhäuser in Northumberland, *Archaeologia Aeliana* 16: 1-9.

GSB PROSPECTION 2003. *Orkney World Heritage Site, Geophysical Survey Report, Phase III, GSB Report 2003/84*, Volume I: Main Report, Unpublished Report held in Orkney SMR, Bradford.

HEWISON W.S. 1985. This Great Harbour: Scapa Flow, *Aspects of Orkney* 3, Stromness.

HISTORIC SCOTLAND 2005. DOWNES J., S.M. FOSTER, C.R. WICKHAM-JONES and J. CALLISTER (Eds.) 2005. *The Heart of Neolithic Orkney World Heritage Site, Research Agenda*, Historic Scotland, Edinburgh.

KNOWLES D. and J.K.S. ST.JOSEPH 1952. *Monastic Sites from the Air*, Cambridge Aerial Surveys, Cambridge University Press.

LÉVA C. 1990. *Aerial Photography and Geophysical Prospection* 2, Brussels.

MACGREGOR A. 2000. An Aerial Relic of O.G.S. Crawford, *Antiquity* 74: 87-100.

MAXWELL G.S. (Ed.) 1983a. *The Impact of Aerial Reconnaissance on Archaeology*, CBA Research Report 49.

MAXWELL G.S. (Ed.) 1983b. Recent Aerial Survey in Scotland. In G.S. MAXWELL 1983a: 27-40.

MORRIS C. and N. EMERY 1986. The Chapel and Enclosure on the Brough of Deerness, Orkney: Survey and Excavations 1975-1977, *Proceedings of the Society of Antiquarians of Scotland* 116: 301-374.

MUIR R. 1984. *History from the Air*, Michael Joseph Ltd, London.

NORMAN E.R. and J.K.S. ST.JOSEPH 1969. *The Early Development of Irish Society. The Evidence of Aerial Photography*, Cambridge Aerial Surveys III, Cambridge University Press.

OMAND D. (Ed.) 2003. *The Orkney Book*, Birlinn Ltd, Edinburgh.

OXLEY I. 2002. Scapa Flow and the Protection and Management of Scotland's Historic Military Shipwrecks, *Antiquity* 76: 864-865.

PHILPOTT R.A. 1998. A Note on New Evidence from Aerial Reconnaissance for Roman Military Sites in Cheshire, *Britannia* 29: 341-353.

RCAHMS (Royal Commission on the Ancient and Historical Monuments of Scotland) 1933. *Eleventh Report and Inventory of Monuments and Constructions in the Counties of Fife, Kinross and Clackmannan*, H.M.S.O. Edition, Edinburgh.

RCAHMS (Royal Commission on the Ancient and Historical Monuments of Scotland) 1946. *Twelfth Report with an Inventory of the Ancient Monuments of Orkney and Shetland. Volume II, Inventory of Orkney*, H.M.S.O. Edition, Edinburgh.

RCAHMS (Royal Commission on the Ancient and Historical Monuments of Scotland) 1956. *An Inventory of the Ancient and Historical Monuments of Roxburghshire* (with the Fourteenth Report of the Commission), H.M.S.O. Edition, Edinburgh.

RCAHMS (Royal Commission on the Ancient and Historical Monuments of Scotland) 1987. The Archaeological Sites and Monuments of Shapinsay, St Andrews and Deerness, Orkney Islands Area, *The Archaeological Sites and Monuments of Scotland* 27. Edinburgh.

REYNOLDS D.M. and J.N.G. RITCHIE 1985. Walter Gordon Grant: an Archaeological Appreciation, *Proceedings of the Society of Antiquarians of Scotland* 115: 67-73.

RICHARDS C.C. 1996. Henges and Water. Towards an Elemental Understanding of Monumentality and Landscape in Late Neolithic Britain, Journal of Material Culture 1(3): 313-336.

RICHARDS C.C. 2005. *Dwelling in the Monuments*, MacDonald Institute for Archaeological Research, Cambridge.

RITCHIE A. 1996. *Orkney. Exploring Scotland's Heritage*, H.M.S.O. Edition, Edinburgh.

SHEPHERD I.A.G. and M. GREIG 1996. *Grampian's Past. Its Archaeology from the Air*, Grampian Regional Council, Aberdeen.

SIMPSON W.D. 1981. *Noltland Castle*, Leaflet produced for SDD.

STEER K.A. 1947. Archaeology and the National Air-Photograph Survey, *Antiquity* 21: 50-53.

ST.JOSEPH J.K.S. 1964. Air Reconnaissance: Recent Results, *Antiquity* 38: 217-218.

ST.JOSEPH J.K.S. 1976a. Air Reconnaissance of Roman Scotland, 1939-75, *Glasgow Archaeological Journal* 4: 1-28.

ST.JOSEPH J.K.S. 1976b. Aerial Reconnaissance: Recent Results 40, *Antiquity* 50: 55-57.

ST.JOSEPH J.K.S. 1980. Aerial Reconnaissance: Recent Results 50, *Antiquity* 54: 132-135.

STORER CLOUSTON J. 1948. *Storer Clouston's Omnibus*, Blackwood, London.

THOMPSON W.P.L. 2001. *The New History of Orkney*, Mercat Press, Edinburgh.

VAUGHAN W.R. 1977. Aerial Archaeology in the North, *Aerial Archaeology* 1: 28.

WICKHAM-JONES C. 1998. *Orkney. A Historical Guide*, Birlinn Ltd, Edinburgh.

WILSON D.R. 1990. *Air Photography in Cambridge University*. In C. LÉVA 1990: 265-276.

WILSON D.R. 1995. John Kenneth Sinclair St Joseph 1912-1994, *Proceedings of the British Academy* 87: 417-436.

WILSON D.R. 2000. *Air Photo Interpretation for Archaeologists*, Tempus, Stroud.

WOOD L. 2000. *The Bull and the Barriers: the Wrecks of Scapa Flow*, Tempus, Stroud.

THE ROMAN LANDSCAPE OF CENTRAL BELGIUM
A VIEW FROM THE AIR

MARC LODEWIJCKX – RENÉ PELEGRIN

Introduction

The landscape in central Belgium is characterised by the fertile loess belt which runs from west to east from Northern France, throughout Belgium, the south of the Netherlands and the Rhineland. It separates the sandy region (Kempen) in the north from the hills of the Ardennes in the south. Due to its fertility and local flint outcrops, this loess zone has always been attractive to settlers and the oldest recorded human occupation goes back as far as the Middle Palaeolithic. The area was first deforested and brought into cultivation by settlers of the Linearbandkeramik Culture of which about 200 dwelling sites are recorded so far, most of them in the south-east area of the Hesbaye, close to similar settlements in the Meuse and Rhine valleys.

Erosion: a huge problem

One of the major problems archaeologists are confronted with is the extensive erosion of the loess soils. This is almost entirely caused by the intensive farming activities and by leaving the land bare for a longer period. That way, on hilltops and on the upper parts of slopes in particular, soil profiles are truncated during periods of heavy rain, while at the same time they are buried in sinks and valley floors by washed-off material (fig. 1). In the last century, the increase of large-scale agricultural operations have also intensified the erosion processes and the destruction of archaeological features.

Many archaeological sites have almost completely disappeared due to the persisting erosion of the topsoil layers.

Fig. 1: A clear example of the huge erosion processes in the fragile Hesbaye region.

Fig. 3: These configurations of rather small scale features are presumably an indication for indigenous dwellings and modest villages from an until now unknown period in the past.

Fig. 2: Much to our surprise, these presumable Celtic Fields appeared in an arboriculture.

Fig. 4: Remains of the Roman wall and turrets at Tongeren.

Nowadays, archaeologists consider themselves lucky if they find the bottom of the deepest elements of the original structures. On many Roman sites on the countryside only the cellar of the original dwelling appears to have been preserved. The rest of the buildings have been reduced to small pieces of debris. Although in recent times more attention is paid to prevent or reduce these erosion processes, mainly in order the safeguard the productiveness of these valuable soils, our surveys show the consistent negative impact of these erosion processes on the preservation of archaeological sites.

Moreover, field surveys and detailed auguring indicate that the original landscape had a varied and hetero-geneous relief that has been transformed into a uniform and largely flattened relief by centuries of unrelenting agricultural activities.

Indications for a pre-Roman occupation

Prior to the Roman conquest, the area was inhabited by the Gaulish tribe of the Nervii in the western part and by the Eburones in the eastern area. Caesar mentions that these tribes did not possess any fortresses (oppidum) but lived in scattered farms and scarce hamlets. During the Gaulish wars, both tribes were defeated by the Roman legions and the Eburones in particular were massacred because their king Ambiorix had slaughtered one and a half Roman legion in an ambush. In the past, most prehistoric sites were discovered by field surveys and hazardous discoveries. However, in recent times, new sites and indigenous farmsteads have been detected by aerial surveys (fig. 2). And although it was not expected due to the erosion, our aerial surveys have even uncovered several systems of Celtic fields in the loess area (fig. 3). It is amazing that these features were still visible, yet in ideal circumstances, although we are not aware of the reason why they appeared (type of crop, varieties in soil substance, rare case of stress ?). We are to continue this aerial research because it brings up new elements about the habitation processes and the long history of land use and farming in the loess zone.

The Roman conquest

After the indigenous Belgic tribes were defeated, the Romans quickly brought the land back into cultivation in order to secure the supply of their troops. They did that by transferring settlers to the loess area, probably parts of amicable tribes from over the Rhine, of which the Tungri were the most eminent. Atuatuca Tungrorum (Tongeren) was founded around 12 BC as a Roman military base on the road from Boulogne, the main port on the Atlantic coast, to the Rhine limes at Cologne. Atuatuca Tungrorum was constructed on a ridge between the basins of the Scheldt and the Meuse and was to become the

Fig. 5: The trackway of the Roman road between the town of Tongeren and the vicus of Tienen.

Fig. 6: Many flights bring to light traces of formal roads but their date is generally unclear.

Fig. 7: These Roman tiles reveal the location of larger villas in the landscape although usually nothing much can be seen from the air due to the removal of their foundations and the erosion afterwards.

capital of the Civitas Tungrorum. Here, at the end of the second decade BC, the Roman army established a regular street grid with square blocks as the substructure for the city to emerge. In the early middle Ages, this typical Roman configuration has been substituted by a more common pattern of centrifugal streets around the medieval basilica in the city centre.

Apart from one temple, the actual habitation has prevented greater areas in the former Roman city centre to be excavated. Nevertheless, the research of the large cemeteries around the city has provided much information on the life of its Roman citizens. In the 2nd century AD, the city became surrounded by a 4,544 m long and partly preserved wall, as attestation of its economic eminence and prosperity (fig. 4). The wall was about 6 m high and 2.1 m wide and retained a set of circular towers. It was preceded by one to three, V-shaped ditches, up to 9 m wide and 6 m deep. In the 3rd century AD, this rampart was reduced to a length of 2,604 m and supplied with additional turrets for a more efficient defence.

Roman roads and allotments

Straight Roman roads opened up the province and gave way to long-term economic prosperity. Roads from and towards the main city of Tongeren in particular are well known because their surface was provided with a layer of

pebbles or hard rock and because they remained the major arteries until far after the Middle Ages. Many of them are still used for agricultural traffic and others are, due to their long-term use in the past, still clearly visible in the landscape (fig. 5). Characteristic for the loess area are the hollow roads, of which the surface has been lowered on hilltops and slopes by centuries of continuous erosion. The Roman roads outside the loess area are hardly known because less care was paid to their construction and maintenance (fig. 6).

For their large-scale agricultural venture, the Romans chose the fertile Hesbaye loess belt as their main radius of action. The undulating landscape was divided into generously proportioned plots and on each parcel a traditional farmhouse was established. The dwellings were usually implanted on carefully chosen places on the allotments. They very often had a marvellous scenic view. The size of these estates varies from rather small in the district of Tongeren to circa 500 ha in central area of the Hesbaye. Consequently, it is most unlikely that these large lots should have been assigned to individual farmers and their families. Several indications point out that the estates were in the hands of the previously Celtic nobility. There is no doubt that many of the members of his tribe or relatives worked on these estates. So far, excavations do not provide enough evidence to find out whether all these people lived within the estate, or whether they had their own dwellings, elsewhere on the allotment.

Fig. 8: A picture with possibly a former Roman road and building next to it. However, their dates remain unclear.

Roman villas

In the 1st century AD, the original farmsteads existed of two-naved constructions, built after the example of the indigenous tradition, i.e. using wood and loam. Normally several constructions succeeded each other, and even though the design cannot always be completely reconstructed, one can distinguish an increasing monumentality of the buildings. We may well assume that the indigenous settlement became prosperous because of the economic boom after the Roman conquest (Pax Romana).

By the 2nd century AD the prominent owners of this production unit, enriched by the profits and the possibilities in market offset for their products, could afford to build a stylish stone house according to the Mediterranean model with hypocaust, painted wall plaster and floor mosaics. Highly appealing is the plan of the average villa estate, consisting of a central dwelling block with two spacious protruding corner rooms, linked by a long porticus on the front side. Bath suites are always present, although they appear to have been added in later periods. Even though excavations are normally restricted to the dwelling houses, we may assume that the premises must have known a similar development and that further utility buildings had at least stonewall footings and a more elaborated plan and construction.

Since natural stone and other building material have always been very scarce in the loess area, Roman buildings are usually completely dismantled in later times and are therefore hard to discover. The major Roman settlements have been identified for a long time but in most cases very little remains of the original constructions. Probably the Roman landscape was spruced up with all sorts of constructions, such as mansions, small shrines and other monuments. Smaller farmhouses in wood or wattle and daub are harder to find and even most tumulus mounds have been flattened in recent centuries. Large-scale agricultural activities and erosion, mainly caused by anthropogenic factors, have turned the original Roman landscape into a uniform and largely flattened relief.

Most of the larger Roman estates were already discovered in the 19th century by the vast amount of debris lying on the surface (fig. 7). In many cases the remnants of the main stone buildings were unearthed in order to reconstruct their plan and to recover some beautiful artefacts. Hardly any attention was paid to other features and buildings on the precinct. These kinds of excavations rarely revealed any information on their origin, their buildings constructed in wattle and daub and later occupations during the Frankish and Merovingian periods. Nowadays, even the debris has sometimes been completely removed by farmers and even from the air no traces can be detected, due to the erosion on many of these sites, located on susceptible hilltops (fig. 8).

Fig. 9: A well preserved Roman burial mound near the road to Tongeren at Koninksem.

*Fig. 10: Most likely an indication for one of the many Roman burial mounds in the Hesbaye region that have
disappeared.*

Roman burial mounds

The owners of these large estates were buried in large coffins underneath immense tombs (tumulus), erected alongside the roads and clearly visible. The exquisite grave goods of these tombs consist of an abundance of samian ware, delightful glass vessels, metal canisters and personal objects of a remarkable extravagancy and represent the wealth of these refined Roman citizens. As many as 100 of these burial mounds are still preserved, sometimes in groups of two to four tombs in a row alongside the road. Many tombs are still as high as 10 to 15 m and although they are often eroded and in a poor state of preservation, due to their towering position with unkempt trees on top, they are still majestic marks in the usually bare landscape (fig. 9). Many others have been levelled to give way to additional fields. Originally most of them appear to have been provided with a circular wall at the base and although the stones have later been removed, the foundation trench often lights up as a circular mark in the field (fig. 10).

Conclusion

Aerial survey is the best way to discover the remains of the Roman occupancy and to at least partially reconstruct the Roman allotments, old road patterns and the dispersion of Roman villas. So far, aerial surveys have completed largely the image that was generated by ground surveys and old findings. The information from our aerial surveys is transmitted as soon as possible to the Agency for Environmental Planning and Cultural Heritage of the Flemish Government which is responsible for the management of archaeological sites. That way we hope to contribute to the preservation of our archaeological heritage.

However, it is without doubt that many remains from the Roman period have been destroyed by later activities and by modern erosion. Large parts of the landscape appear to be empty or filled with only blurred patterns. One can only estimate the amount of archaeological information that is lost. The reaction to our investigation by the local population and policy makers only underscores the increasing significance of archaeology. We are hoping for a more systematic protection of the archaeological information, hidden underground, through an appropriate archaeological legislature and ditto approach, to safeguard the future of this heritage.

Marc LODEWIJCKX – René PELEGRIN
University of Leuven (K.U. Leuven)
Dept. Archaeology, Art History and Musicology
Blijde-Inkomststraat 21, bus 3313
3000 LEUVEN
Belgium

Apologizes

This article was written by the authors in 2005-06 but due to various difficulties it was only published in 2011, for which I want to apologize sincerely – Marc Lodewijckx (editor).

Bibliography

LODEWIJCKX M. 1995. Essay on the Issue of Continuity applied to the Northern Hesbaye Region (Central Belgium). In M. LODEWIJCKX (Ed.), *Archaeological and Historical Aspects of West European Societies*, Acta Archaeologica Lovaniensia, Monographiae 8: 207-220.

LODEWIJCKX M. and L. OPSTEYN 1999. An Early Roman Ditch at Wange (Central Belgium), *Journal of Roman Military Equipment Studies* 10: 95-101.

OPSTEYN L. and M. LODEWIJCKX 2001. Wange-Damekot Revisited. New Perspectives in Roman Habitation History. In M. LODEWIJCKX (Ed.), *Belgian Archaeology in a European Setting II*, Acta Archaeologica Lovaniensia, Monographiae 13: 217-230.

MEGANCK M., J. BOURGEOIS, I. ROOVERS and M. LODEWIJCKX 2001. SMR in Flanders. The Havik-Project: Archaeological GIS-based Inventory of Archives at the Universities of Ghent and Leuven. In C.Ph. CLARKE (Ed.), Protecting the Past in the Present for the Future. The Developments of SMRs in the Planarch Project Region and Beyond, *Papers from the Planarch Chelmsford Seminar, May 2001*, Chelmsford, Essex County Council: 26-32.

BOURGEOIS J., I. ROOVERS, M. MEGANCK, J. SEMEY, R. PELEGRIN and M. LODEWIJCKX 2002. Flemish Aerial Archaeology in the Last 20 Years: Past and Future Perspectives. In R.H. BEWLEY, W. RACZO-KOWSKI (Eds.), Aerial Archaeology, Developing Future Practice, *Proceedings of the NATO Advanced Research Workshop on Aerial Archaeology, Leszno (Pl), 15-17 November 2000*, Swindon: 76-83.

OPSTEYN L. and M. LODEWIJCKX 2004. The Late Roman and Merovingian Periods at Wange (Central Belgium). In M. LODEWIJCKX (Ed.), *Bruc ealles well, Archaeological Essays Concerning the Peoples of North-West Europe in the First Millennium AD*, Acta Archaeologica Lovaniensia, Monographiae 15: 125-155.

LODEWIJCKX M. and R. PELEGRIN 2005. First Results of Aerial Surveys in the Eastern Part of Flanders (Belgium). In J. BOURGEOIS and M. MEGANCK (Eds.), *Aerial Photography and Archaeology 2003. A Century of Information*, Archaeological Reports Ghent University 4, Gent: 341-348.

INTERPRETING A FUNERARY LANDSCAPE: THE DESERT CEMETERIES AT DAYR AL-BARSHĀ (EGYPT)

CHRISTOPH AND HELEN PEETERS

1. The site: a short introduction

The site of Dayr al-Barshā is located approximately 270 km South of Cairo on the east bank of the Nile, just to the north of the well known site of El-Amarna. The site of Dayr al-Barshā was used as a necropolis for millennia. The oldest burials we have evidence of now, are dated to early Old Kingdom being about 2600 BC and part of the site is still being used as a cemetery to this day.

On top of that, the site has seen a lot of quarry activity. These quarry activities peaked around 600 BC. From the 5th century AD, a Coptic monastery was built in the village and Coptic monks used the old rock tombs and quarries as habitats.

Although the site was summarily investigated a few times at the end of the 19th century and the beginning of the 20th century, no publication, apart from a scant publication of some texts in the big tombs, was ever made, before the Katholieke Universiteit Leuven started its Dayr al-Barshā project in 2002. For an overview of archaeological research of the site and its wider geographical situation the reader is referred to WILLEMS 2007.

2. Geography and geology of the site

The site is geologically made up from 3 major units. In the west there is the fertile Nile valley traditionally a place of agriculture and human habitats. Just to the west of the site is the low desert. This desert lies barely above the level of the fertile Nile valley, yet in the past, before the Aswan dam was built, this part of the valley was not flooded by the yearly Nile flood and has until recently remained barren.

A few hundred meters to the west of this divide lies a series of rock cliffs roughly parallel to the Nile and the valley/low desert interface. These cliffs are up to 120 m high and constitute the foothills of the Egyptian Eastern Desert plateau, that continues up to the Red Sea. At the site of Dayr al-Barshā these cliffs are intersected by a deep wādī: the Wādī Nakhla. This wādī drains a large desert area in the very rare occasions of rain in the Eastern Desert and then forms a flash flood which drains in the lower desert. The Wādī Nakhla divides the cliffs in a northern and southern part, both of which contain rock tombs and quarries.

3. The use of the site at the beginning of the second millennium BC

Of all the eras of human interaction with the site that in the beginning of the second millennium BC is the most interesting for this article. At that time, the governors of the Hare province built large rock tombs in the northern cliffs. Their predecessors had built their tombs close to the contemporary course of the river Nile.

Between these two sites a mud covered road was laid. The mud presumably being wetted for lubrication on the occasion when a very heavy burial coffin was dragged on a sledge from the Nile to the cliff tombs. On an excavated part of this mud road sliding traces of sledges have actually been found (WILLEMS *et alii* 2005).

To the north and the south of this mud road, walled burial complexes were built. These consisted of a wall of sun dried clay bricks surrounding a rectangular area which usually contains several tombs. The tombs themselves range from very shallow burials near the surface to well built structures almost 6 meters deep and lined with clay brick. Of the larger tombs, the most common type seems to be a shaft tomb with a burial chamber opening to the south at the bottom of the shaft. This shaft is at the most only supported in its upper 1 to 2 meters by a lining in clay brick. Below this both shaft and burial chamber were simply dug out in the subsoil of rough wādī deposited compacted sands (PEETERS 2009).

For our project, we decided to evaluate the possibilities of satellite imagery and bought a CORONA image taken in 1968.

4. CORONA imagery

The CORONA project represents the first generation of U.S. photo intelligence satellites. They were launched between 1960 and 1972. These satellites are of the types KH-1 to KH-4B, with each type apart from the KH-1 representing several launches of satellites.

Fig. 1: CORONA image of Dayr al-Barshā in 1968. On the lower right the wādī mouth. To the left of it in order from left to right: the ancient cemetery in the desert, the modern cemetery (represented by the spotted area), the village and cultivated land.

All CORONA imagery is in the visual band only and mostly black and white.

Since at the time of the CORONA program high resolution electronic imagery was impossible, the CORONA satellites took their pictures on traditional still photography film. At the end of the mission the film was transferred to a capsule which descended to the earth. The resulting film(s) could then be developed and researched in ground based facilities.

For high resolution imagery the KH-4B types are the best with a resolution of 1.8 m. Images with this resolution are also available as stereo pairs. The KH-4B series were launched between 9/1967 and 5/1972. The older types of CORONA satellites are useful if one wants to get older pictures of a landscape. They range from KH-1 in 1960 with 12 meter resolution to the KH-4A type active between 1963 and 1969 with 3 meters resolution.

In 1995 the imagery was no longer considered vital to U.S. security and the value of high quality imagery of such age meant that they were made available to the general public via the United States Geological Survey.

On the website of the United States Geological Survey one can search, preview and order the images on-line. When we bought our image for the Dayr al-Barshā Project, the delivered product was still a negative copy of a first generation copy of the original image negative. This could then be scanned by the end user according to his specifications. Since some time the USGS only delivers the data in scanned format and it is not guaranteed that the maximum resolution of the original image is thus met.

We chose for an evaluation of the possibilities of satellite imagery to buy a CORONA image taken in 1968. The low price and the early date of this picture were appealing and ideal to get a first indication of the usefulness of remote sensing of the site of Dayr al-Barshā.

Apart from this CORONA image a SPOT image of lower resolution but with infra-red range was used and also Landsat 5 and Landsat 7 images that can be downloaded for free at the United States Geological Survey Website. The SPOT image was provided to us by Gert Verstraeten of the Katholieke Universiteit Leuven for which we wish to thank him.

Fig. 2. Areal view of a walled tomb complex. On ground level most of these structures were barely noticeable.

Due to the different dates of all these imagery, we could reconstruct the encroachment of human activities on the low lying desert, the place where most Egyptian antiquities are found, in the last 40 years: Whereas in the CORONA image the low desert is still almost free from modern human activity, in the most modern image (SPOT), most of the low desert has been transformed into fields, modern habitats or tombs.

5. Using the CORONA imagery

The CORONA image was of great use in interpreting the lay-out of our site. Given that the available maps lacked in detail for the desert areas, the CORONA picture gave us our first detailed view of the desert on a large scale. Also on the CORONA imagery lots of features were visible that have since disappeared due to human interaction with the landscape. Since the CORONA image was taken large part of the low desert has been overbuilt or irrigated thus destroying the ancient landscape that was well preserved in 1968.

One of the main questions we had about the placement of the cemetery along the road was its placement in the landscape: namely right in front of a wādī mouth. Given that the ancient Egyptians equalled the possibility of an afterlife with the physical survival of the corpse and its associated funerary equipment in the world of the living it didn't make much sense at first sight to build a cemetery in a place that is prone to flash floods

A look on the CORONA picture showed that all the modern villages and their cemeteries in the vicinity of Dayr al-Barshā lie in front of a wādī. A closer look at the imagery revealed that the outflows of the wādīs was not straight but flowed besides these villages in front of a wādī mouth.

Was is the explanation for this ? It lies in a desert type phenomena called an 'alluvial fan'. Where the wādī is constricted by cliffs the flow of water has a very high debit and speed and hence a high carrying capacity for small rubble and sand. When the wādī appears from the cliffs, the flow is not constricted anymore, the velocity and carrying capacity diminish a lot and a sort of dry river delta is formed. The sand and rubble carried by the wādī gets deposited. Over the millennia this results in a triangular fan of deposited sands and rubble. The wādī will over the ages re-route its main flow away from this heightened triangle. Thus a roughly triangular 'island' is formed which is a bit less prone to flashfloods than the surrounding flat desert.

This is exactly what happened at Dayr al-Barshā: both the modern village, modern cemetery and ancient cemetery lie on a roughly triangular spit of slightly higher land. (the modern village and cemetery are built over parts of the ancient cemetery). The outflow of the wādī runs to the north and south of this spit of land. Also visible on the CORONA image is a multitude of small dry rivulets in front of the cliffs where there is no wādī. Thus these parts of the desert are also more prone to flooding than the heightened alluvial fans.

Thanks to the CORONA imagery we thus can explain the apparently counterintuitive placement of the ancient cemetery and the modern villages and cemeteries in relation to desert phenomena. Given the very large impact of human activities on the landscape since 1968 it is doubtful that we could easily have come to the same conclusion using modern imagery.

6. Kite Aerial Photography

Kite aerial photography, colloquially known as KAP, is simply the use of a dragon kite to loft a camera to a suitable height in order to make aerial pictures with it. This technique is very old and was used from the late 1880's to make aerial pictures. The interest in the technique diminished sharply with the advent of heavier than air aircraft. With the coming of very light cameras and micro electronics to operate them in recent decennia, the interest in this form of aerial photography has resurfaced, almost exclusively amongst amateur photographers.

The system consists of 3 main components: A dragon kite, large enough to lift the line and camera rig and adapted to the prevailing wind conditions. Given the wide range of possible wind conditions it is usually advisable to have at least two dragon kites: for hard and low wind conditions. The camera rig is hung from the dragon kite on the line some 10 to 15 meters below the kite. The camera rig consist of a pendulum or a system of small pulleys that keep it horizontal automatically by the action of gravity. Also on the rig is the camera itself and all the necessary components to remotely control the camera. There are basically two types of camera rigs. Most rigs allow you to pan and elevate the camera so you can take pictures under any angle. This works nice for low altitude photography where you can see the camera and estimate its viewing angle. For higher level (in the realm of KAP)

photography a simple camera pointing down might be preferable.

The height the camera can reach in KAP is theoretically only limited by the length of the line the kite is attached to and the size of the kite needed to loft the weight of this line and the rig. In practice one is generally restricted to heights of about 75 to 100 m. This last height is also in many countries the legal limit for dragon kite flying heights.

The great advantage of KAP is its promptness: after a little assembly one immediately has a tool to make low height areal pictures. Thus they are very suitable to illustrate the progress of an excavation. In our excavation, we used it to image structures that were barely visible from the ground level on photographs. We used a ladder approximately 3 meters high to photograph the excavated 5 by 5 meters squares. But from this height the larger structures are barely visible on photographs. It was for that end that we used KAP to illustrate larger structures spanning several 5 x 5 m squares. The example given will demonstrate to the reader the usefulness of KAP.

Christoph and Helen PEETERS
Katholieke Universiteit Leuven
Blijde-Inkomststraat 21, bus 3318
3000 LEUVEN
Belgium

Bibliography

PEETERS C. 2009. Work in Zone 9. In H. WILLLEMS *et alii* 2009, Report of the 2004-2005 Campaigns of the Belgian Mission to Deir al-Barsha, *Mitteilungen des Deutschen Archäologischen Instituts* 65: 401-408.

WILLEMS H. 2007. Dayr al-Barshā Volume I. The Rock Tombs of Djehutinakht (No. 17K74/1), Khnumnakht (No. 17K74/2), and Iha (No. 17K74/3), with an Essay on the History and Nature of Nomarchal Rule in the Early Middle Kingdom, *Orientalia Lovaniensia Analecta* 155, Leuven.

WILLEMS H., Chr. PEETERS and G. VERSTRAETEN 2005. Where did Djehutihotep erect his Colossal Statue ?, *Zeitschrift für Ägyptische Sprache und Altertumskunde* 132: 173-189.

WILLEMS H., A. DELATTRE, M. DE MEYER, D. DEPRAETERE, T. DUPRAS, T. HERBICH, G. VAN LOON, C. PEETERS, S. VEREECKEN, G. VER-STRAETEN and L. WILLIAMS 2009. Report of the 2004-2005 Campaigns of the Belgian Mission to Dayr al-Barshā. *Mitteilungen des Deutschen Archäologischen Instituts* 65: 377-432.

THE NMP IN ESSEX: MAPPING OF EARLY PREHISTORIC SITES

HELEN SAUNDERS

1. Introduction

The National Mapping Programme (NMP) in Essex was begun in 1993 and was one of the first English Heritage projects established as a response to the Monuments Protection Programme (MPP). The background and ideology of the programme was set out in B. Bewley (BEWLEY 2001) with the principles and procedures for the recording of the archaeology presented by J. Edis and others (EDIS *et alii* 1989). The main aim of the NMP is to map all visible archaeology from all available aerial photographs to a set standard and to a common scale of 1:10,000, and then to record the morphology of each site. In Essex this recording was carried out using the MORPH2 database developed by English Heritage (EDIS *et alii* 1989). This ensures consistency across recording of sites thus facilitating analysis at both a local and national level.

Essex is located in the south east of Britain (fig. 1) on the east coast and is one of the largest counties in England. Its position close to London and the coast has ensured a varied history that is reflected in its extensive archaeological remains. The NMP in Essex drew upon the vast oblique aerial survey collection gained from a reconnaissance programme that had been carried out in the county since 1978, along with the collections held in the National Monuments Record (NMR) and at the Cambridge University Collection of Aerial Photographs (CUCAP), as well as other collections of vertical photography held both in Essex and elsewhere. It was the first time that any consistent and coherent programme of mapping and interpretation had been carried out in the county using all the available aerial collections.

This article presents the results of analysis carried out on some of the 10,700 sites recorded during the course of the project. It is part of the formal publication material that is being prepared and which will be published as an East Anglian Archaeology (EAA) monograph. The sites and case studies discussed below are part of a larger corpus of work looking at the prehistoric ritual landscape of Essex. Other themes addressed in the publication will include later prehistoric and Roman settlement, medieval landscapes, coastal exploitation and military landscapes of World War II.

2. Prehistoric Essex and Ritual Landscapes

Over the last 30 years Essex has seen much research into the prehistoric period, often resulting from good cropmark evidence (BROWN 1999 and 2001; HEDGES-BUCKLEY 1978). Recent publications on work carried out in Essex have highlighted areas of potential research. Projects such as the Stour Valley Project have used aerial photography and GIS to aid the understanding of the variety and complexity of monuments within their landscape context (BROWN *et alii* 2002: 5). Due to the size of the county, extensive agricultural practice and the geological potential of large areas of Essex for the development of cropmarks, the NMP has produced a large corpus of data, particularly on the responsive soils. This, combined with extensive fieldwork and excavation material, has ensured that there is a broad evidence base for the study of the later prehistoric in Essex. While settlement evidence for the early prehistoric period is lacking there are many monuments that attest to activity of this date.

It is perhaps misleading to distinguish between ritual and domestic landscapes. A clear distinction between ritual/religion and domestic activity in the landscape is essentially a modern attitude. The landscape in the prehistoric period would have been suffused with ritual practice and symbolic meaning; and the issues regarding the divide between domestic/ritual have been discussed elsewhere (for example: BRADLEY 1998; THOMAS 1999). Furthermore, landscape context is the same whether used for domestic or ritual purposes, and is not static, but constantly changing. Two people would experience the same landscape in a different way (DARVILL 1997: 4) and this can be problematic for us to reconstruct how a monument fitted into its surroundings and how structures were perceived by the people who built them.

Aerial photographic evidence is inevitably biased as to the types of sites that can be recognised, for example size, physical form and location all effect whether a site would be visible on certain aerial photographs. Within the early prehistoric landscape many sites identified on aerial photographs appear to be of a ritual nature. This may be due to the monuments developing out of the routines of

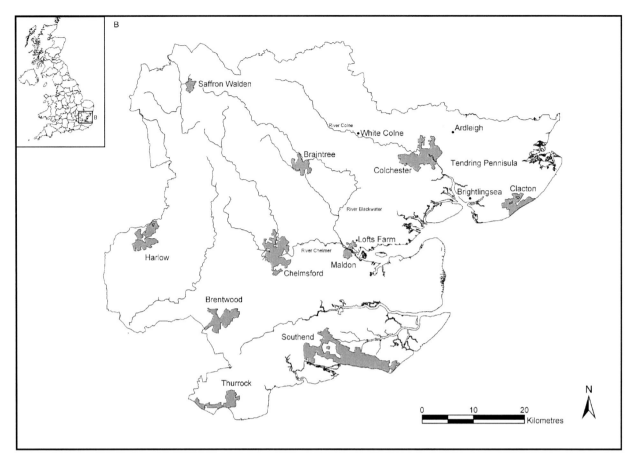

Fig. 1: Location map.

daily life and perhaps they should be considered not, as a by-product of an elusive farming culture for which we have little evidence, but as significant in their own right (BRADLEY 1998: 14, 17). This leads to the question of how the monuments were related to each other and how their presence in the landscape was both a by-product of people and, in turn, influenced people.

2.1. Distribution of Prehistoric Sites

In Essex, NMP mapped and dated 2990 sites to Prehistoric period. At a county level distinct distribution patterns can be detected, with the vast majority of prehistoric sites being located along the major river valleys, especially those of the Stour, Chelmer and Blackwater (fig. 2). However, this distribution maybe influenced by the biases inherent within aerial photographic evidence which are discussed elsewhere (RILEY 1979; RILEY 1983; WILSON 2000).

Several major classes of early prehistoric monuments have been found and mapped within Essex, including cursus monuments, mortuary enclosures, causewayed enclosures, long barrows, henge monuments and round barrows. Many of the monuments mapped fit into standard classification categories and can be interpreted with reasonable confidence on morphology alone.

Small prehistoric sites such as barrows are much more frequently found whereas large Neolithic monuments are considerably rarer, but they still appear in significant numbers. For example, two cursus monuments have been mapped within the county with at least three further sites that have a similar morphology to known cursus and have been interpreted as such. Two causewayed enclosures were mapped over the course of the project, Orsett (Essex Historic Environment Record (EHER) number 5158) and Matching Green (EHER 17064); although a further two, Springfield Lyons (EHER 5788) and St. Osyth (EHER 2970), have since been identified through a combination of excavation and aerial photography.

There have been problems with interpreting some features with confidence. For example, circular monuments of various sizes are quite common and it has proved to be notoriously difficult to give an accurate interpretation on morphology alone. This has proved particularly true with the interpretation of henge monuments within the county. The Essex Cropmark Enclosures Project (BROWN-GERMANY 2002) four sites were examined, all of which had been considered to be possible henge monuments. The sites, all circular enclosures with one or more entrances, at Colemans Farm, Rivenhall, Sturrick Farm, Great Bentley, Hall Farm, Little Bentley and Clare Downs Farm, Belchamp

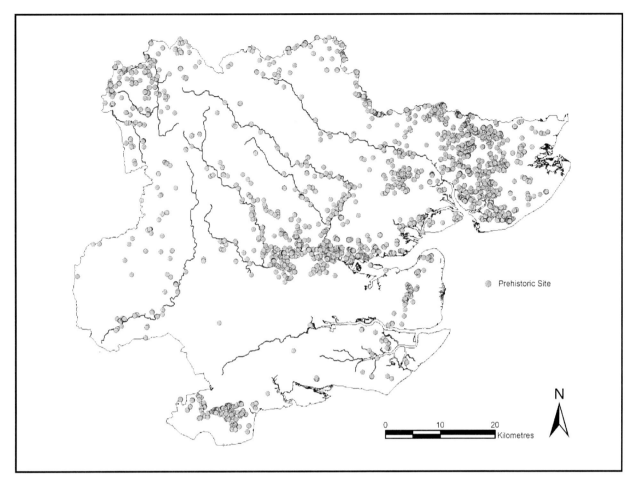

Fig. 2: Distribution of mapped prehistoric sites.

St. Pauls, were investigated by excavation and the surrounding area was field walked. The results of this work showed that the two sites at Great and Little Bentley were the remains of medieval windmills. The Great Bentley site, prior to the project, was considered to be one of the best examples of a Neolithic henge monument in the east of England. The finds at Rivenhall indicated that the enclosure was of prehistoric date and had an extensive period of use (BROWN-GERMANY 2002: 47) but was probably not a henge monument and the enclosure at Belchamp St Pauls was considered to be more than just a simple barrow, but the interpretation could not be taken further. This project illustrated the problems with characterising sites; even with extensive fieldwork a confident interpretation may not be possible based purely on morphology.

Ring ditches are the most prolific site type identified, and many have been interpreted as round barrows, probably of Bronze Age. There is a tendency, within aerial interpretation in Essex, to allocate all ring-ditches, with or without entrances, to the round barrow category. This is often due to the size and location of the sites, although many ring-ditch sites have characteristics similar to many excavated examples of round barrows and so are classified as such. The vast majority of round barrows in

Essex are attributed to the Bronze Age. The use of round barrows as a burial monument has a long history and some may have been constructed earlier than the Bronze Age, for example, Westbury 7, Wiltshire (THOMAS 1999: 151-152) and the ring-ditch excavated within the cursus monument at Springfield (BUCKLEY *et alii* 2001: 155). Others may be considerably later in date as the use of this monument type lasted from the Neolithic through to the Roman and Saxon periods (as shown in figure 1.2 in OSWALD *et alii* 2001: 3). This hampers the identification of prehistoric round barrows and while many individual sites probably are round barrows further interpretation is not possible without more complete investigations.

Morphologically a round barrow is a sub circular or circular (though few are strictly circular) enclosure that can range in size from 3m-65m in diameter (ENGLISH HERITAGE 1988). Within Essex 1605 circular or sub-circular enclosures have been mapped by NMP, of which 1599 are less than 65m in diameter. It cannot be assumed that all of these sites represent the vestiges of prehistoric burial activity. Analysis of these monuments is made easier when looking at clusters of sites, as it is less likely that other forms of monument would be clustered together in the same way. Spacing at round barrow

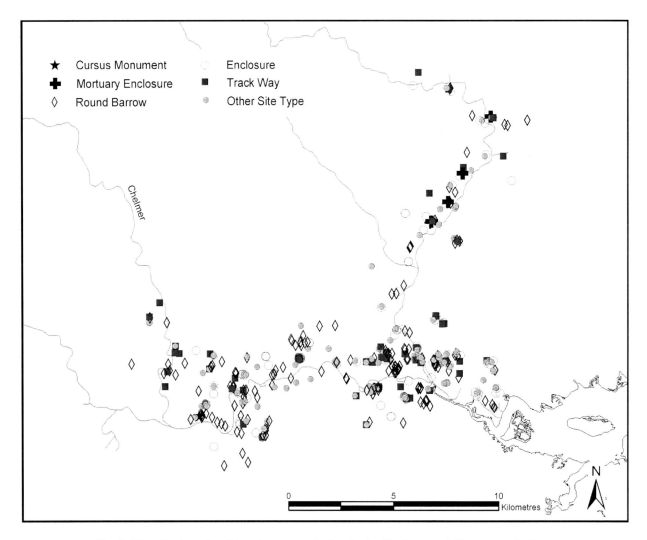

Fig. 3: Distribution of prehistoric cropmark sites in the Chelmer and Blackwater Valleys.

cemeteries varies considerably but few sites have spacing greater than 150m (ENGLISH HERITAGE 1988). A total of 754 circular enclosures are in clusters no more than 150m from their nearest neighbour. These sites form 107 clusters around the county. It would seem sensible to suggest that these are more likely to be round barrow cemeteries of possible Bronze Age date.

Several of these ring-ditch clusters, known about within Essex, have been excavated. Fieldwalking over several decades at Ardleigh has resulted in one of the most extensive investigations of a cropmark complex and one of the largest concentrations of Bronze Age burials in East Anglia (BROWN 1999: 1). There is some evidence for Neolithic activity here, but it is fragmentary. Excavation revealed many more monuments than were identified from the aerial photographs. This excavation has led to suggestions as to how the cemetery was laid out and its structure, which could be applied to other non-excavated sites. It has been suggested that the barrows were constructed in pairs with the larger examples being

built first and then the gaps filled in later with cremation burials. Some of these cremations are very close to the ring-ditches with some within 1m. None of the round barrows were particularly big with the largest excavated only 25m in diameter; it was found that there was often more than one burial or pit within the monument (BROWN 1999: 162-172).

A number cemeteries of this type are known across north east Essex. At a site at White Colne (EHER 8627) a number of urns were recovered during the 1920s but no aerial photographs exist and similar sites exist at Brightlingsea, Little Bromley and St. Osyth. The excavations at Brightlingsea showed that the site was strikingly similar to Ardleigh (LAVENDER-CLARKE forthcoming). The site comprises of a mixture of larger round barrows with smaller ring-ditches and cremation burials. Whilst it is not necessarily the case that all the densest concentrations of ring-ditches are Bronze Age (BROWN 1999: 175) it would seem likely that most are.

3. The Chelmer and Blackwater Valleys

3.1. The Upper Chelmer Valley

The Chelmer and Blackwater valleys have been a major focus of archaeological investigations for many years with both survey work and excavation (e.g. HEDGES-BUCKLEY 1987; BROWN 1997; WALLIS-WAUGHMAN 1998). Some areas with dense cropmark complexes were under threat from development, so sites such as the Springfield cursus near Chelmsford (BUCKLEY *et alii* 2001), Chigborough Farm and Slough House Farm near Maldon (WALLIS-WAUGHMAN 1998), have been excavated. This river valleys offer one of the highest cropmark concentrations in the county; is there a good reason for this, other than the valley has suitable conditions for producing cropmarks ?

There is a change in the nature of the monuments along the river valleys. To the east of Chelmsford there is a complex of major prehistoric monuments including the Springfield Cursus, a mortuary enclosure and many round barrows, but there is very little evidence for settlement. While moving east towards Maldon there are fewer major monuments, but an increase in the number of possible settlement enclosures and associated round barrows.

The river Chelmer drains the boulder clay plateau which dominates the geology in the north west of the county, and moves through the glacial gravels towards the Blackwater estuary; the Blackwater valley is very similar in nature. Both valleys provided routes linking the coast and the boulder clay plateau (BROWN 2001: 92). The Springfield cursus and other monuments lie at the major geographical boundary where the clay plateau meets the gravels. There are concentrations of important sites along both rivers, implying that this area was a focus for activity for long periods of history. Some of the monuments to the east of Chelmsford have been investigated individually (BROWN-LAVENDER 1994; BROWN 2001; BUCKLEY *et alii* 2001) and the Neolithic period of the Chelmer valley was addressed in N. Brown (BROWN 1997).

Within this landscape lay the Neolithic causewayed enclosure at Springfield Lyons. This site was built at a location that may have had an earlier significance to those who built it and, although is located on the edge of a spur of land, the site appears to face downhill towards the river. Viewshed analysis demonstrates a semi-circular panorama which includes the Springfield cursus and the River Chelmer (BROWN 2001: 93-94). This location may have been chosen for this view and this might imply that the land was fairly clear of woodland at the time, which might differ from evidence further down the valley. Although the environmental evidence suggests a reliance on woodland for fuel at the cursus site (BUCKLEY *et alii* 2001: 149), the woodland cover may have been heavier for the earlier stages of construction at the causewayed enclosure and then may have been gradually cleared.

The causewayed enclosure consisted of a single circuit, constructed with deep pit like ditches (BROWN 2001: 95) and this could imply that a large amount of bank material was upstanding which may have made the monument more visible on the horizon as the vegetation was cleared. Although there is little evidence for the activities that occurred at the causewayed enclosure there was an obvious importance within the landscape. This leads to the question of how this monument related to the others in the area.

The cursus monument lies within 250m of the river Chelmer, in the valley bottom, defined by the 20m contour. This means that it is the lowest of all the major monuments in the area, along with the possible mortuary enclosure that is found approximately 350m to the north east. Unlike other cursus monuments the entire interior would have been visible from anywhere along its length (BUCKLEY *et alii* 2001: 155); however, other elements within the landscape may not have been visible.

The causewayed enclosure and the cursus were broadly contemporary, although the construction of the causewayed enclosure was earlier. This means that both these major monuments would have been visible elements within the landscape. It has been argued that cursus monuments are fixing a part of a route way by enclosing it (LAST 1999: 87). The Chelmer valley was a routeway from inland to the sea and it has been argued that the cursus was fixing a small part of this route, it is also true that the cursus also reflects and is influenced by, the local topography. The cursus appears to 'cut off' a broad meander in the Chelmer River and this is a common feature of this site type. N. Brown (BROWN 1997) suggests that during the winter the cursus could have had water in close proximity on three sides. This is significant, as the location must have been chosen carefully enough that the monument was surrounded by water but was not flooded. It would appear that the causewayed enclosure was not visible from the cursus, but was from the mortuary enclosure that was aligned with the cursus. The visibility from the cursus monument was restricted in other directions too. For example, although the visibility down the valley to the east was very good towards a small ring-ditch aligned with the cursus, it would have only been possible to see a few hundred metres to the west; this puts the emphasis on the view towards the mortuary enclosure. This could suggest that while the cursus was a formalisation of a route or path it was actually leading towards another significant place in the landscape. The activities associated with the cursus appear to be very different to those at the causewayed enclosure as there is evidence linking the disposal of the dead with the cursus and there is no evidence for this at Springfield Lyons. Both monuments were used until the later Neolithic and then they went out of use.

Even when the monuments went out of use they would have still been prominent features in the landscape and

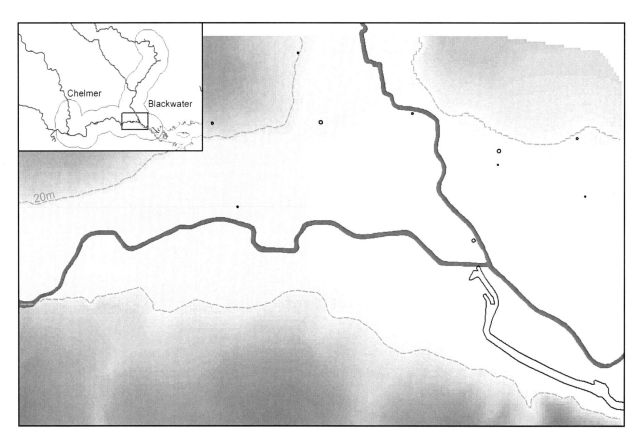

Fig. 4: First phase of cropmark development with location of study area.

there is no evidence that either monument was altered or destroyed immediately. However, other monuments became increasingly more important. A large circular enclosure 60m in diameter was constructed at Springfield Lyons in the late Bronze Age, partially over the Neolithic causewayed enclosure and, when excavated, was found to be a settlement enclosure with at least six entrances (BUCKLEY-HEDGES 1987). This settlement was constructed on a site already singled out as important and the causewayed enclosure would still have been highly visible. Likewise an occupation site at Great Baddow 1.5km to the south east had striking similarities to the Springfield Lyons settlement site. Both these sites overlook the valley (BROWN-LAVENDER 1994: 10) and the monuments within it. It would appear that the occupation sites were located on either side of the valley and with the monuments associated with the dead located on the valley bottom. Within 500m of the cursus there are seven possible round barrows as well as the mortuary enclosure. One of these barrows is aligned with the cursus and another is within the cursus ditches, which, during the excavations of the ditches produced evidence that indicated a Neolithic date (BUCKLEY *et alii* 2001: 114). This demonstrated the importance of the area for the location of round barrows. Interestingly they do not appear to continue to 'cut off' the Chelmer meander as the earlier monuments do; instead the round barrows are almost perpendicular to the eastern cursus terminal. Unlike other parts of the county there are no visible large

round barrow cemeteries, the monuments in this area appear to be relatively small scale in a dispersed linear pattern, which is common along much of this valley.

Even in this small area the landscape appears to have been evolving continuously and there are several linear features immediately surrounding the cursus. Many of them respect the cursus ditch and are probably much later, while others actually cross the cursus. It could be assumed that the cursus ditches and bank had been filled and it has been suggested that once the cursus went out of use the ditches silted up quite rapidly due to the loose gravely nature of the sub-soil (BUCKLEY *et alii* 2001: 115), this means that the area may have held a different significance once the physical evidence of the larger monuments was lost.

3.2. The Lower Chelmer Valley

Moving east along the Chelmer valley there appears to be extensive activity from all periods, while there is evidence for landscape organisation with extensive linear features, some of which may represent prehistoric settlement activity, it is difficult to classify. As is common elsewhere there is evidence in several places for settlement incorporating monuments associated with the dead. The lower part of the Blackwater valley appears very similar to that of the lower Chelmer valley with some of the possible round barrows being 'enclosed' by

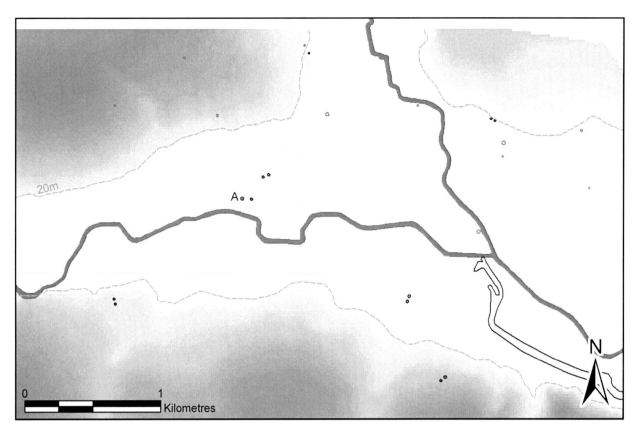

Fig. 5: Second phase of cropmark development (earlier phases in gray).

Fig. 6: Third phase of cropmark development (earlier phases in gray).

settlement activity. While the larger monuments such as mortuary enclosures and long barrows are further up the valley away from the confluence of the two rivers and the estuary.

West of Maldon near to the confluence of the Chelmer and Blackwater rivers there is a vast array of cropmark evidence ranging in date and morphology. There are some prehistoric 'ritual' monuments such as round barrows but no major Neolithic or Bronze Age monuments unlike further up the Chelmer valley (WALLIS-WAUGHMAN 1998: 218). Often round barrows were built in close context with earlier and bigger monuments, but this is not the case in the lower Chelmer valley. It may be because the meaning of the landscape was different in this area because it was not settled in the same way. It could be suggested that by the time this area was settled permanently the larger monuments such as causewayed enclosures, cursus monuments and henges had gone out of use and hence are absent from the cropmark record in this area.

Some cropmark complexes have been excavated, as at Woodham Walter (HEDGES-BUCKLEY 1987). This has produced dating and morphological evidence that can be used to compared and interpreted other cropmark sites. An area, to the east of Maldon, covering approximately 12km^2 shows that an interesting array of monuments are visible as cropmarks and appear to influence the positioning of other archaeological features. Figure 3 shows the distribution of cropmark sites within the area. There is an apparent development within the cropmark landscape and the relationship between ritual monuments and domestic needs to be addressed.

There are 176 prehistoric monuments within this area with a high concentration of smaller monuments. The vast majority of these monuments are round barrows, enclosures or trackways. The morphology of some of these sites is very similar, and groups of features can be identified.

Geologically this area is largely Pleistocene terrace gravels associated with the rivers. The soils that develop make this an area with good potential for the development of cropmarks. Most of the cropmarks are between 5-30m OD with approximately sixty sites below the 10m OD contour. As is often the case, occupation evidence for the Neolithic and early Bronze Age is sparse (WALLIS-WAUGHMAN 1998: 220), however, the evidence for Bronze Age burial is more apparent. The Chelmer and Blackwater valleys have some of the densest concentrations of ring-ditches in Essex (PRIDDY 1981: 99) and this small area is no exception, with fifty-six sites interpreted as round barrows.

There is a tendency to think of round barrows as uniform and produced to a standard form with a single tradition; this is clearly not the case. When a small area is examined more carefully and position, form and topography are considered spatial patterns become apparent. All the round barrows within this area are relatively small measuring 5m – 23m in diameter with an average of 12m. The visible evidence suggests that the monuments are made up of between one to three ditches or pits.

Environmental evidence suggests that the later Neolithic and early Bronze Age was a period of forest regeneration in the area with little or no cultivation. The pattern in the Lower Blackwater suggests that seasonal domestic occupation with the more intensive activity closer to the estuary (WALLIS-WAUGHMAN 1998: 218) with small scattered settlements in woodland clearings, leaving very little evidence of settlement visible on aerial photographs. It could be suggested that single isolated round barrows were the first to be constructed, located around the river valley some within 200m of the rivers and others on higher ground overlooking the rivers (fig. 4). While the vegetation might not have enabled visibility between round barrows, it is possible that the earliest monuments were placed in woodland clearances that may have been used for earlier activities or seasonal settlement. It would seem likely that the chosen site for burial monuments was in a landscape strewn with the visible presence of 'known history' (GARWOOD 1991: 17) of which we can now only see a small part. The monuments must have been placed into the landscape for a reason of which we can now only surmise, but it would seem logical that past activity and use of the land would have influence future activity and monument construction.

The visibility of sites is highly restricted within the area and using line of site (LOS) analysis it can be suggested that even without the complication of vegetation very few of these initial sites were visible to each other, despite the local topography being relatively flat, though this does not take into account the issue of reciprocity where one point can be seen from another but not vice-versa (WHEATLEY-GILLINGS 2002: 210-211). Viewshed analysis confirms this with only three of the initial twelve sites being intervisible. This would suggest that visibility was not the main concern for the location. Garwood's spatial associations and developments of round barrow groups would suggest that once single monuments were established some would have been chosen to be the 'core' of groups. Existing mounds might have been made more elaborate, while secondary 'pairs' were constructed and this sequence of development can be applied in the Chelmer valley.

Based on their size, morphology and spatial relationship several 'pairs' of round barrows seem to have been constructed (fig. 5) and these would appear to be slightly smaller than the original isolated mounds. At least five new sets of pairs are visible while there are at least two further instances of another mound being added in close proximity to an original, while the original may have had a ditch added. These 2 more elaborate monuments would not have been visible to each other; however, four of the five new sets of pairs would have been visible from A.

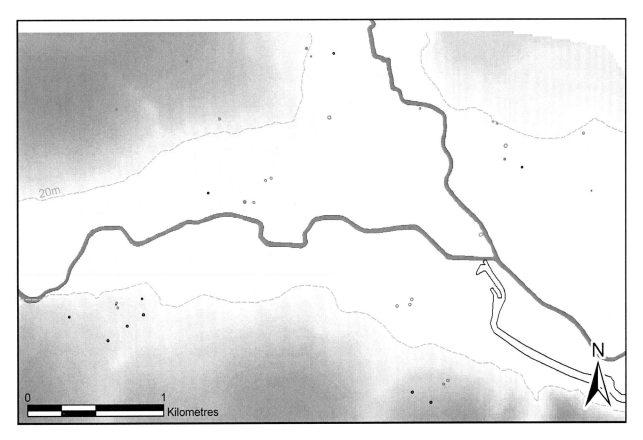

Fig. 7: Fourth phase of cropmark development (earlier phases in gray).

Fig. 8: Fifth phase of cropmark development (earlier phases in gray).

If the construction of pairs of monuments with a direct association with one another was becoming increasingly more important, it would also appear that intervisibility from one central site was becoming more important. It could be that landscape clearance was becoming more common so enabling increased visibility. Environmental data from Lofts Farm further up the Blackwater supports this as it shows that there was increased land clearance during the Bronze Age (BROWN 1988).

Next in sequence could have been the monuments of a similar size that are located slightly further away from the original groups. For example, one of these monuments is approximately 100m from the original groups (fig. 6). This may have been closely followed by the construction of dispersed groups of similar size mounds found away from earlier monuments. Often these monuments are 150-250m from each other and other potentially earlier monuments (fig. 7). There could be a number of reasons why these barrows were being constructed away from earlier monuments including the desire to be 'individual' while still maintaining a link to ancestry and therefore a claim to the land. Though some of the monuments are still quite dispersed, clusters of monuments are beginning to form.

Based on the evidence found at Lofts Farm, N. Brown (BROWN 1988: 295) has suggested that a pastoral economy probably existed at this time in the Lower Blackwater, and given the close proximity and similar topographic and geological nature, the Chelmer valley. This type of economy would have necessitated the clearance of trees and scrubland, possibly increasing visibility. While sites in the river valley would still have had a relatively restricted view towards sites further away from the rivers. The sites on the higher contour appear to have a good all round view of both the sites located on the valley floor and the sites on the opposing side of the river. It could be suggested that at this time a greater degree of landscape organisation was taking place and it is quite likely that some of the linear cropmarks visible are associated with this period of monument building but, at present, is too fragmentary to understand.

It would seem sensible that the smaller or perhaps partial round barrows were the last in the monument sequence (fig. 8: 5th phase). These would appear to be the most numerous type, but are also the smallest. In several instances there appears to be pairs of these smaller barrows (some measuring less than 10m in diameter) barrows and are located in very close proximity to the larger and possibly earlier ones. P. Garwood suggests that sections of the community might have manipulated burial practices to their advantages (GARWOOD 1991: 17). By relating new burials with older ones a clearer association with both the land and ancestors could be established and an expression to be part of a living landscape continued.

There is little doubt that there was settlement in this landscape from the Mesolithic but there is little aerial photographic evidence until the later Bronze Age when the occupation of the river terraces was widespread (WALLIS-WAUGHMAN 1998: 220) a picture supported by the cropmark evidence. Within the study area there are several non-burial related cropmark complexes that are probably prehistoric (fig. 9: 6th phase). Three enclosures are of particular interest in relation to the ritual landscape. Enclosure A (EHER 7870) (fig. 9) is 130m by 130m, with several features, including a trackway leading from it. The enclosure appears to have been built around an earlier round barrow, with the west ditch of the enclosure clearly diverting around to avoid the monument, which implies that this large circular feature was not a hut circle. This essentially encloses the round barrow while cutting between the larger monument and a smaller one. This would imply that the larger one had more significance.

There would appear to be a desire to incorporate earlier monuments that may have given the occupants an identity and connection to the past, much the same as building the smaller mounds in close proximity did. R. Bradley suggests that it is no coincidence that round barrows were selected for reuse in this way as they are often approximate the same size as houses built during the middle Bronze Age and this link can be found in areas such as Cranbourne Chase, Dorset (BRADLEY 1998: 157). There could be a similar link here; there are lots of round barrows in the area and some of the largest appear to be similar in size to some round houses built during the period. R. Bradley goes on to suggest that the two landscapes of domestic and ritual in Cranbourne Chase are closely linked (BRADLEY 1998: 158). Within this small area this link between burial mounds and apparent occupation enclosures occurs elsewhere. Enclosure B (EHER 7963) shows where a later enclosure again incorporates a round barrow (fig. 9). The north side of the enclosure appears to have been diverted around the earlier monument. Again the larger round barrow appears to hold a greater significance and the smaller ones, while not removed, are not incorporated within the main enclosure.

A third site at Woodham Walter (fig. 9: C) also incorporates ritual and domestic landscapes and has been partially excavated (HEDGES-BUCKLEY 1987). While this site also integrates a round barrow, various phases of enclosure construction would have, at different times, made the round barrow both internal and external to the main enclosure, implying that the importance of the monument changed during the period that the mound was extant. Unlike the other enclosures elsewhere in the valley its construction ensured the destruction of at least one of the smaller mounds. What may have also been important within this landscape was that all three examples would have been visible to each other, so not only were the settlement enclosures incorporating immediate round barrows, but the others would also have been visible. All these examples show basics of 'binding' two elements of life together. It shows the importance of lineage which was also represented within the sequence of initial barrow clusters.

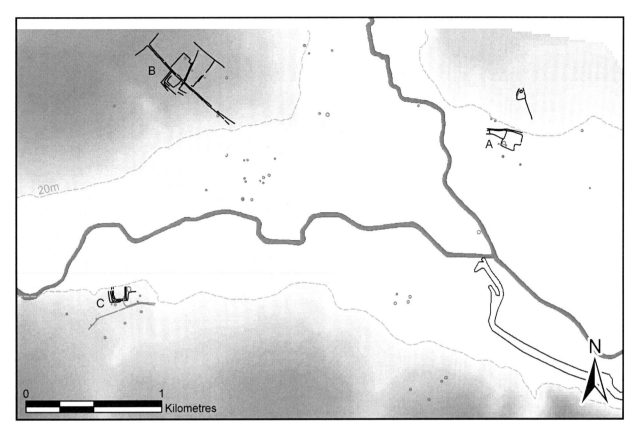

Fig. 9: Sixth phase of cropmark development (earlier phases in gray).

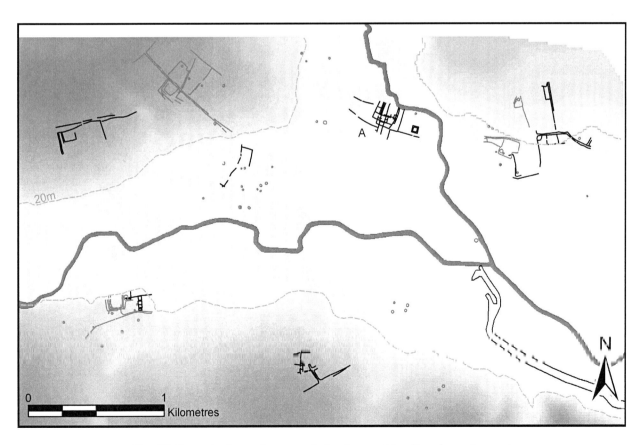

Fig. 10: Seventh phase of cropmark development (earlier phases in gray).

The final stage in this prehistoric landscape would appear to be the elements of development clearly away from this perceived 'ritual' landscape (fig. 10). These are areas of settlement not as closely associated with existing monuments and round barrows; this does not mean that there are no round barrows close to the developments. Cropmark complex A (EHER 7872) has been constructed away from other monuments in the area and appears to be very regular in its lay out. This leads to the question as to why the areas of occupation and burial are in different locations and why are certain round barrows enclosed ? This may be more to do with location than the actual monuments. The round barrows in the lower part of the river valley may have been affected by sea level changes. While it is not being suggested that these lower level sites were ever completely inundated or waterlogged they may have been within more marginal areas of land and therefore occupation sites developed on slightly higher ground, consequently these lower sites were never chosen to be enclosed or settled. There is evidence for this shift elsewhere around the coast (WILKINSON-MURPHY 1995: 132) and this might also explain why later settlement areas are in different locations as the river valleys may have made suitable locations once sea levels had dropped.

4. Conclusions

This re-use of the prehistoric landscape is common in many areas of Essex and the cropmark evidence shows that the locations for ritual monuments was then often used in later periods for settlement. This has lead to the assumption that there was not the same level of ritual activity in later prehistory. However, it could simply be that the ritual activity was not as easily distinguishable from the domestic and there was still the same level of symbolism in activities performed they were just not performed in large monuments that we can now easily identify.

While it is unlikely that many more large prehistoric monuments will be found within Essex, recent experience has shown that there are still areas of potential discovery, through a mixture of aerial photography, field work and excavation. This has been demonstrated recently with the discovery of a causewayed enclosure at Lodge Farm near St. Osyth, where excavation of a complex cropmark landscape prior to the construction of an agricultural reservoir revealed large pits and ditches of Neolithic date (GERMANY 2003). In retrospect some of these features can be identified on the aerial photographs of the site, though size and nature of the features lead to them being interpreted as geological features. This has shown that even with aerial photographic programmes important discoveries are still made through a range of techniques. This said, the NMP has also demonstrated that interesting sites can be recorded through reconnaissance pro-grammes. For example, two large elongated enclosures, with similar morphological characteristics to cursus

monuments were mapped for the first time through the NMP in the north west of the county near Saffron Walden. No previous large prehistoric monuments were known in this area of the county and without the systematic mapping that the NMP provides they may have remained unrecorded.

It is possible that there are other similar monuments still to be recorded in other areas of the county and with continued reconnaissance and, just as importantly, continued mapping then there is always the possibility that monuments will be lost to development and mineral extraction, even with the expertise of archaeologists and development control.

Helen SAUNDERS
Essex County Council
HER, County Hall
CHELMSFORD CM1 1QH
Essex
United Kingdom

Apologies

This article was written by the author in 2005-06 but due to various difficulties it was only published in 2011, for which I want to apologise sincerely – Marc Lodewijckx (editor).

References

BEWLEY B. 2001. Understanding England's Historic Landscapes: An Aerial Perspective, *Landscapes* 2: 74-84.

BRADLEY R. 1998. *The Significance of Monuments*, Routledge, London.

BROWN N. 1988. A Late Bronze Age Enclosure at Lofts Farm, Essex, *Proceedings of the Prehistoric Society* 54: 249-302.

BROWN N. 1997. A Landscape of Two Halves: The Neolithic of the Chelmer Valley / Blackwater Estuary, Essex. In P. TOPPING (Ed.), Neolithic Landscapes, *Neolithic Studies Group Seminar Papers* 2, *Oxbow Monograph* 86.

BROWN N. 1999. The Archaeology of Ardleigh, Essex Excavation 1955-1980, *East Anglian Archaeology* 90.

BROWN N. 2001. The Late Bronze Age Enclosure at Springfield Lyons in its Landscape Context, *Essex Archaeology and History* 32: 92-101.

BROWN N. and M. GERMANY 2002. Jousting at Windmills ? The Essex Cropmark Enclosures Project, *Essex Archaeology and History* 33: 8-53.

BROWN N., D. KNOPP and D. STRACHAN 2002. The Archaeology of Constable Country: the Cropmarks of the Stour Valley, *Landscape* 24: 5-28.

BROWN N. and N.J. LAVENDER 1994. Later Bronze Age Site at Great Baddow and Settlement in the Chelmer Valley, Essex, 1500 to 500 BC, *Essex Archaeology and History* 25: 3-13.

BUCKLEY D.G., J.D. HEDGES and N. BROWN 2001. Excavations at a Neolithic Cursus, Springfield, Essex, 1979-85, *Proceedings of the Prehistoric Society* 67: 101-162.

BUCKLEY D.G. and J.D. HEDGES 1987. *The Bronze Age and Saxon Settlements at Springfield Lyons, Essex,* An Interim Report ECC Occasional Paper 5.

DARVILL T. 1997. Neolithic Landscapes: Identity and Definition. In P. TOPPING (Ed.), Neolithic Landscapes, *Neolithic Studies Group Seminar Papers* 2, *Oxbow Monograph* 86.

EDIS J., D. MACLEOD and R.H. BEWLEY 1989. An Archaeologist's Guide to the Classification of Cropmarks and Soilmarks, *Antiquity* 63: 112-126.

ENGLISH HERITAGE 1988. *Bowl Barrows General Description,* www.eng-h.gov.uk/mpp/mcd/sub/bb3.htm

GARWOOD P. 1991. Ritual Tradition and the Reconstitution of Society. In P. GARWOOD, D. JENNINGS, R. SKEATES and T. TOMS (Eds.), Sacred and Profane, *Oxford University Committee for Archaeology, Monograph* 32: 10-32.

GERMANY M. 2003. A Causewayed Enclosure at St. Osyth, near Clacton, *Essex Journal* 38/2: 39-43.

HEDGES J. and D. BUCKLEY 1978. The Causewayed Enclosure, Orsett, Essex, *Proceedings of the Prehistoric Society* 44: 219-308.

HEDGES J. and D. BUCKLEY 1987. Excavation of a cropmark enclosure complex at Woodham Walter, Essex, 1976, *East Anglian Archaeology* 33.

LAST J. 1999. Out of Line: Cursuses and Monument Typology in Eastern England. In A. BARCLAY and J. HARDING (Eds.), *Pathways and Ceremonies: The Cursus Monuments of Britain and Ireland,* Oxbow Books. Oxford.

LAVENDER N.J. and P. CLARKE *forthcoming. Excavations at Brightlingsea,* East Anglian Archaeology.

OSWALD A., C. DYER and M. BARBER 2001. *The Creation of Monuments: Neolithic Causewayed Enclosures in the British Isles,* English Heritage, London.

PRIDDY D. 1981. The Barrows of Essex. In A.J. LAWSON, E.A. MARTIN and D. PRIDDY, The Barrows of East Anglia, *East Anglian Archaeology* 12: 89-105.

RILEY D.N. 1979. Factors in the Development of Cropmarks, *Aerial Archaeology* 4: 28-32.

RILEY D.N. 1983. The Frequency of Occurrence of Cropmarks in Relation to Soils. In G.S. MAXWELL (Ed.), The Impact of Aerial Reconnaissance on Archaeology, *Council British Archaeology Res. Rep.* 49.

THOMAS J. 1999. *Understanding the Neolithic,* Routledge, London/New York.

WALLIS S. and M. WAUGHMAN 1998. Archaeology and the Landscape in the Lower Blackwater Valley, *East Anglian Archaeology* 82.

WHEATLEY D. and M. GILLINGS 2002. *Spatial Technology and Archaeology: The Archaeological Applications of GIS,* Taylor and Francis, London/New York.

WILKINSON T.J. and P.L. MURPHY 1995. *The Archaeology of the Essex Coast. Volume One: the Hullbridge Survey, East Anglian Archaeology* 71.

WILSON D. 2000. *Air Photo Interpretation for Archaeologists,* Batsford, London.

COMBINING IMAGE- AND MODEL-BASED RENDERING OF AN HISTORICAL LANDSCAPE FROM AERIAL IMAGERY

Maarten VERGAUWEN – Geert WILLEMS –
Frank VERBIEST – Luc VAN GOOL – Daniël PLETINCKX

Abstract

Preservation of cultural heritage through digital technology can only be successful if people can experience sites and reconstructions in an intuitive, yet convincingly realistic manner. A way to get people interested in the past is highlighting the link of the past with the present.

In this paper, an entire pipeline is discussed that augments an existing Quicktime VR object movie of the virtual reconstruction of an archaeological site with images of the site as it exists today. The new images are generated using an Image-Based Rendering approach.

1. Introduction

Aerial recordings of archaeological sites have the advantage that they can show a much clearer overview of the site than ground-based recordings. If one wants to employ the aerial imagery in an exhibit or public application, however, it is important that the image data be presented in a clear and user-friendly way that makes it easy to navigate through the scene. Furthermore, if one can highlight the link between the current situation of the site and its history, including previously existing buildings, artefacts, etc this link intensifies the experience of the visitor.

This paper proves that it is possible to show the evolution of a landscape until the present day, without making a virtual model of that present day situation. In this paper, we discuss a way to create interactive applications to explore the evolution of a landscape and register a visualization of the current landscape with existing virtual reconstructions. In this way, we obtain an optimal combination of real and virtual images that shows the evolution and history of the site. This paper outlines the pipeline from data acquisition by oblique aerial photography, over camera calibration and registration of the virtual with the real landscape, to image-based rendering techniques to create the appropriate views.

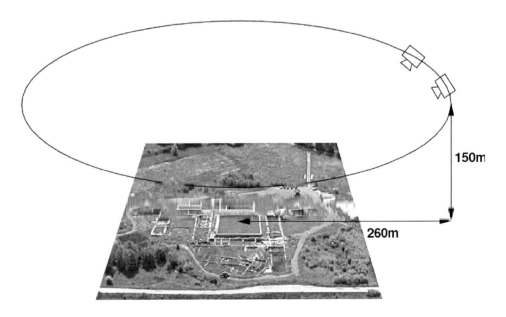

Fig. 1: The setup of the virtual cameras. They are distributed every 10 degrees on a circle with a radius of 260 meter at 150 meter altitude.

Many applications make use of the QuickTime technology provided by Apple, especially to create interactive applications through the QTVR suite (APPLE 2006). One element of this technology is QTVR object movies that allow interactive access to a two-dimensional matrix of images. One of the ways to use this is to show an object from several different angles.

A more sophisticated use of the QTVR object technology is to build interactive 4-dimensional objects, by rotating the object through a horizontal cursor movement, and evolving the object through time through a vertical cursor movement. Since 1999, the Provincial Archaeological Museum of Ename has used 4-dimensional QTVR objects to show the evolution of the entire village over the last ten centuries (PLETINCKX-SILBERMAN-CALLEBAUT 2001).

In this interactive TimeLine application, virtual models of 12 consecutive periods are visualized. In the TimeLine application a virtual camera spins at a fixed height around a fixed point, yielding 36 regularly spaced views on the geo-referenced virtual model, and this for all 12 historical periods. In this way, the columns of the 36x12 matrix of views show the evolution of the landscape from 1020 to 1780 AD from a specific point of view, with the columns evenly spaced on a predefined circle with a height of 150 m and a diameter of 260 m. The circle where the virtual camera was positioned is shown in figure 1. This figure also shows the Ename site.

To extend this matrix to the present, as illustrated in figure 3, we need to take images from exactly the same 36 viewpoints and this at a height of 150 m. This is virtually impossible with straightforward photography however, and the paper proposes an alternative way, based on image-based rendering. The result is rewarding. In more than one way, this most recent, modern row of the TimeLine matrix (see the 4th row in figure 3) is the most intriguing one, as it links the present – experienced by the visitor – to the past. Every element in the current landscape gets a meaning, a story, a reason why it is the way it is. By linking the past to the present, a general audience can be addressed by telling the story of how a place in time came to be.

2. Overview of the pipeline

A processing pipeline has been devised to create modern views that are aligned with those already in the TimeLine matrix, as shown in figure 2.

First step

In essence, this pipeline produces interpolated views, starting from a series of photographs of the site. Therefore, a first step consists of acquiring the latter. Since the virtual TimeLine images show the archaeological site from above, a helicopter was used to shoot the photographs. Section 3 explains this in more detail. The use of a helicopter is only part of the solution. Even when combined with state-of-the art technology such as DGPS or steadycams, it is highly unlikely that one would manage to let any of the images coincide perfectly with one of the 36 target viewpoints as used in the TimeLine views. We have used image-based rendering (IBR) for that purpose. IBR takes a series of close photographs taken from known directions and a 3D model of the scene as input, and then creates a kind of interpolated views, taking account of the 3D geometry.

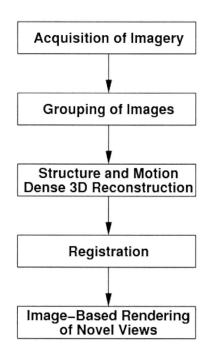

Fig. 2: Five steps in the pipeline will realize our final goal of making a QTVR object movie of the real site, registered with the virtual views of the existing TimeLine.

Second step

Typically IBR is applied based on images taken from many and widely spread directions, so as to be able to generate synthetic views from all around an object. Here, we are only interested in a very limited set of such synthetic views. Hence, we can actually split the task into a series of smaller IBR problems. For each target viewpoint images are selected that were taken in its vicinity. This image grouping step is explained in section 4.

Third step

In the previous step, the helicopter images have been subdivided into groups, where each group is to be used as the input to an IBR process for some of the target viewpoints. On average four target viewpoints could be rendered per selected group. For the images within each group, the camera parameters are extracted (calibration) and a 3D reconstruction is computed from their point of view, exploiting all the images in the group.

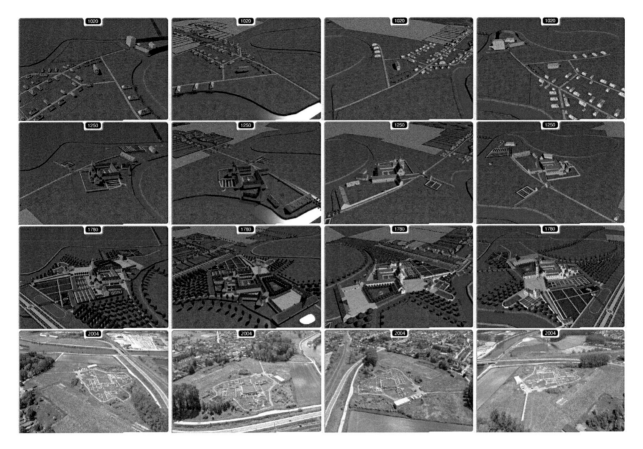

Fig. 3: These 16 images are a small part of the 36x13 TimeLine image matrix, upgraded with present day images (last row), using methods described in this paper. Each column represents one of 36 different viewpoints (in this case arranged along a circular path), and the 12 first rows represent different eras from the past. The last row contains images from our own time, for the same viewpoints and in the form of photo-realistic images, so that visitors can directly relate to them. In this cut-out of the complete TimeLine matrix only 4 eras are shown, namely 1020, 1250, 1780 and 2004.

These processes – camera calibration and 3D geometry extraction – are jointly referred to as Structure and Motion (SaM). They are the subject of section 5.

Fourth step

In order to determine the actual target viewpoints in terms of the IBR images that have to be formed, the new images must be registered to the virtual target images.

Since only few structures visible in the virtual TimeLine views are still easily recognizable in the real images of today, we opted for a manual process in which an archaeologist indicates points on the virtual reconstructions of the different eras and on the ortho-photo of the actual site. This process is described in section 6.

Fifth step

Finally, once data from all previous steps have become available, newly rendered images can be produced using the IBR approach explained in section 7.

3. Acquisition of imagery

The Ename TimeLine was created with views on a set of geo-referenced virtual models of the complete village. If we want the real component of the movie to seamlessly match the virtual images, we need images of the real site that are recorded from approximately the same positions. For every time instance, there are 36 images, evenly distributed over a circle with a radius of 260 meter. The virtual cameras are positioned 150 meter high and looking towards the centre of the circle on the ground.

Figure 1 shows this setup. The easiest way to record images in the real world, taken approximately on this same circle, is by using a helicopter. On a day with perfect weather conditions in June 2004, the helicopter (fig. 4) arrived at the site.

The helicopter pilot was asked to fly the white circle (with a radius of 260 m) at an altitude of 150 meter as shown on the ortho-photo of figure 5.

An additional navigator made sure the pilot could follow these requirements safely. While the helicopter followed this path as precisely as possible, a photographer – as a third crew member – used a digital photo camera to record the scene, focusing his camera all the time on the centre of the circle, somewhere in the middle of the archaeological site.

As the helicopter needs a certain speed to fly the circle and the digital camera needs a certain time to store the high resolution image, an average of 15 images were taken per tour, so the consecutive images were quite far apart. Therefore, the helicopter flew the circle several times at slightly different altitudes and images were taken constantly. Fig. 6 shows some of the 130 digital images that were acquired during the helicopter flight.

Fig. 4:   Helicopter from where the photographs were shot.

Fig. 5: The navigator of the helicopter was asked to follow the flight path shown in this figure.

Fig. 6: Some of the 130 images taken during the helicopter flight.

4. Grouping of images

The images that were acquired as described in section 3 show the site from different angles. Consecutive images can be far apart and are therefore not always suited for SaM algorithms. Since the images were recorded during multiple fly-bys, the same content reappears regularly. As explained in section 2 it is not our goal to calibrate the cameras of all images or of the entire circle in one SaM process (rather several, smaller IBR problems are solved). We want to combine different images taken from viewpoints that are quite close to a target viewpoint and apply SaM to this group of images. The camera range spanned by the selected group of images is large enough to solve the IBR problem for the targeted viewpoint and some of its neighbours. It turned out that an average number of four viewpoints could be rendered for every group of images. The process of selecting the group of images for a target viewpoint was therefore repeated nine times. The major task in the grouping process consists in detecting images that were taken close to each other. Manual selection in the 130 images is, while possible, a very tedious task. A simple but effective algorithm has been implemented which does the job.

The algorithm boils down to a comparison of all pairs of images. The centre part of one image is selected. An area with the same size is extracted from the other image and slides over this image. For every position, both windows are compared using Normalized Cross Correlation. The highest correlation gives us a measure of how well these images resemble each other. The images are subsampled to decrease processing time.

Figure 7 shows the resulting, symmetric matrix of these values. White points represent a high correlation; black points denote no correlation between the two images given by the x and y coordinate in the matrix. The diagonal is of course perfectly white. One can clearly see the different passes of the helicopter appearing as white lines, connecting consecutive images.

The selection process becomes a much easier task now. If we want to reconstruct the cameras and 3D scene from a certain viewpoint, all we need to do is select one image that is taken near the viewpoint we want. The matrix of figure 7 then lists the best candidates to match this image with.

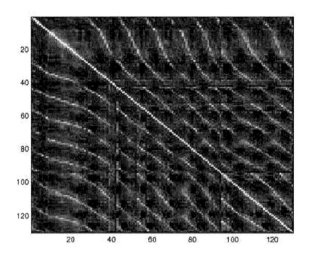

Fig. 7:   Matrix with NCC values. White points represent a high correlation, black points mean that there is no correlation between the two images given by the x and y coordinate in the matrix. This matrix can be used to determine a set of images that were taken close to a given image.

5. Structure and motion and dense 3D

The ultimate goal of the pipeline described in section 2 is to generate new images from specific viewpoints. We have chosen an image-based rendering approach to do so. As will be explained in section 7, this approach produces a kind of high quality interpolation between a set of images recorded in the vicinity of the required viewpoint. As mentioned earlier, our version of this approach also extracts the calibration parameters (both extrinsic and intrinsic) of the camera views and the 3D geometry of the scene – i.e. the scene 'Structure' and camera 'Motion' – and does so directly from the same set of images.

In the last decade tremendous progress has been made in the computer vision community on solving the problem of structure and motion recovery from uncalibrated image sequences. It is beyond the scope of this paper to go into the details of this problem and its solutions. A short overview will be given in paragraph 5.1. Paragraph 5.2. will deal with one specific aspect that was important in this work, namely how to deal with the degenerate case of a nearly planar scene. Some results of the structure and motion recovery are shown in paragraph 5.3.

5.1. Structure and motion

The general problem of structure and motion recovery can be stated as: Given a set of images or a video sequence, compute the intrinsic and extrinsic camera calibration parameters for all views and the 3D reconstruction of the scene that is visible in these views. A possible solution to this problem that computes the result completely automatically has been developed in our lab (POLLEFEYS *et alii* 2004) and comprises the following steps:

- First the images are pair wise related to each other. Feature points are extracted in every image and matches are found between consecutive images by comparing these features using a comparison function like Normalized Cross Correlation.

- For every consecutive pair of images the epipolar geometry is computed from the previously computed matches. Outliers (which normally correspond to wrong matches) are detected and removed with the help of the epipolar geometry.

- The 3D structure of the scene and the calibration of the camera is initialized for the best suited pair of images. All other cameras are consecutively computed in the same coordinate frame and the 3D pose of the feature points is computed. The resulting reconstruction is valid up to any projective transformation.

- The projective reconstruction is upgraded to metric (Euclidean up to scale) using self-calibration and a bundle adjustment procedure minimizes the total reprojection error of all points in all cameras.

- Since the calibration is now computed, the cameras can be rectified and a dense 3D reconstruction of the scene can be computed, using stereo and a fusion algorithm that combines information from all stereo pairs into a depth map for every original view.

5.2. Planar degeneracy

Standard structure and motion algorithms, as described in the previous paragraph, first relate all images in a projective frame and then upgrade this frame through self-calibration. Unfortunately this approach suffers from the existence of critical motions (KAHL-TRIGGS-AASTROM 2000) and surfaces (HOFMANN 1953). This means that there are cases for which sequences are recorded in a specific fashion such that multiple solutions to the self-calibration procedure exist. Since only one of these solutions corresponds to the real world and since this solution can not be distinguished from the other solutions, the result of the pipeline of paragraph 5.1. will in general not be correct. Examples of critical motion sequences are a motion on a line or a circle. A typical example of a critical surface sequence is one in which only a single plane is visible. The archaeological site of Ename is not exactly planar but when viewed from a distance of about 300 meter there is hardly any 3D information outside the ground plane, which will certainly cause problems for standard structure and motion.

In recent years different solutions have been proposed to deal with planar structures. They vary from merely surviving the plane by detecting when only a plane is visible in the images, calibrating and reconstructing in parts where more than this plane is visible and extending this structure to the planar part (POLLEFEYS-VERBIEST-VAN GOOL 2002), to effectively dealing with the planar structure (or other critical motions and surfaces for that matter) by taking into account more

Fig. 8:   Four of the seven images that served as input for one structure and motion process. The images were taken during different passes of the helicopter and are selected automatically using the matrix in figure 7.

information about the camera intrinsic parameters than in the general structure and motion algorithm (NISTER 2003). The first approach will not help us in this case because it needs some cameras of the sequence to observe more than a plane which is not the case in the recordings from the helicopter. Therefore the second approach has been implemented. Since it assumes the intrinsics of the camera to be known, one can estimate the essential matrix instead of the fundamental matrix when relating two views. This essential matrix takes into account the intrinsic camera parameters and, unlike the fundamental matrix, is unique for all practical cases, even if all observed points lie in a single plane. Pose estimation of the cameras (the third step of paragraph 5.1.) can then be done in a metric frame which alleviates the problems we had with general structure and motion.

In order to retrieve the intrinsic parameters we recorded some other, non planar scenes with the camera that was used in the helicopter, using the same settings. These sequences could be processed with our normal algorithms. The calibration we used for the planar scene

was inferred from the resulting camera calibration of these extra sequences.

5.3. Structure and motion results

For the automatic structure and motion algorithm to succeed, the input images should not differ too much from each other. Techniques exist to deal with wide-baseline cases but these are not applicable here since the result of the structure and motion pipeline will be used by the image-based rendering process of section 7. This process needs images with viewpoints that are close. Figure 8 shows four of seven images in a group used for one of the 9 structure and motion computations mentioned in section 4. The images are selected by choosing one manually and retrieving the six best matching views from the matrix in figure 7.

The resulting point reconstruction and camera calibration can be seen in figure 9. Top and side views are shown. It is clear that the structure of the scene is very close to planar. Figure 10 shows some views of the dense 3D model that was reconstructed from the images. The dense

Fig. 9:   The camera calibration of the images and a set of 3D points, representing the scene, retrieved by our structure and motion algorithm. Both a top and a side view are shown. The planar nature of the scene can clearly be recognized.

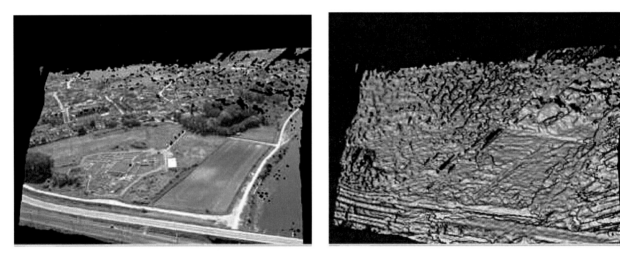

Fig. 10: Dense reconstruction of the scene. The quality is not perfect, certainly in homogeneous areas or in areas that are far away.

3D is far from perfect, due to large homogeneous areas like the fields or due to the large distance to the cameras, like the houses in the background. The quality might not be good enough for ordinary, geometry-based rendering but is sufficient for image-based rendering.

6. Registration

At this stage in the pipeline of section 2 we have available separate sets of images – on average one set per four target views – with corresponding 3D reconstructions and camera calibrations. We want to employ these results to create synthetic viewpoints that coincide with the corresponding target viewpoints. Unfortunately, every 3D reconstruction has been computed in its own metric frame. So far, each reconstruction is related to the site coordinate system of figure 1 via an unknown metric transformation consisting of a rotation, a translation and a scale factor. If we want to use the reconstruction for image-based rendering, we need to compute these metric transformations. This process is called registration. A possible strategy to find the metric transformation described above consists of the following two consecutive steps:

- Bring one camera of the structure and motion reconstruction into the target frame, effectively computing the rotational and translational part of the transformation.

- Compute the scale factor between the two frames from one or more indicated distances.

Fig. 11: Pose estimation with manual interaction. Corresponding points (in red) are indicated both on the ortho-photo (left) and on the image taken from the helicopter (right).

Step one boils down to a pose estimation process of one camera that has been computed in the SaM-frame in the target frame. This can be done if at least 3 3D points in the target frame and their corresponding 2D points in the image are known (GRUNERT 1841). If more than three correspondences are available, a better approach is to compute an initial solution and then minimize the total reprojection error of all available points with a non-linear optimization step. For the 3D coordinates, we employed a geo-referenced ortho-photo of the archaeological site.

A member of the Ename archaeological team was asked to indicate points on this ortho-photo and their corresponding points in the image as well. Figure 11 shows such a process. In the top image the relevant part of the ortho-photo is shown. The bottom part shows the image taken from the helicopter. The labelled indicated points are shown superimposed.

Step two still needs to determine the scale factor between the two frames. If two 3D points are known in both coordinate systems, the ratio of both distances is the scale factor we are looking for. One of the points could be the centre of the camera that has been computed with pose-estimation, since we already know this in both frames. We just need one more 3D point with known coordinates in both frames. The scale factor can be computed from any of the indicated points. The coordinates in the target frame are known from the ortho photo and the position in the SaM frame can be found through a lookup in the corresponding depth map that was computed in section 5.

7. Image-based rendering

Image-Based Rendering (IBR) generates novel views by interpolating information from images that are close to the requested view. The advantage over traditional 3D

scene model-based rendering is that an exact geometrical description of the scene is not necessary in this approach (LEVOY-HANRAHAN 1996) although approximate geometrical information can be used to improve the results (GORTLER *et alii* 1996; CHAI *et alii* 2000).

In our lab we have developed an image-based rendering pipeline (HEIGL *et alii* 1999; KOCH *et alii* 1999) and have recently extended it further to incorporate elements from the work of different authors, such as Buehler (BUEHLER *et alii* 2001), Pajarola (PAJAROLA-SAINZ-MENG 2003) and Evers-Senne (EVERS-SENNE-KOCH 2003). This extended pipeline is used to create each of the 36 target views of the present site (i.e. the last row of the TimeLine matrix), each time exploiting a set of relevant, grouped images (step 2).

In contrast to the first Lumigraphs, the pipeline developed in our lab can deal with an unstructured set of images. All source images have their associated camera pose estimates, which we have computed using Structure and Motion and which were registered with the target frame. The algorithm behaves like an extension of view-dependent texture mapping and uses depth maps generated through SaM as an approximation of the 3D geometry (KOCH *et alii* 1999). Not all cameras that we have at our disposal are equally suited for rendering from a certain virtual viewpoint and therefore a set of cameras is selected. In our implementation the cameras which will be used to render the virtual view are selected in a similar fashion as described in (EVERS-SENNE-KOCH 2003). During operation the user can set the number of selected cameras, the relative importance of the selection criteria, etc.

Rather than using a fixed 3D geometry, Pajarola *et alii* (PAJAROLA-SAINZ-MENG 2003) propose a technique to approximate the 3D information in a non-uniform way.

Fig. 12: A virtual image, rendered from three helicopter images (left). The corresponding blendfield (right) clearly shows the relative importance of each camera at each pixel. For visualization of this blendfield, a colour is assigned to each of the three images used to generate this virtual view: red, green and blue. A reddish pixel for example denotes a pixel where the influence of the first image in the final rendered image is high.

Fig. 13: The difference image between the reference and one other camera before (left) and after (right) minimization. Black pixels indicate a high intensity difference, white pixels a low difference. The overall intensity error is reduced by a factor of 2.4.

For every depth map a restricted quadtree is built. This quadtree holds the hierarchical representation of the depth map and has the additional property that, no matter which hierarchical level is chosen, the topology of the scene is preserved. The construction of this quadtree can be done beforehand in an off-line step, reducing the on-line processing time significantly.

The key property of image-based rendering techniques is the combination of different images to render a new virtual view. Not every image that is used for the rendering has the same impact in all areas of the new image. It is desired that the importance of each image depends on the quality of its camera, its 3D reconstruction, etc. evaluated at every pixel of the virtual view.

To this end a blendfield is constructed. This blendfield describes the relative importance of each camera for every pixel in the virtual view. In order to generate the resulting image, each selected camera projects its own image onto its own quadtree and is rendered from the requested viewpoint. All renderings are combined into one image using the weights in the blendfield.

Although the 36 necessary views can be rendered off-line, one can easily think of other applications where interactivity is important. That is why we have implemented as many operations as possible on the GPU. Fig shows a virtual view, reconstructed from three selected cameras with its corresponding blendfield.

178

Fig. 14: Four of the newly generated images of the archaeological site.

8. Refining cameras

During processing it became apparent that the calibration of the cameras sometimes needed improvement. For the Structure and Motion process to deliver accurate results feature points need to be tracked throughout the entire sequence of images. The longer the feature tracks, the better the result will be. Unfortunately in this specific case images contain a lot of homogeneous areas, like the green and brown fields and the river. These areas are a nightmare for feature detectors. In order to improve the calibration result a refinement process has been implemented that updates the camera calibration. One camera and its corresponding 3D information is selected as the reference and a virtual viewpoint is chosen.

All other images are projected sequentially on the reference 3D scene through their corresponding camera. This result is projected onto the virtual view. The difference between this rendering and the one obtained from the reference view is computed. A non-linear optimization algorithm aims at minimizing this difference by allowing each camera to adjust its position and viewing direction. Figure 13 shows the difference before and after the optimization for one camera. The resulting camera calibration is more accurate than the original

because also the homogeneous areas will have their impact. All projection and difference operations are performed on the GPU, speeding up this minimization process significantly.

9. Results

The pipeline of section 2 was executed for 9 sets of helicopter images. The reconstructions of these sets allowed us to generate the necessary 36 views for the QTVR object movie, yielding an average of four newly generated images per set of helicopter images. Fig. 14 shows four of these new views, evenly distributed along the circle.

The new images fit very well with the virtual images of the TimeLine. This can be evaluated by comparing the position of the remaining foundations of the buildings with the walls of the virtual images. Figure 15 shows the last two time periods in the updated TimeLine. The first image is a virtual reconstruction, representing the site as it was around 1780. The second is a photograph of today's situation, generated with the IBR pipeline. Figure 16 shows two viewpoints where the virtual reconstruction of 1780 has been merged with the newly generated images.

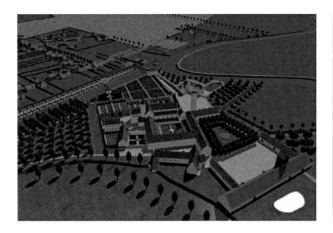 

Fig. 15: The newly rendered image for position 10 and its virtual counterpart. The fit is very good in the area of the archaeological site. The areas near the border of the image, like the church, have a larger error.

Fig. 16: Two viewpoints of the time period around 1780 have been merged with the corresponding image-based rendered images of the current situation. The fit is remarkably good.

The buildings of the archaeological site clearly correspond to the foundations in the real images. The area in the background, including the church (visible in figure 15), does not fit so well. This can easily be explained by errors in the registration step. The reference data in this step consisted of an ortho-photo of the archaeological site. This data corresponds to an area in the helicopter images of about 25 percent of the total image. The registration is therefore good for this area but the error in other image parts increases rapidly.

10. Conclusion

Several novel techniques have been implemented to obtain the resulting QTVR matrix of figure 3. Image-Based Rendering (IBR) techniques are used to generate the 36 requested views. IBR is typically used on data acquired in laboratory conditions. Some previous experience existed in bringing IBR outside the lab, using hand-held cameras instead. In this paper this approach has been lifted to yet another level where images are used

taken from a helicopter flying around the scene. One can hardly imagine a setup with less control on the recorded image data. The contrast with the very controlled laboratory circumstances of typical IBR systems is obvious. An approach for finding the available pictures taken from neighbouring viewpoints for a selected viewpoint has been implemented. Traditionally, IBR assumes that the input pictures come in a pre-ordered fashion. This is hardly acceptable when images have been taken with a handheld camera.

A lifelong experience in the cultural heritage field has taught the Ename Centre for Public Archaeology and Heritage Presentation that in order to get visitors interested in the past, its link with the present must be clear. That is why they came up with the idea of creating an extra time-layer showing the current situation for their existing QTVR TimeLine application. The result turned out to be very rewarding and useful, to the extent that the new QTVR movie is now on display in the museum (ENAME-974 2006). Many historical features can be recognized in the newest period of the TimeLine.

Visitors immediately spot the old pond of the abbey which is now visible as a dark patch of humid ground in the same position. Also roads, remains of the abbey, parts of the river, etc can be very clearly recognized. Other correspondences are not quite as apparent to the untrained eye but, when outlined by a conservator, an old bend of the river can now be found back in the curve of a set of large trees or, in another place, a narrow lane in the field.

The pipeline we implemented for the generation of the 36 novel views is automated to a large extent. In fact the only remaining manual interaction in the process lies in the registration step in which the transformation from the Structure and Motion reconstruction to the Ename coordinate centre is computed. An operator is asked to indicate some points on one of the images in the sequence and on the ortho-photo of the site. Possible future development might make this user interaction unnecessary. This could for instance be done by registering the helicopter image with the ortho-photo automatically. The difference between two images (viewpoint, intensity, even projection) makes this a far from trivial task. The technique described in (FRANSENS-STRECHA-VAN GOOL 2004) might be of use for this.

Maarten VERGAUWEN – Geert WILLEMS – Frank VERBIEST – Luc VAN GOOL
K.U. Leuven ESAT-PSI
Kasteelpark Arenberg 10
3001 LEUVEN
Belgium

Daniël PLETINCKX
Ename Centre for Public Archaeology and Heritage Presentation
Abdijstraat 13-15
9700 OUDENAARDE
Belgium

Acknowledgments

The authors gratefully acknowledge support from the European IST project INVIEW (IST-2000-28459) and the European Network of Excellence EPOCH (IST-2002-507382). Thanks also to Noel Colman, aerial photographer for providing the helicopter service and for giving advice on the aerial photography issues of this project.

Apologies

This article was written by the authors in 2005-06 but due to various difficulties it was only published in 2011, for which I want to apologise sincerely – Marc Lodewijckx (editor).

Bibliography

APPLE 2006. *Developer Connection: QuickTime VR*, http://developer.apple.com/documentation/QuickTime/InsideQT_QTVR.

BUEHLER C., M. BOSSE, L. McMILLAN, S. GORTLER and M. COHEN 2001. Unstructured Lumigraph Rendering, *Proceedings SIGGRAPH 2001*: 425-432.

CHAI J.X., X. TONG, S.C. CHAN and H.Y. SHUM 2000. Plenoptic Sampling, *Proceedings SIGGRAPH 2000*: 307-318.

ENAME-974 2006. *Ename Archaeological Site*, http://www. ename974.org.

EVERS-SENNE J.F. and R. KOCH 2003. Image Based Interactive Rendering with View Dependent Geometry, *Proceedings Eurographics 2003, Computer Graphics Forum*: 573-582.

FRANSENS R., C. STRECHA and L. VAN GOOL 2004. Multimodal and Multiband Image Registration Using Mutual Information, *Proceedings ESA-EUSC 2004*.

GORTLER S., R. GRZESZCZUK, R. SZELISKI and M.F. COHEN 1996. The Lumigraph, *Proceedings SIGGRAPH 1996*: 43-54.

GRUNERT J.A. 1841. Das pothenotische Problem in erweiterter Gestalt nebst über seine Anwendungen in der Geodäsie, *Grunerts Archiv für Mathematik und Physik* Band 1: 238-248.

HEIGL B., R. KOCH, M. POLLEFEYS, J. DENZLER and L. VAN GOOL 1999. Plenoptic Modeling and Rendering from Image Sequences Taken by Hand-Held Camera, *DAGM*: 94-101.

HOFMANN W. 1953. *Das Problem der gefährlichen Flächen in Theorie und Praxis – Ein Beitrag zur Hauptaufgabe der Photogrammetrie*, PhD Thesis, Fakultät für Bauwesen, Technische Universität München.

KAHL F., B. TRIGGS and K. AASTROM 2000. Critical Motions for Auto-Calibration when Some Intrinsic Parameters can Vary, *Journal of Mathematical Imaging and Vision* 13(2).

KOCH R., M. POLLEFEYS, B. HEIGL, L. VAN GOOL and H. NIEMANN 1999. Calibration of Hand-Held Camera Sequences for Plenoptic Modelling, *ICCV* (1): 585-591.

LEVOY M. and P. HANRAHAN 1996. Lightfield Rendering, *Proceedings SIGGRAPH*: 31-42.

NISTER D. 2003. An Efficient Solution to the Five-Point Relative Pose Problem, *Proceedings of the Conference for Computer Vision and Pattern Recognition*, vol. 2: 195-202.

PAJAROLA R., M. SAINZ and Y. MENG 2003. *Depthmesh Objects: Fast Depth-Image Meshing and Warping, Technical Report* 03-02.

PLETINCKX D., N. SILBERMAN and D. CALLE-BAUT 2001. The Saint Laurentius Church in Ename and its Role in the Francia Media Heritage Initiative, *Proceedings VAST, Virtual Reality, Archaeology and Cultural Heritage*: 197-204.

POLLEFEYS M., F. VERBIEST and L. VAN GOOL 2002. Surviving Dominant Planes in Uncalibrated Structure and Motion Recovery, *Proceedings ECCV*, Part II: 837-851.

POLLEFEYS M., L. VAN GOOL, M. VERGAUWEN, F. VERBIEST, K. CORNELIS, J. TOPS and R. KOCH 2004. Visual Modelling with a Hand-Held Camera, *International Journal of Computer Vision* 59(3): 207-232.